ANGEL DUST

Befriend and Betray: Infiltrating the Hells Angels,
Bandidos and Other Criminal Brotherhoods

The Fat Mexican:
The Bloody Rise of the Bandidos Motorcycle Club

Charlie and the Angels:
The Outlaws, the Hells Angels and the Sixty Years War

ANGEL DUST

HOW THE OUTLAW BIKER GANG BECAME A CRIMINAL EMPIRE

ALEX CAINE

WITH JOHN LAWRENCE REYNOLDS

VIKING

VIKING
an imprint of Penguin Canada Books Inc., a Penguin Random House Company

Published by the Penguin Group
Penguin Canada Books Inc., 90 Eglinton Avenue East, Suite 700, Toronto, Ontario, Canada
M4P 2Y3

Penguin Group (USA) LLC, 375 Hudson Street, New York, New York 10014, U.S.A.
Penguin Books Ltd, 80 Strand, London WC2R 0RL, England
Penguin Ireland, 25 St Stephen's Green, Dublin 2, Ireland (a division of Penguin Books Ltd)
Penguin Group (Australia), 707 Collins Street, Melbourne, Victoria 3008, Australia
　(a division of Pearson Australia Group Pty Ltd)
Penguin Books India Pvt Ltd, 11 Community Centre, Panchsheel Park, New Delhi – 110 017, India
Penguin Group (NZ), 67 Apollo Drive, Rosedale, Auckland 0632, New Zealand
　(a division of Pearson New Zealand Ltd)
Penguin Books (South Africa) (Pty) Ltd, 24 Sturdee Avenue, Rosebank, Johannesburg 2196, South Africa

Penguin Books Ltd, Registered Offices: 80 Strand, London WC2R 0RL, England

First published 2014

1 2 3 4 5 6 7 8 9 10   (RRD)

Manufactured in the U.S.A.

LIBRARY AND ARCHIVES CANADA CATALOGUING IN PUBLICATION

Caine, Alex, author Angel dust : how the outlaw biker gang became a criminal empire /
Alex Caine with John Lawrence Reynolds.

Includes index.
ISBN 978-0-670-06708-4 (bound)

1. Hell's Angels. 2. Hell's Angels—History. 3. Motorcycle gangs. 4. Organized crime.
I. Reynolds, John Lawrence, author II. Title.

HV6486.C34 2014   364.106'6   C2014-902416-9

eBook ISBN 978-0-14-319292-3

Visit the Penguin Canada website at **www.penguin.ca**

Special and corporate bulk purchase rates available; please see
www.penguin.ca/corporatesales or call 1-800-810-3104.

FOR JOHN AND JUDY,
THE NICEST PEOPLE I'VE NEVER MET

CONTENTS

1

BEHIND THE BEARDS,
THE PATCHES, AND THE IMAGE

Whenever people ask me if the Hells Angels are as tough and nasty as they appear in movies, TV shows, and books like this one, I answer, "Damn right. They started off bad, and they stayed bad." Some things mellow with time, but not the Angels. Not in the ways that count. If you believe that someday you'll find a bunch of bearded and tattooed guys—who look like they haven't had a bath in two months and smell like they haven't had one in six—selling apples on a corner for some charity, forget it. The Angels have always been out for the only people who really matter to them: themselves. And they still are.

But time has a way of changing things and people, and it's even changing the Angels. As much as they refuse to admit it, they're getting old, fat, sloppy, and slow. No surprise there. Many of them were always fat and sloppy. Now most of them are also old, and old means you start slowing down. Besides, they may have stayed bad, but many of the guys they deal with or try to avoid are even worse.

The point is, they're no longer a biker club. They're criminals and thugs whose primary interest is in making money, intimidating people, and using every means, including legal and political, to get what they want. The motorcycles? They're basically just a symbol.

WHEN YOU'RE IN YOUR TWENTIES and thirties, and if you dress for and practice the part, it's easy to walk into a bar and stare at people until they start pissing their pants. But when you hit your fifties and sixties, you can't scare a baby squirrel with that kind of stuff, because you look too much like Santa Claus wearing dirty Levi's that even the Goodwill store wouldn't accept.

And that's just the way you look. The way you do business changes, too. You don't buy anything today in the same way you or your parents did ten, twenty, thirty years ago. Companies you never heard of last year do business in the billions now. Who do you think they stole the business from? They stole it from people who sat on their butts too long, believing that business would always be good, that they could always be fat and lazy, that no one would ever challenge them. Just like the Angels. Now a lot of them are getting their butts whipped by Johnny-come-lately bikers who view the Angels as a bunch of guys who sometimes cut the lawn at their grandparents' house.

Don't believe me? Let me paint you a picture.

We're in North Hollywood, at a place called Occidental Studios. The place has twelve different film and TV stages where you can shoot whatever you want if you've got the money, the equipment, the crew, the actors, the script, but especially the money. Stage 5 is the biggest of them all: thirty-three thousand square feet under one roof. They're shooting a cable TV series here called *Sons of Anarchy*, and it must be a success because it's been running for six years now.

Everything you need for a big production is here in the studio. Dozens of people are busy doing things that you and I don't know about and couldn't understand if we did. You see this stuff in movie and TV credits if you look closely. I mean, what's a *gaffer* and who's a *best boy*? Doesn't matter. My point is, this is serious show business.

So it's the summer of 2012 and they're getting ready to shoot an important scene. They're waiting for one of the actors to come out of the makeup room, a guy who'll play Lenny "The Pimp" Janowitz. You can tell by his name that this is going to be some badass dude. The actor is in there reading over his lines, maybe listening to the director or the dialogue coach or someone else tell him how to say the words right.

The actor's an old guy. He's lost most of his hair and his skin is loose with his veins showing through it. He walks with a limp, is blind in one eye and reportedly deaf in one ear, and his voice is weird because he had his voice box removed years ago, the result of throat cancer. When he finally comes out of the makeup room and starts dragging his butt in front of the camera, some people elbow each other and nod in his direction. Other people just keep doing what they were doing, getting on with their job.

Finally the old guy is where the director wants him. He forces a smile, closes his eyes to remember his first lines, and the director says, "Ready, Sonny?"

Sonny Barger, the soul of the Hells Angels, the meanest mother of the meanest gang of toughs that ever came out of the home of the brave and the land of the free, is acting in a cable TV show. Hell, why not? He's already the author of six books. Why not add some acting to his résumé? So who is this dude—the guy who set the tone for motorcycle rebels all over the world, or a geriatric Robert De Niro?

That's how far the Angels have come. The ultimate Hells Angel, the only guy who almost any biker anywhere in the world would call Sir if he was told to, is playing a pimp and being told where to stand, what to say, how to say it, and when he can take a break and go to the john.

SONNY IS NOBODY'S PATSY and never would be, of course. But seeing him looking like a street person who found some friends to clean him up for a day is a measure of how the Angels have changed. They're no longer who they were, or who they *thought* they were. They're what other people think they are or should be. So who are they being true to? Good question.

The Angels, and all the other motorcycle clubs (or MCs), started out with a fuzzy warm image. They were going to be brothers, knights of the open road, warriors of the highway and all that. Whether you liked or feared the Angels, you had to admire them for spitting in the eye of straight society, for not giving a damn what other people thought, and especially for riding hours on end just to be together, lost in the hum of their Harley-Davidsons.

You think that's the Angels today? Not the guys at the top. Not even close. A lot of the guys at the top of the Hells Angels Motorcycle Club (HAMC) are grandfathers, and they act like it. Will they ride for three days straight on a run so they can swill beer, sleep in a tent, and trade stories with other Angels? Like hell they will. They'll get a prospect—a Hells Angel wannabe—to load their Harley on a trailer and drive it where they want to go. Then they'll fly to wherever the run is being held, check into a Hilton or a Marriott, slip on their club colors, roll their bikes off the trailers, and spend a couple of days looking like badasses before flying home again.

Here's my point: the Angels are no longer bikers who commit crimes. They're criminals who ride bikes.

SO IF THE ANGELS have changed so much, why do they still wear their colors in public? Isn't that like waving a red flag at every cop they pass, not to mention rival gangs? Why do they still show that death's head on their backs and on clubhouse flags? Because it commands fear and respect. At least, that's what HAMC members think. The truth is, it creates less fear and respect than it did in the past. And all the stuff the Hells Angels did, or thought they did, was never as scary as the media and the cops claimed. That's at least one thing the Angels and the Mafia have in common—they built their image not just on reality but on perception.

The media love gangster stories. You want people to read a front-page story in a newspaper or jump their smartphones to a new website? Just use "Mafia Massacre" or "Biker Bloodbath" as a headline. Works every time. And every police department in the country knows that it can polish its image with Jack and Jill Middleclass by raiding the clubhouse of a local Hells Angels chapter and making sure the media take lots of pictures of the bikers sneering at the camera: your law enforcement tax dollars at work.

Eventually you couldn't tell the difference between cause and effect. Were the Angels harassed by the law because they were rough and dirty and dangerous? Or were they rough and dirty and dangerous because they were harassed by the law? Look into this long and deeply enough and you'll find yourself in a house of mirrors where you can't tell what's real and what's reflected back at you.

The other side of this media-frenzy law enforcement focus was to give straight people the impression that they knew what the Angels were all about: they rode bikes, they drank beer, they intimidated people, and they did what they wanted to whatever woman was stupid enough to hop on an Angel-owned Harley or wander into a Hells Angels clubhouse. The straights picked this up from those who claimed to know all about the inner workings of an HAMC, and even from researchers who took their pencils and clipboards with them when they interviewed Angels. Maybe one guy—Hunter S. Thompson—came close to getting it right when he wrote *Hell's Angels: The Strange and Terrible Saga of the Outlaw Motorcycle Gangs*,* but that was nearly fifty years ago. A lot of things have changed!

Nobody is going to walk into an MC's clubhouse and expect to get anything except a lot of bullshit and maybe a well-kicked ass, even if he's been invited. Bikers are notoriously secretive. It's a way of binding them together. If two people share a secret, they're careful about who they talk to and what they say. When thirty or forty bikers have secrets, they depend on everyone around them to keep their mouths shut.

It worked for the Angels. For a while. But as I said, time changes things. Pretty soon, there was a two-way street between law enforcement types and the Angels and biker clubs generally. Not a busy freeway, maybe; more like a country lane. You had bikers who didn't share the same feelings of brotherhood the early members had, when life was more about being free riders on the open road than about lining their pockets with cash. They started moving toward the police, usually to save their own butts. On the way, they'd pass some new MC recruits going in the other direction, police informers infiltrating the clubs to shine a light

---

* Thompson didn't get the name right. It's not *Hell's Angels*; it's *Hells Angels*. Bikers don't give a damn about apostrophes.

on the real action happening in the clubhouses or on the bikes during a run.

So the police had two sources of information about bike gang activities, which meant paper trails and testimony in court. On their own that's powerful stuff, but by the 1970s the cops also had RICO, the Racketeer Influenced and Corrupt Organizations Act, which provided serious penalties for anyone convicted of performing illegal acts on behalf of a criminal organization.

RICO meant that anyone at the head of an organization who ordered someone lower down to do something illegal—to blow somebody's head off with a double-barreled shotgun, say—was as guilty as the guy who pulled the trigger.

This gave law enforcement a big club to swing in nearly any direction and at almost any head it wanted.* The cops weren't always successful with RICO—California's Oakland HAMC chapter and Sonny Barger himself were targeted back in 1979 and beat the charges. Still, RICO was enough to persuade MCs to be a little more careful about what they did, how they did it, and who they let know about it.

RICO didn't slow down second-tier MC gangs, like the Devils Disciples and the Highwaymen, from wanting a share of the big money to be made from drugs and prostitution. And this is where the break between the old bike clubs and the newer organizations was made. In the 60s and 70s the question was, You want to ride free and take no shit from anybody? Join an MC. Sometime in the 1990s the question changed to, You want to make some easy money by kicking ass and maybe selling it? Join an MC.

---

* It wasn't just your everyday organized crime groups who were targeted, either. Among the various groups charged under RICO statutes were the Montreal Expos baseball club and American pro-life supporters who blocked access to abortion clinics and threatened clinic staff.

That's when the bikers' "colors" became mostly one color: green, like the back of an American dollar bill.

In effect, the Angels can be seen as two different organizations. One is a biker club ready to ride hard and raise hell. The other is a criminal organization with its eye on profit margins, competition, and expansion opportunities. The former is slipping away to oblivion. The latter is growing and prospering.

MOST PEOPLE WHO want to learn more about outlaw MCs than the media or the cops will tell them, read books by Hunter S. Thompson or Daniel Wolf or Sonny Barger. These give some idea of the way things used to be, but they won't tell you much about the beginnings of the Angels because everyone has a different view and nobody at the time thought about writing anything down.

Sonny Barger's book* should give the best insight into the Angels' beginnings and development, but unfortunately Sonny writes mostly about Sonny. His book tells us little about how the club grew into a worldwide organization.

This much we know is true: the media's fascination with MCs generally and the Hells Angels in particular grew first out of something called the Hollister Riot in July 1947. Hollister is a California town about a hundred kilometers south of San Jose, and the riot was a story that got more out of hand than the bikers ever did. *Life* magazine ran a full-page photograph of a drunk leaning back on a Harley-Davidson knucklehead engine, a bottle of beer in each hand and empty beer bottles lying on the road around him. The headline read "Cyclist's Holiday: He and Friends

---

* *Hell's [sic] Angel: The Life and Times of Sonny Barger and the Hell's Angels Motorcycle Club* (Avon, 2001).

Terrorize a Town," and the story claimed that gangs of motorcycle riders had wreaked havoc in Hollister all through the July Fourth weekend. The image was probably staged by the photographer, and the "terrorizing" consisted mostly of guys riding up and down the streets, sometimes whooping and hollering. They were also sleeping in parks and on the streets themselves, but that's because more riders showed up than had been expected. With no motel rooms available, they slept where they could.

All the riders—about four thousand, apparently—were welcomed by the bar owners and almost everyone else who ran a business, since they probably spent more money in one weekend than the businesses made all summer long. But a few beer bottles and punches got thrown, and when that picture appeared in *Life* with a readership numbering in the millions, the impact was enormous. Today, we'd say the story went viral. Whatever term they might have used back in 1947, it led to much of Middle America believing that barbarians were taking over.

The story became a snowball running down the side of a mountain. Once it started rolling, everything clung to it. Somebody—a law enforcement officer or an executive with the American Motorcyclist Association, nobody's sure—declared that 99 percent of people on motorcycles are good law-abiding citizens, a claim that created the "one percenters," the riders who said they were out to raise hell. *True Detective* magazine soon ran a fictional treatment of the Hollister "riot," with some sex tossed in amid the beer-drinking and fistfights, and *Harper's* kept the snowball rolling with a Hollister-based short story that became a Hollywood movie. When *The Wild One* premiered in theaters all over the world, featuring Marlon Brando in a black leather jacket astride a Triumph 650 cc Thunderbird (bad guy Lee Marvin rode a Harley-Davidson), the fable was fixed in the minds of people everywhere.

The idea that all these beer-swilling, leather-jacketed bikers were gang members was based at least a little on reality—more reality than *Life* and the rest of the media relied on. A few clubs already existed in California, including the Pissed Off Bastards of Bloomington (POBOB), the Boozefighters, the Market Street Commandos out of San Francisco, and the Galloping Goose MC, which began in Kansas but by then had spread to California.

The point is, the Hells Angels didn't exist back in 1947. The earliest claim about the formation of the club is that it happened in 1948 when a bunch of POBOB members and some others got together, probably inspired by the *Life* story, to lead the kind of life it depicted. The name "Hells Angels" had been used by one of the United States Air Force squadrons serving in China and Burma during World War II. Long before that, Howard Hughes titled a 1930 movie using the same name.

Sonny Barger claims he launched the HAMC in Oakland, but admits that other clubs with the same name popped up around the same time in San Francisco, Gardena, Fontana, and other places. About the only things we know for sure are that the San Francisco chapter, which some say was launched in 1953 by Rocky Graves, started using the familiar death's head logo designed by Frisco MC president Frank Sadilek, and that in 1959 Sonny Barger's Oakland chapter began sporting a larger rendition, which naturally became known as the Barger Larger version, the one still used today. Nobody calls it a logo. It's a *patch*. It helped make Barger the personification of everything the Angels stood for: guys who spit in the eye of "normal" society, take whatever the hell they want, and dare anybody to stop them.

So it all started coming together for the Angels in the early 1960s. They had a name, a logo/patch, a national leader, an image, and a reputation. They got famous enough and big enough to attract academics, people who figure that anything so famous and influential must be a good subject for a PhD thesis.

Like William Dulaney. No, wait a minute—there's nobody else like Bill Dulaney. For one thing, he's a professor at Western Carolina University. For another, he rode a 1953 Harley-Davidson Panhead as an outlaw rider for ten years, so he's had a foot in both worlds, the ivy-walled academic one and the greasy-fingernailed biker one.

Dulaney broke the history of motorcycle clubs into three sections, or periods. He called the first one the Preformative period, lasting from 1901 to 1944. It began with the launch of the Indian Motocycle (*sic*) Company. Harley-Davidson started selling motorcycles two years later, in 1903, which happens to be the same year that the Federation of American Motorcyclists began. FAM's goals were pretty straightforward and could have been written at a Rotary Club meeting:

> [The Federation's] objects shall be to encourage the use of motorcycles and to promote the general interests of motorcycling; to ascertain, defend and protect the rights of motorcyclists; to facilitate touring; to assist in the good roads movement; and to advise and assist in the regulation of motorcycle racing and other competition in which motorcycles engage.

The second, Formative, period lasted from 1945 to 1957, according to Dulaney. He explained that a lot of young servicemen returning home from the war were bored with civilian life and turned to riding motorcycles for recreation and excitement. Some of them had been trained to handle motorcycles in the war, but the biggest attraction may have been the bonds soldiers had made in combat. Think about it: you spend two or three years having people shoot at you, during which you learn to trust and protect your buddies. They have the same attitude toward you. When the war is over and you come back home, you miss the excitement and the connection you shared with your brothers-in-arms. Plus, you probably raised a little hell during the war, and maybe you'd like to keep doing it for a while.

Or maybe some of the things you saw and did shook you up so much that you need a way of dealing with the memories and nightmares. Today we call it post-traumatic stress disorder, or PTSD, and if you look around you can find people to help you deal with it, sometimes with medication, sometimes with counseling, and usually with both. But back in 1945–57 no one had heard of PTSD and no one was around to help you get over it. So what were your options? You could use booze or you could go riding on your Harley, and it was especially good when you could do both with a bunch of buddies who looked after you the way the guy in the next foxhole or tail-gunner hatch or lifeboat station would have just a couple of years earlier.

Is it any wonder so many young guys jumped at the chance to join an MC? And that a lot of them—probably more than the "one percent" law enforcement people claimed—decided to have a little fun while doing it? And when enough of them got together and organized themselves with rules, regulations, and eventually trademarked club logos, the world would become aware of Dulaney's third, Transformative, period of MC evolution, which began in 1958.

BY THEN MOTORCYCLE CLUBS recruiting one percenters were nearly as common as Boy Scout troops. Through the 1950s and 1960s new clubs popped up here and there, old clubs disbanded, and existing clubs either absorbed or merged according to what they did and how they described it.

Some new clubs survived, some didn't. In the mid-1960s the Sons of Silence grew out of Colorado, the Bandidos came out of Texas, and the Pagans were born in Pennsylvania. Meanwhile the Boozefighters, one of the original outlaw clubs, started fading away, and several members of the Pissed Off Bastards of Bloomington either joined or launched, depending on whom you believe, the Hells Angels in Frisco.

One of the things that kick-started the growth of outlaw MCs in the late 1960s was similar to the event that started everything rolling in 1947's July Fourth weekend in Hollister. When veterans came home from Vietnam they experienced many of the things their fathers had gone through a generation earlier. A lot of them were bored, suffering from PTSD, and missing the comradeship they'd relied on in 'Nam. But things were actually worse. Whereas their dads had come home as heroes, these guys came back from an unpopular war to be spat on and called baby killers. Also, the hardest drugs experienced by most Americans in World War II were alcohol and nicotine—beer and cigarettes. Big deal. Vietnam vets were familiar with a whole drugstore of narcotics—heroin, mescaline, hashish, you name it. They knew them, they used them, and many of them sold them.

Oh, and one more thing: sex. The Pill and other 60s developments had loosened up America and the rest of the world. Things that hadn't been talked about or were swept under the carpet, or in the case of the Mann Act, which prohibited "the interstate transport of females for immoral purposes," were either no longer valid or out in the open. So when "raising a little hell" by an MC meant grabbing a girl when and where available, it all fell into place for bikers.

Or not.

The thing is, the world was ready to buy anything that was said or printed about cycle gangs, especially if it involved violence, law breaking, and, thanks to Sonny Barger, the Hells Angels.

In 1964, when two young women in Monterey, California, claimed they'd been abducted and raped at an Angels club rally, everyone on the outside was ready to believe it. They *wanted* to believe it, because these hairy, greasy, unwashed guys looked and acted the part of drug-crazed rapists. Statements like "It's about time these hoodlums were put in their place!" were made by a lot of people who didn't know what the hell was going on. They especially didn't know, or didn't care, that the charges were eventually dropped owing to a lack of evidence. Which didn't stop the cries to "do something!"

California State Attorney Thomas C. Lynch responded to these demands the way all politicians do when voters want blood: he launched an investigation into outlaw motorcycle clubs. The 1965 Lynch Report confirmed the worst nightmares of good folk everywhere. Outlaw motorcycle clubs, the report declared, represented a clear and present danger to local, state, national, and even international constituencies. The report also launched various urban legends, including the alleged gang raping of young women and the plundering of some California townships.

Reactions to the Lynch Report depended on who and where you were. If you were a media outlet, you could run a week of features based on the report's allegations and know that every word would be devoured by shocked readers who demanded more details. If you were a politician, you could call for new laws to rein in these hoodlums, and earn a few extra votes in the next election. And if you were in law enforcement, you could make a point of harassing the hell out of the clubs at every opportunity.

But if you were a guy in his late teens or early twenties who sure as hell didn't want a nine-to-five job with wife, mortgage, kids, and dog, an outlaw MC started looking like a way to have a lot of fun, earn a lot of respect, and, eventually, make a lot of money.

And no one seemed to promise more of it than the Angels.

2

CAUGHT IN THE MIDDLE WITH YOU

You always hear them before you see them, and when you see them you wish you hadn't.

When a Hells Angels chapter is on a run, sometimes with other chapters riding with them, those dozens of Harley-Davidsons blast out a pulsating roar that precedes them down the highway. It works just as an overture does in a Broadway play: get ready, people, the curtain is about to go up on a scary show filled with characters and costumes, drama and danger. People in the front rows should be prepared to duck out of the way of bullets, knives, blood, and various other disgusting stuff.

Then they're in your rear-view mirror, coming up fast behind you. If you're a charter member of Middle America, proud of your split-level house and regular pay check, you'll probably advise others in the car not to stare as they pass, not to make any gestures, and especially not to do something *really* stupid, like give them the finger or show disrespect.

They fly by your car in the next lane, two abreast and in

close formation even at a hundred kilometers an hour, looking as relaxed as if they were sitting back in an easy chair instead of guiding a quarter-ton of metal and rubber on two wheels. You glance over and see only beards, shaggy hair, greasy denim, angry expressions, dark glasses, and, on their backs, a grinning skull with wings.

If only half the gang passes you before oncoming traffic forces some to remain behind, you're caught in the middle of thirty, forty, fifty, or more men (and in some cases, their "old ladies"). You grip the steering wheel a little tighter and coast along uncomfortably until they vanish up the road, their thunder flooding back. Then you take your first deep breath since you heard them approach from behind.

In a way, a Hells Angels run really is just street theater. You're the audience and you're meant to be intimidated, because intimidation is part of their overall strategy, even down to the sound of their motorcycles.

It's impossible to think of a Hells Angel motorcycle and not think of Harley-Davidson. Its sound is unique, and thanks to the Hells Angels' almost exclusive use of Harleys, the two have become synonymous.

The sound originated with the design of the Harley engine. Other motorcycle manufacturers long ago went from two- to four-cylinder designs for extra smoothness and power. Not Harley-Davidson. Adding more cylinders means adding more parts and more complexity. And smoothness is for pussies. Harley-Davidson engines have always had two cylinders set in a V arrangement at a forty-five-degree angle. It's a fine design for a bike meant to travel through cities or on short trips. But it's a bone-shaker when the engine displacement is 1700 cc, or 103 cubic inches.

It's not just the size, however; it's the design—one that hasn't changed substantially in seventy-five years. When the cylinders are set horizontally with a common crankcase and separate pins on the crankshaft (BMW motorcycles are the best-known brand to use this arrangement), it's easy to set them up so that each cylinder fires alternately, giving the engine a balanced feel. But the Harley-Davidson engine, designed to pack the maximum amount of potential power in the smallest space, uses an unbalanced placement of the pistons on the crankshaft, so the pistons can't fire at even intervals. That's why Harleys don't sound smooth-running when they're idling. Instead of a steady hum, a Harley-Davidson sounds as though it's saying "potato, potato, potato." Something about it sounds vaguely threatening to the ear, which, thanks to the Hells Angels' preference for Harleys, became a real selling point for the brand. Not everyone could grow a beard and look as mean and menacing as an Angel, but hey, we could all ride the same motor-cycles and get something of a rush that way.

The sound of a Harley became so important that when Japanese motorcycle manufacturers like Honda and Kawasaki began marketing their heavy-duty bikes in the 1980s, Harley-Davidson set out to trademark the Harley's distinctive sound. The Japanese opposed the idea and won, but Harley-Davidson had made its point: the sound of their bikes was a selling point in itself.

Other aspects of Harley-Davidson bikes weren't always as appreciated. For much of the 1970s the company suffered from serious quality-control problems that were solved with only partial success. Even today, many people believe Harley-Davidsons to be overpriced and under-engineered—including Sonny Barger himself, who has criticized their quality. "I ride them because I'm in the club," he's written, "and that's the image, but if I could I would seriously consider riding a Honda ST1100 or a BMW. We really missed the boat not switching over to the Japanese models when they began building bigger bikes."*

None of this matters. Hells Angels ride Harleys, and if you thought the Harley-Davidson company might be scandalized or even a little embarrassed by being associated with such criminal riffraff, you'd be wrong. They love the connection and have even sought to exploit it. After Angels began referring to Harley-Davidsons (usually modified to make them leaner and louder) as hogs, the company attempted to register the nickname at the same time as they tried to trademark the sound. They failed here as well.

SO WHEN THE SOUND of the Harley-Davidsons and the beards, denim, and attitude finally vanish somewhere up the road, it's tempting to feel at least a little smug. *You* don't ride a heavy, underpowered, overpriced motorcycle spewing oil and noise across the land; you've got your safe, comfortable SUV complete with air conditioning, satellite radio, rear-facing camera, DVD player for the kids, and a dozen or so airbags for safety. They may have intimidated you and your family without even acknowledging your presence, but they're still a ragged batch of bums. When it comes to success, you're doing a lot better than they are.

Or maybe not.

The chapter of the outlaw motorcycle gang that just passed you—Hells Angels, Bandidos, Mongols, Rock Machine, or any of more than a dozen others—may well make more money in a week than you make in a year. They do it without working very hard,

---

* Sonny Barger, *Hell's Angel: The Life and Times of Sonny Barger and the Hell's Angels Motorcycle Club*, p. 53.

without punching a clock every day, and without worrying about withholding tax or social security payments or early-morning meetings or a carefully chosen wardrobe. And across North America there are hundreds of such chapters.

The very image of a Hells Angels clubhouse sets some people's teeth on edge. They assume that finding yourself within shooting range of such a place could put your life at risk. Or that, if you're a female virgin, you'd risk losing something else.

The reality is somewhat different. The Angels clubhouse in El Cajon, California, where I spent many hours hanging out, was no better and no worse than the average sports bar in towns all across the southwestern United States. In many places, those living near an Angels clubhouse note that petty crime in their neighborhood is practically nonexistent: after all, the Angels won't tolerate hoodlums spreading graffiti or mugging local residents, and the hoodlums know it. It's a relatively small but significant way of explaining how the Angels manage to survive and thrive despite the fact that law enforcement, social opinion, and media depiction all appear to be against them.

In fact, it's the idea that the world is against them that gives the Angels and their brethren things they wouldn't otherwise get and usually haven't experienced anywhere else—things like brotherhood, security, friendship, and in the widest sense of the word, love. It's difficult to talk about such things in a milieu where the wrong word, the wrong look, or the wrong patch on the back of your vest can get you shot, stabbed, or maimed. But it's true—and it's vital in explaining so much of the mystique and success of the Angels, the Mongols, the Bandidos, and others.

William Queen, a special agent with the U.S. Bureau of Alcohol, Tobacco and Firearms (ATF), went underground for two years to infiltrate the California Mongols MC. He proved so successful that he was fully patched and then elected secretary-treasurer of the San Fernando Valley chapter of one of the toughest bike gangs in the country, all the while building a mountain of evidence that would result in charges laid against forty-two club members and long prison terms handed out for offenses ranging from possession of stolen property (usually motorcycles) to first-degree murder.

In his book on the experience,* Queen describes one of the most difficult experiences he encountered as a member of the club: it involved not the raft of assaults and drug deals he witnessed, but his return to the gang following the funeral of his mother.

Queen, who grew up in North Carolina, told both his law enforcement handlers and his Mongol brothers about his mother's death and how he'd need three days to travel to her home and attend the funeral. It was an emotional journey for him, and when he returned to Los Angeles to resume his dangerous work, the first Mongol member he met, Philip "Evel" Alarcon, hugged him, said he was sorry to hear about his mother, and told him he loved him. "And at that moment I didn't want to send him to prison," Queen wrote. "I slumped into his tattered beer-stained sofa, holding back tears."

Some "ancient wall" inside Queen began to crumble at that point, and it continued to fall as each Mongol expressed his concern and affection for the man who, within a few months, would be instrumental in seeing that they spent the next several years in a prison cell. Meanwhile, "No one from the ATF realized I was just another number to the ATF. I wasn't Bill Queen, a flesh-and-blood man; I was ATF badge number 489."† Queen's experience revealed the power that resides within these MCs: the bond between gang members that gives them a means of dealing with and separating

---

* William Queen, *Under and Alone* (Random House, 2005).
† Ibid, pp. 187–188.

from the rest of the world, whose attitude toward them is openly hostile.

Of course, the MCs work at maintaining that attitude, and they are remarkably successful at it.

ONE OF THE BEST WAYS to understand both the phenomenon and the influence of MCs, and Hells Angels in particular, is to look back in history—about two thousand years back. That's when the so-called civilized world was ruled by the Romans.

For at least five hundred years, no one challenged the Romans on their own turf, and they kept expanding that turf. At its height, around 100 AD, the Pax Romana covered five million square kilometers, extending north to Scotland, south to Egypt, west to Spain, and east to Iraq and beyond. There has never been a bigger empire in history, and the Romans did it without cars, trains, planes, or powered ships. They travelled by foot and by horseback for the most part. So what was their secret? Organization, discipline, determination, and ruthlessness. As soon as word spread that the Romans were arriving, people either got out of Dodge or gave up entirely. Any army that chose to take on the Romans soon found itself obliterated. Eventually, the Roman army's reputation was as effective in controlling its enemies as its legions of well-trained fighters. The Romans didn't have to swing their swords or thrust their spears to win. They just had to show up.

Nothing lasts forever. The Roman Empire ended around 500 AD, although it wasn't a now-you-see-it-now-you-don't event. Depending on which historian you believe, its decline began about two hundred years earlier, when all kinds of things started going wrong, including political infighting and economic depression. Those were bad enough, but during all this time the empire and the city itself were being attacked by barbarians who lacked the discipline and organization of Rome at its best.

Other factors played a role as well, but I'm not about to do a historical analysis of Rome's fall. There must be thousands of PhD theses on the breakup of the biggest empire in world history, written by those who studied it for years and still came up with different conclusions. The reasons ranged from the Black Death and lead-dish poisoning to the impact of Christianity and infighting among military leaders.

If you were looking for a single cause that could encompass all of these factors, you might turn to Edward Gibbon, who in his book *The Decline and Fall of the Roman Empire* put it like this: "The decline of Rome was the natural and inevitable effect of immoderate greatness. Prosperity ripened the principle of decay, and the causes of destruction multiplied with the extent of conquest." Or, to put it another way, the Romans just didn't give a damn as much as they used to.

From the mid-1950s to the mid-1990s the Hells Angels ruled the biker world every bit as much as the Romans ruled the civilized world of their time. And like the Romans, the Angels developed a sense of entitlement. When a Roman general marched his troops into a village in Europe or Britain two thousand years ago, all he had to say was "We are Romans. Put down your weapons, give us your valuables, and stay out of our way." This worked for Rome for five or more centuries. It worked for the Angels for about forty years.

The release of the Lynch Report coincided with other events, including Hunter S. Thompson's book and *Hells Angels on Wheels*, a so-so 1967 movie starring a young Jack Nicholson and the real Sonny Barger in his first scripted role as an actor. By 1969 the Angels myth was born. They were the New Romans whose very presence caused fear among those aware of their reputation, earned or not. Instead of dispensing peace via the Pax Romana, the Angels dispensed drugs and protection for a price.

One of the great ironies of the Angels is that they built their earliest and most impressive reputation as two-wheeled barbarians in the middle of California's Peace and Love culture. By now almost everyone knows about the December 1969 concert at Altamont Speedway near San Francisco, when, despite warnings from Michelle Phillips of the Mamas and the Papas, promoters hired the Hells Angels for security. "The Angels were fighting with everybody for no reason," Phillips said. "They were throwing full cans of beer, bouncing them off people's heads." The Angels, Phillips suggested, wouldn't add security to the event; they would generate insecurity. Someone didn't listen. In exchange for $500 worth of beer, the Angels cordoned off the front of the low stage to prevent anyone reaching the musicians.

From the beginning, it was a disaster waiting to happen. Even before the Rolling Stones took the stage as the headline act, Phillips was proven correct when Marty Balin of the Jefferson Airplane was knocked unconscious when he tangled with a Hells Angels security guard.

Almost with the first note of the Rolling Stones' set, violence began breaking out in the crowd, all of it involving the Hells Angels, who set upon anyone they deemed unruly or just disrespectful with pool cues and fists. When they encountered teenage Meredith Hunter, who tried to defend himself with a gun, he was stabbed from behind, then beaten (or more correctly, stomped) to death.* Alan Passaro, the Angel charged with stabbing Hunter, was acquitted

---

* One faction familiar with the case claimed that the Angels, who've been associated with white supremacist groups, chose to attack the African-American Hunter because his date was an attractive blond girl.

of a murder charge after pleading self-defense. Passaro himself was found drowned in a water reservoir under what local police called "kind of suspicious" circumstances, but no one was ever charged.

With Hunter's death, Mick Jagger, who'd been calling for peace throughout the few songs the Stones had been able to perform to that point, said the concert was over. The band fled in helicopters.

Later, when Sonny Barger demanded more payment for the Angels' services and the Rolling Stones rejected the claim, Barger spread the word that he was putting out a $50,000 contract on Jagger's life. Whether he was serious about it or not, the announcement concerned the Stones enough that they paid Barger and his gang the $50,000 to call off the hit.

Barger, of course, accepted the deal.

And the Power of the Patch was born.

IT'S DIFFICULT TO DETERMINE whether the Angels' expansion was a rolling wave moving under its own power or a conscious effort by Sonny Barger to build an empire of chartered branch plants. More likely it was a combination of the two—the idea of establishing a local HAMC chapter in towns and cities east of San Bernardino, California, had begun in the early 1960s, and both Altamont and Sonny's subsequent threat helped it build speed.

But it wasn't always easy. Many parts of the United States outside of California were enemy territory. Motorcycle clubs, after all, had predated the Angels by a few years, and members of the Outlaws, the Pagans, and other clubs tended to resist the Angels' invasion. Nonetheless, one way or another the Angels became established and, in most locales, dominated the biker gang culture there. The most notable exception was, of all places, Kansas City, Missouri.

Kansas City? The home of good steaks and decent blues? What did KC have that might trip up Sonny Barger's hell-raising boys?

The Galloping Goose MC.

That name isn't likely to sound familiar. Other clubs, including the Angels, have a much higher profile and a wider reputation. Besides, as a club name, "Galloping Goose" just doesn't have the same threatening ring as do the Outlaws, Pagans, Bandidos, Rebels, and Warlocks. This, along with their compact area of influence, limited their notoriety as far as the general public was concerned. But, as the Angels discovered, it did not restrict their attitude toward newcomers.

The Galloping Goose MC was born, like the Angels and virtually every other outlaw MC, in California. About a dozen members were listed in the early 1940s, at least some of whom appeared at the infamous Hollister "riot" in 1947. Soon after Hollister, members worked out a deal with the El Forasteros MC, and the Goose focus shifted to Kansas City. It was a strange arrangement. Each club kept its own colors, and even shared the same clubhouse while defending each other's interests. They also proved effective by focusing on four elements: bikes, strippers, guns, and drugs.

In that respect the Galloping Goose may not have differed from dozens of other clubs across the country. But their sense of independence and isolation on the Great Plains of America may have fostered a different outlook on the Angels than other clubs and other communities had. Rather than welcoming or at least tolerating HAMC's arrival in Kansas City, the Goose basically told them to get lost. And in 1980, when membership reached two hundred, the club made two critical decisions that formally strengthened their power and position.

The first was to shut down the club to new members. No one would be allowed to join or even to apply for membership for the next twenty years. It was a decision that almost every MC executive, from Sonny Barger down, would find confusing, even maddening. Close the club to new members? For twenty years? How was the club supposed to grow and build power, not to mention make bigger profits?

Goose members didn't care. Shutting the club down to new members meant they didn't have to worry about infiltrators— police plants who would spy and report on the club's activities. As a result, no one managed to get a real handle on any secret activities by the Galloping Goose for a very long time, leaving them with an almost free hand to do whatever they felt they had to do.

The other decision was to establish and enforce the Hundred Mile Rule, which meant the Goose wouldn't tolerate any other outlaw MC within that radius of their clubhouse. This presented a solid benefit to Goose members. No other outlaw gangs meant no serious competition in the rackets they were running. But it also presented a challenge: Kansas City sits at the crossroads of two major interstate highways near the geographical center of the continental United States, making it the ideal place to launch an outlaw MC. And for a time, a few of them tried.

Any effort to start a competitor to the Galloping Goose within the hundred-mile circle would kick off a three-stage process. In the first stage, a couple of Goose members would visit the new MC to say it was time to move on—drop the idea of a club and get the hell out of town. If the lesson wasn't learned, the second stage consisted of a beating or two with an "or else!" attached to it. Stage three was serious, just in case the new guys still didn't get the message. It consisted of extreme violence, sometimes causing death.

After a few years of applying their Hundred Mile Rule, stages two and three became unnecessary.

The Galloping Goose evolved into a gang that rejected the all-attitude approach of many Angels chapters who, often correctly, believed they had only to show up and swagger to get what they wanted. Goose members had the same swagger, but they also had a deeper approach to getting things done. Best example: the club patch includes the initials MF. Most people believe it stands for Mother Fucker. That's what other MCs assume.

In reality, it stands for Mute Forever.

ELSEWHERE, THE SPREAD of the Angels across North America was complex and uncompromising. Here's an example.

In the early 1970s, Sandy Alexander, in a New York HAMC chapter, got Pastor James "Oats" Oldfield to create an Angels chapter in Charleston, South Carolina. (The "Pastor" title is real; Oldfield would bless any motorcycle, whether the owner was an Angel or not.) Several high-ranking Angels from Fayetteville and Durham abandoned their chapters to join the new Charleston chapter, including influential members Spook Sosebee and Artie Ray Cherry.

Sosebee and Cherry represented the orthodox Angel type—the type that the Angels wanted everyone to believe populated every HAMC chapter. When Spook Sosebee was almost sixty years old he encountered Jim Moye at Wallbangers, a Charlotte bar considered Angels territory. Moye, a member of the Iron Cross MC, had stopped in for a drink, unaware that it was an Angels bar. Sosebee proceeded to beat Moye with the handle of his Bowie knife. Then he placed the blade of the knife to Moye's throat and demanded that the Iron Cross member hand over his colors. When Moye refused, and asked to leave the bar, Sosebee thrust the blade of the knife into the other biker's body.

Moye survived, after undergoing emergency surgery. Saying the stabbing had been "a motorcycle thing," he refused to identify Sosebee as his attacker. Someone did, however, and in December 2011 Spook was found guilty of attempted armed robbery, kidnapping, possession of a knife during a violent crime, and first-degree assault and battery, all of which got him a ten-year prison sentence without any chance of parole.

Artie Ray Cherry was even less lucky. Cherry, who'd been on the run for two years after stabbing a soldier who failed to show him sufficient respect, got himself into a barroom brawl in Rock Hill, South Carolina, in early 1982. It was a bad decision; one of the other brawlers had arrived armed, and sometime during the brawl Cherry was shot four times.

DESPITE THESE MINOR SETBACKS, the expansion continued, an eastbound wave rolling out of California. And when it reached the East Coast, it kept rolling right across the Atlantic.

In the same year as Altamont, the first chartered Hells Angels club outside North America appeared in London, England. It had taken some time for the Angels to spread beyond California and through the Midwest to New York and elsewhere. That spread might have been considered inevitable, given the Angels' jingoistic, pro-American posture and their dedication to ideals that sound as though they were lifted directly out of some unfamiliar corner of the Constitution—one that promoted freedom, independence, and unfettered access to the joys of the open road.

But stiff-upper-lip Brits, with their teapots, pomp, and ceremony? What was the appeal?

There were several attractions, no doubt, but the one that probably dominated all others was the same one that Sonny Barger had recognized and exploited years earlier: the power to take whatever you wanted, under the right circumstances and from the right people, just by establishing a reputation and threatening to live up to it.

If it worked in London as well as it had worked in San Berdoo, it could work elsewhere as well. And it did. By 1980 Europe boasted over a hundred Angels chapters, with more in Australia and New Zealand. In 1984 a Hells Angels chapter appeared in Rio de Janeiro, and within another ten years a chapter opened in Johannesburg. Soon after the fall of the Iron Curtain, the Angels' death's head symbol appeared in countries all across Eastern Europe, replacing the hammer and sickle as an emblem of power and intimidation.

Sonny Barger's small Berdoo chapter had effectively spawned the biggest motorcycle brotherhood in the world. And it was intent on being known as the baddest.

3

ANGELS IN DIFFERENT HEAVENS

We tend to link organized crime with its country of origin. The Mafia will always be associated with Italy, the Triads with China, the Yakuza with Japan, the Russian mob with somewhere east of Moscow, and so on. Each organization reflects the culture it grew out of. Change the culture and you change the organization's focus, goals, and chances of success. In the case of the Hells Angels, becoming an international organization did not prove as successful as they expected. After all, Düsseldorf is not San Diego, London is not Chicago, and Amsterdam is not Kansas City.

Biker gangs reflected the American postwar culture, the one that said "Don't mess with us because we're tough, we're free, we're independent, and we take no shit from anyone." You can attach this kind of thinking to prominent Americans ranging from Billy the Kid to John Wayne, with maybe a little Bonnie and Clyde tossed in.

The basic qualities are admirable. Who can object to a sense of independence and freedom? The Declaration of Independence was literally built on the idea, and it has inspired people all over the world for more than two hundred years. The problem comes when no moral code is attached to the concept. For the Hells Angels, the model of freedom and independence isn't John Wayne. It's Billy the Kid.

SONNY BARGER and his followers across the United States had their own clear vision of what the Angels stood for and what they should become. International chapters of the HAMC, especially in Germany and Scandinavia, liked the Angels' media image but disagreed with the day-to-day approach. For example, the U.S. represents the world's biggest market for illegal drugs like cocaine and heroin. The rest of the world serves that market. The Americans are consumers; people elsewhere are more likely to be producers and distributors.

Geography has an influence as well. The United States, especially its southwest region where the Angels were born, is a wide-ranging landscape where bikers can ride for hours without encountering major metropolitan areas. It opens their horizons and reminds them of what bike riding is all about. When you go for a biker run in California, Nevada, Arizona, and almost anywhere else on the Great Plains states, it's a real *run,* not a commute. You need a good bike, a lot of stamina, and the support of your brothers to get it done. In most of Europe, meanwhile, you're never more than twenty or thirty kilometers away from the next community, the next place where you have to gear down and cruise slowly, weaving through marketplaces and school zones. It's a closed-in approach to biking, and it's one more way the differences are measured among MCs, especially the Angels.

So when people in the media and law enforcement speak of

the international influence of the Hells Angels, the first question to be asked is "Which Hells Angels are you referring to?" The next question may even be "Influence? Just who is influencing whom?"

NO MATTER HOW you measure it—by miles or kilometers, by language, by history, or by culture—it's a long way from San Bernardino, California, to Jakarta, Indonesia. It's almost impossible to find any common ground between them, although it's easier if you start by looking at those living in poverty, and specifically at young men growing up full of anger and ambition. They're everywhere, and given the right conditions, they all behave in similar ways in response to similar incentives.

Guys like Aditya, for example, who would do anything to escape the slums. Aditya had felt that way since he was a young boy, hanging around the docks in Muara Angke, the coastal section of Jakarta bordering the worst of the Jakarta slums.

He had lots of time on his hands to think about getting away from Muara Angke, with its constant smell of fish, the noise of boats and vendors that went on all night, the hopeless future that most young people believed it held. Their fathers and grandfathers had worked the dock for a subsistence income, and they were expected to do the same.

Aditya was a little different. His father didn't work the docks. He spent the day drinking with other men who lacked work and didn't give a damn. Aditya's mother worked shelling mussels for local residents, bringing in barely enough money to keep the family alive. Neither parent gave much thought to how their son spent his day. By the time Aditya was a teenager, he had given up on school and vice versa. The boy had found something more interesting and, in its own way, more educational.

He began to follow people. He would choose someone, anyone, at random, pretending he was a spy and they were his target, following them home, learning their routine, becoming their shadow without their even knowing he existed.

He acquired notebooks to record all that he saw and heard about his targets, down to the clothes they wore from day to day, the foods he watched them eat, and the friends they met with.

In his mid-teens, his father abandoned the family, and while Aditya's uncle in Amsterdam sent a little money from time to time, it was hardly enough. Which is when Aditya began cashing in on his notes and his expertise at watching and following without being seen. He knew who lived alone, and who had things likely worth stealing—jewelry or appliances he could sell for cash on the street.

It worked. Who needed a regular job? He could enter any home or apartment he chose, take what he wanted, and leave like a houseguest. It was easy.

In fact, it was too easy. He began to miss the challenge. He needed a way to spice things up, to enhance the fun and the profit. So by his late teens he began following and robbing women exclusively. Women who lived alone. Pretty young women who lived alone, breaking in while they were home. That way, he could take the jewelry they wore during the day. In fact, he could take anything he wanted, and he did. He even began giving them names and pretending they were his women.

Then, at some point, burglary, robbery, and sexual assault were no longer enough.

HE CALLED HER Pretty Girl, which wasn't original but it described her well. In fact her name was Eka, but this never interested him.

Naming her became part of his means of possessing her. He'd call her what he wanted, and he'd do what he wanted with her.

He'd been following her for weeks. He never saw anyone else enter her apartment, and he knew that she arrived home from work at eight every evening and turned out her lights at nine-thirty.

At seven in the evening he stood on the garbage bin beneath her kitchen window, pulling himself into her small apartment. He chose a large butcher knife from the drawer, telling himself it was for his own protection, although he didn't believe it. Then he settled himself near the apartment door and waited in the dark.

She was late getting home that evening, twenty minutes late in fact. But when he heard the key enter the lock and saw the doorknob turn, he was ready. When she walked into the apartment and turned her back to close the door he seized her by the hair with one hand, pulling her body against him. With the other hand he drew the knife across her throat, severing her arteries and windpipe. Blood spewed against the wall like water from a fountain, and when he released her she fell to the floor on her back, looking up at him, her eyes open and her severed windpipe making a gurgling noise.

She seemed to be staring at him in amazement. Was she dead already, or at least unconscious? He didn't know. He recalled being told that the eyes retain the last image their owner sees at death, and Pretty Girl's last image would be of him. This wouldn't do. He knelt beside her and plunged the knife into and through her eye sockets, pushing it all the way until the point reached the back of her skull, first one, then the other. Then he sat next to her and held her hand. She had never looked prettier to him than she did at that moment.

He jumped at the knock on the door and the sound of a woman's voice. "Nyonya," (Madam) the woman called. "Are you all right?" She tried the door, which Pretty Girl hadn't locked. She pushed the door open against Pretty Girl's body and stood frozen for a moment, trying to make sense of the dead girl and the blood. Before she could react, Aditya stepped forward and thrust the knife into the older woman's stomach, seizing her around the waist with his free hand to pull her to him, then withdrawing the knife and driving it into her over and over again. With each thrust the woman appeared to leap from the floor. He kept doing it in an erotic frenzy, finally dropping the woman onto Eka's body before locking the door and staggering into her bedroom. He was exhausted. He stripped off his blood-soaked shirt and managed to slip into one of Eka's sweatshirts. Then he lay down on her bed while her fragrance enveloped him, and fell asleep there.

HE WOKE AN HOUR LATER in total darkness, sensing immediately that he needed to get to work. But first he needed food. He was famished.

He made a sandwich in the kitchen, drank a glass of water, then spent a few minutes washing blood from his face and hands.

He left the apartment the same way he entered it, through the kitchen window onto the garbage bin, down the stairs and on his way. The two bodies he left behind were butchered so violently that the sight horrified the most hardened of the Jakarta police who investigated the crime.

WHEN ADITYA ARRIVED HOME his mother needed only one glance at him to know that he'd committed some dreadful crime. She didn't know what it was. She didn't want to know. But she knew what needed to be done.

The first thing she did was to bury her son's clothes in a yard behind the apartment house. The next thing was to call his uncle in

Amsterdam and explain that Aditya needed to get out of Indonesia as soon as possible. The uncle understood. He immediately wired Aditya an electronic air ticket, and his nephew was soon on his way to Amsterdam, the city of canals, diamond cutters, Rembrandt, the Rijksmuseum ... and the Satudarah motorcycle club.

SATUDARAH MC—the word means "One Blood" in Indonesian—was founded in the Netherlands in 1990 and has since expanded into Belgium, Spain, Indonesia, Malaysia, and Germany. Unlike most one-percenter MCs, Satudarah welcomes all races as members. It's not unusual to find bikers from Morocco, Surinam, Turkey, the Dutch Antilles (Aruba, Bonaire, Curaçao), and elsewhere riding with Satudarah patches. This openness to other nationalities and races has helped the Satudarah grow much bigger in the Netherlands than the Hells Angels, who are far more restrictive about who they admit as members. It also helps them grow much richer and substantially more violent.

The violence grows in part from the Satudarah's relationship with the Bandidos of Germany, who hate the Angels with a passion. Many of the German Bandidos are ethnic Turks, who can find buddies from their own country among the Satudarah but none among the Angels. In MCs as everywhere else, blood is always thicker than water, and the Turks tend to band together no matter whose patch they're wearing.

All those different cultures within the Satudarah give them more opportunities to make contacts in money-making businesses, like dealing drugs through Western Europe. Check a map for those ABC islands of the Dutch Antilles and see how close they are to South America. Aruba is less than two hundred kilometers off the coast of Colombia. Drugs can be obtained almost anywhere in the world these days, and thanks to some serious efforts by its government, Colombia is no longer the world's largest source of cocaine. But for many years, having a buddy, or a buddy's brother, living a half hour's flight from the country simplified the import business.

HELLS ANGELS HOLLAND got off on the wrong foot when a guy named Willem van Boxtel and his friends decided to name their MC Hells Angels without receiving permission from the main chapter in San Bernardino. This got them in trouble with both Sonny Barger and the local police. Barger snarled and threatened until finally granting them a charter ten years later. Shortly after Barger granted his approval, the Netherlands police arrested van Boxtel and eleven other members for assault. Nothing stuck, and in October 2003 Angels arrived in Holland from various countries to celebrate the chapter's twenty-fifth anniversary.

But things weren't all that friendly between the Netherlands HAMC members and the Satudarah, who were intent on proving they were tougher and more ruthless than the Angels. This was the can of worms that Aditya walked into when he arrived in Amsterdam looking for assistance from his uncle. He needed money desperately, he told him. If he had to, he would kill for it. He confessed that he already had.

The uncle had a close relationship with the Satudarah, who, as it turned out, were looking for a fresh face who would follow orders and didn't have too many scruples about killing people. With an offer of US$5000 cash and a chance to build a reputation as a hit man, Aditya was handed a contract. And just to stroke his ego a little more, he would be whacking not just any guy on the street but a top-level member of the Hells Angels. This, Aditya figured, would establish him as a guy to be respected. And the US$5000 would be more money than he'd ever seen.

He could hardly wait to get started.

The men putting out the contract were members of the Satudarah MC. They showed Aditya a photograph of the target, ordered him to use a gun, told him where to do the job and what to do when it was completed. They would take care of him.

So a few days later, Aditya, confident that he was about to become Europe's most feared hit man, leaned against the wall of a train station on Hollands Spoor, a spur line in The Hague. Not the best station in the city. A little dark and shabby compared with the bigger and brighter Central Station, which, of course, made it all the more suitable.

He stood watching his target, the gun in his pocket. He would have preferred a knife. Knives are more personal: you use them up close, you can feel the ease of the blade entering flesh and the resistance when it encounters bone, feel the target jerk and tremble. But he was excited anyway. Killing, he decided, was his passion. And to be paid for doing something he loved to do anyway … well, life didn't get any better than that.

Had he been more in touch with reality, Aditya would not have been as confident in his new career. He'd been dropping clues like breadcrumbs since leaving Jakarta. Interpol had been alerted to suspicions of a brutal murderer in the city, and to his connections. The Amsterdam police were familiar with his uncle—who, as well as his association with the Satudarah MC, was a prominent drug dealer and pimp—and were taking an interest in his newly arrived nephew. And there was more for Aditya to worry about, had he known enough to worry.

ADITYA'S TARGET was a large man, a respectable-looking man despite his neatly combed ponytail. He wore designer jeans, and his leather jacket was nicely tailored—not a biker jacket at all, just a pricey fashion garment. The duffel bag swung over his shoulder confirmed that he was about to board a train for parts unknown, just as thousands of other Netherlanders or tourists at railroad stations do all across the country.

When he was younger and more vulnerable, careful of every move he made, he might have been aware of the dark-skinned guy who'd followed him from the hotel to the railroad station. He might have noticed that his shadow did not buy a train ticket and yet trailed him down the ramp toward the boarding platform. He might have watched the other man more closely, considering the dark-skinned guy's suspicious appearance: baseball cap, raggedy jeans, sad-looking worn windbreaker, oversized sunglasses.

But he didn't. Along with the other passengers, he stepped forward as the train approached. Behind him the dark-skinned younger man moved briskly toward the edge of the platform, withdrew the small .38 handgun from his jacket pocket, placed the muzzle to the back of the bigger man's head, and pulled the trigger. With his other hand he seized the duffel bag as the target's legs began to buckle, then pushed him off the edge of the platform directly in front of the oncoming train.

Then he stepped back while horrified onlookers screamed, most of them turning away from the sight of the target's body being crushed by the train. He turned and walked calmly away.

"He must have jumped," someone said, meaning what was left of the big man with the well-combed hair and the classy leather jacket. Aditya smiled when he heard that. He was still smiling as he dropped the gun in a waste container and left the station, stepping into the cool air of a winter's day.

Right on cue a car pulled to the curb in front of him, the rear window rolled down. He tossed the duffel bag through the window, pleased with himself and thinking of how he would spend the five thousand American dollars. He was about to stretch his hand into the car to receive his payment when the driver turned and said, "Here's your reward."

He must have seen the gun, although it would have taken a millisecond or two to understand what it was and what it meant. He would surely have seen the flash from the muzzle, but only just as the bullet hit him square in the face and drove him back against the dozens of bicycles parked against the station wall. He lay against them, the wheels and spokes and rubber tires, as the car pulled into traffic and disappeared.

Everything had been captured by video cameras and recorded. The Netherlands police looked at the sequence over and over. They were watching a classic Hollywood gangster movie, except that this one was shot in the Netherlands and the actors and the action were real.

THE SHOOTING in The Hague was just one in a series of killings that occurred between 2003 and 2010. In almost all of them, Hells Angels were the victims. The killings were bad enough. The Angels' dumb moves and the number of times they were double-crossed just made them worse—and destroyed forever the image of the Hells Angels Netherlands as the toughest MC in Europe. Compared with the Satudarah, they looked like a crowd of little boys trying to play an adults' game without knowing the rules.

It had all begun with a classic double-cross led by Paul "The Butcher" de Vries, who headed the Nomads chapter of Hells Angels Netherlands located in Limburg, about 150 kilometers east of

Amsterdam near the border with Germany. De Vries picked up his nickname not by killing people but by cutting them up after getting someone else to kill them. Or so the story goes.

Whatever de Vries did in his spare time, he was central to the Limburg chapter's drug dealing, which meant he helped organize the shipment of three hundred kilograms of Colombia-sourced cocaine through Curaçao to Portugal and eventually to the Netherlands. It was a joint deal between the Hells Angels and another non-biker bunch of criminals, but somewhere along the line the entire batch of cocaine vanished. Given de Vries's past reputation as a rip-off artist, he and two partners were suspected of seizing the shipment for themselves, which seriously upset both the Colombians who expected to be paid and the partners who expected to peddle the cocaine for a substantial profit.

Double-crossing your partners and putting your club brothers at risk in the process is not a good way to ensure a long and happy life, especially if the brothers are Angels and the partners include members of a Colombian drug cartel. When the Caribbean contact for the deal, a sometime fisherman from Curaçao named Angelo Diaz, was fingered as the guy who'd ripped off the Colombians, it confirmed that de Vries, along with Serge Wagener and Cor Pijnenburg, had taken the cocaine for themselves. All three were doomed.

The entire caper suggests some pretty foolish thinking on the part of de Vries and his friends. How did they think they'd get away with it? Did they really believe that when their Nomad brothers heard about their leader's haul they'd simply nod and shuffle their feet and say, "Okay, Paul, whatever you say"?

In February 2004 de Vries and his two double-crossing partners attended a meeting at the Nomads clubhouse in Oirsbeek, a quiet little village not far from Limburg. A dozen outraged Nomad brothers started by looking for an explanation and ended by getting revenge.

It's pretty clear that de Vries and company were tortured before being killed. All three had been shot in the arms before receiving dozens of bullets in the head and chest. That's what the Netherlands police surmised after the bodies were found dumped into a stream near the town of Echt.

The police arrested and charged twelve Angels with the three deaths. They were tried a year later and all twelve were found guilty of—get this—manslaughter. If you look up the legal definition of manslaughter, you'll find that it means "criminal homicide without malice aforethought." So based on the court decision, the Angels didn't really mean to kill de Vries, Wagener, and Pijnenburg. Perhaps they were just having a little target practice in their clubhouse and those three guys got in the way of the bullets, and since their double-crossed buddies were already pissed off they acted without thinking. Whether or not the court decided this was how things happened, it's one way of interpreting the verdict.

The manslaughter convictions got the dozen Angels six years each in jail. They also inspired a new level of outrage against the Angels by Netherlands citizens and the Korps landelijke politie-diensten (the national police services, or KLPD). Soon after the twelve Angels were locked away, the police began planning a series of coordinated raids on HAMC clubhouses. On a Monday morning in October 2005, about a thousand police officers, armed with automatic weapons as well as bulldozers to knock through walls, raided sixty-four Angel clubhouses and hangouts across the country. The KLPD arrested forty-five Angels.

More frightening to the public than the jailed Angels were the weapon arsenals seized from the clubhouses. They included a grenade launcher with ammunition, a flame-thrower, two hand grenades, a smoke grenade, a submachine gun, and various other weapons. Also seized were about seventy thousand euros in cash, marijuana plants, and expensive watches.

Included among the Angels arrested was Willem van Boxtel, who had wandered down a very different path from that of Paul "The Butcher" de Vries. The contrast is interesting. De Vries had wanted to rip off his buddies for a few million dollars in cocaine. Van Boxtel had agreed to kill a buddy of the Angels on a murder-for-hire basis by blowing up an Angels clubhouse, which could have involved wiping out a few fellow Angels as collateral damage. De Vries was brutally murdered. Van Boxtel was merely disgraced. That's Angels justice, Netherlands style.

Van Boxtel was the longest-serving leader of an Angels chapter in all of Europe, having served as president of the HAMC Amsterdam since the club received its official approval in 1978. He'd done a good job of building the Angels in various ways over the years, including launching and managing two Angels-managed cafés in the Amsterdam red-light district (although he kept the businesses in his name) and making Amsterdam a kind of crossroads for Angels' activities on the continent. Anything the Angels wanted done in Europe had to be rubber-stamped by Big Willem first.

All went well until Willem Endstra asked van Boxtel to kill yet another Willem, this one a major underworld character and friend of the HAMC Amsterdam chapter named Willem Holleeder. The three Willems shared the same view of life—namely, why work to make a living when you can get rich faster by breaking the law?

Endstra and van Boxtel were a study in contrasts. Big Willem van Boxtel had come from the streets. He was impressed with motorcycles and was determined to make as much money with as little effort as he could. Running the Amsterdam HAMC had given him many opportunities to line his pockets, most of them associated with drugs. Except for his obvious leadership and business-management abilities, he was just another big guy on a big bike.

Endstra, on the other hand, had been able to take the high road to enormous wealth. The son of well-off parents in the real estate business, he earned himself a law degree. His legal work brought him into contact with a gang making loads of money by dealing in ecstasy. They made so much money from the drug, in fact, that they needed a means of laundering it. Endstra used his legal business to get the job done.

And he appears to have done it well, until Dutch authorities grew suspicious. When they began seriously investigating Endstra's activities, he managed to work out a deal in which he paid a fine of €450,000 to avoid criminal prosecution. The deal proved to be a good one: ten years later Endstra's net worth was estimated at €350 million.

Endstra didn't make that much money that fast by following the straight and narrow. He was almost certainly involved in money laundering to some extent, although the police were never able to assemble a solid case against him. Whatever game he was playing, it involved the third Willem, an interesting character named Holleeder.

Willem Holleeder was the son of a worker at the famed Heineken breweries. His father may have sampled the brewery's product too often, though, because when Willem was still a young boy Holleeder Sr. was fired for alcoholism. Possibly thinking his father had been ill-treated, Holleeder gave up on the idea of legal employment and formed a gang of young toughs who hired themselves out to landlords needing strong-arm treatment of unwanted tenants. Holleeder and his boys used whatever it took to persuade the residents to vacate the premises, including threats, intimidation, physical force, and vandalism. Most got the message.

In 1983, the twenty-five-year-old Holleeder came up with an idea for both a bigger score and suitable revenge: he and his boys would kidnap Freddy Heineken, CEO and majority shareholder of the same firm that had fired his father years earlier. They managed to pull it off in early November 1983, seizing Heineken and his chauffeur and demanding a ransom of €16 million. Despite opposition from the police, the Heineken family paid it and both men were released. Within a few weeks, the police had tracked down Holleeder and his gang. All were given prison sentences.

After serving eleven years for his kidnapping caper, Holleeder arrived back in Amsterdam like a movie star, shopping for high-end goods in the city's best fashion outlets and showing up at parties thrown by the biggest pop stars. Rumor had it that Holleeder had managed to squirrel away a few million of the ransom money that had escaped the police, and that he was ready to enjoy it. If so, he supplemented it with an extortion operation that he ran in conjunction with his brother-in-law, and that employed as many as twenty-four "associates" to bring the money in.

He also managed to hook up with Willem Endstra as a partner in Endstra's money-laundering business. Somewhere along the line the two men disagreed on things. The disagreement grew more serious—no surprise—when Holleeder kidnapped one of Endstra's children. The child was unhurt, Holleeder was found guilty and was awaiting sentencing, but as far as Endstra was concerned, jail would not be sufficient punishment.

Endstra offered van Boxtel a contract to kill Holleeder, who was living at the Angels' clubhouse, known as Angel Place, in the Watergraafsmeer district of Amsterdam. Among other things, this raised a small problem in van Boxtel's mind. Holleeder was a friend, a business partner of the Angels, and a temporary house-guest. What would it take to blow him away?

Endstra had the answer: a million euros in cash, with €250,000 cash down.

Problem solved.

Holleeder would not be an easy target. He was as streetwise as anyone else, and he was often in the company of other Angels, whose first response to an attack on their friend would be to protect him and themselves. A hit on the street was out of the question. But since Holleeder's presence was known and predictable, why not use another weapon—like a bomb? Van Boxtel decided to plant an explosive device inside his own clubhouse and be a safe distance away when it was detonated.

This raised another problem, of course. At any given time other Angels were likely to be present in the clubhouse and just as likely to suffer the same fate. This didn't seem to trouble Big Willem, but it sure as hell troubled his Angel brothers, who learned of the plot and took immediate action.

And yet, even though their president had been willing to wipe out other Angels as mere collateral damage, the Amsterdam HAMC acted like an army issuing a dishonorable discharge to one of its officers. They removed van Boxtel from running the club and took away his colors, his patches, and his motorcycle before ordering him to burn off his Angel tattoos. He also had to give up any claim to the two cafés in the red-light district as well as his Amsterdam home, although the Angels permitted his wife and children to remain there.

Van Boxtel escaped with his life, although losing all the perks and identity that came with being the most powerful Angel in all of Europe. Holleeder survived as well, serving time in prison before being released in January 2012.

Endstra wasn't nearly so lucky. On May 16, 2012, he appeared on an Amsterdam television program complaining that after years of investigation the Netherlands police had yet to come up with enough evidence to try him, and that they should give up and leave him alone. The very next day, while walking near his office, Endstra was shot and left to die in the street. The shooter was never identified.

4

TERROR IN PARADISE

Vancouver is a beautiful place, I'll admit. Mountains, seaside, big trees, mild climate—what's not to like? But there's something about this part of the world that seems to bring out the worst in people. And where biker gangs are concerned, there's a long history of outrageous acts that just don't seem to happen elsewhere. Take the fate of Eugene Uyeyama and his wife.

The Uyeyamas lived in the Vancouver suburb of Burnaby. In 1995 Eugene became involved in a mobile drug lab being run by the Angels in East Vancouver, and when the lab was busted and Uyeyama was linked to it, the police offered him a deal: help us get the real power behind this operation and we'll go easy on you.

Whether Eugene should or should not have agreed to become an informant isn't the issue. It was his choice to make and, let's remember, being a police informant is not against the law. Meanwhile, producing vast quantities of meth and other narcotics that eat up people's money and their very lives definitely is against the law.

The police naturally told Eugene to be careful about who he spoke to and who he let into his house, and he was. But four days before Christmas two impeccably dressed men knocked on the front door with gaily wrapped packages complete with ribbons, bows, and Santa Claus stickers.

Eugene's wife, Michele, who'd married him just a few months before and may or may not have known about his activities, answered the front door, leaving the safety latch attached. When the men said they had presents from "the boys," she asked that they leave them on the front porch. But it had begun to snow, and the well-dressed men suggested that the gifts would get wet and politely asked if they could leave them inside. Michele reluctantly removed the safety latch, opened the door, and found herself staring at a gun in the hand of Bobby Moyes. His partner grabbed Michele and together they went in search of her husband, who was sleeping. Moyes strangled the husband and wife before unwrapping one of the "gifts," which was a can of gasoline. Pouring the fuel over the bodies, he left a trail leading to the front door before lighting the fuel and leaving.

Moyes, who had a history of violent crime that Tony Soprano might have envied, was on day parole at the time, and was still on day parole the following year when he massacred five people in a farmhouse near Abbotsford. Like the gruesome murders of the Uyeyamas, he neither knew nor had any problem with his victims. He performed the murders on orders from others, including the Angels, and is currently serving life in prison with no parole eligibility for twenty-five years.

One guy who might have nodded in approval at Bobby Moyes—and who undoubtedly knew him and perhaps did some dirty work with him—was Anthony "Big Tony" Terezakis. Another Hells Angels associate, Big Tony pushed cocaine, crack, and heroin out of the Cobalt and American hotels in East Vancouver. He wasn't the only one, of course, but Big Tony wanted more than money. He wanted notoriety, he wanted respect, and he wanted fear.

He got it whenever someone was holding out on him for payment or lying to him about almost anything or maybe just because Tony felt like it. Pulling his victim into a basement room of the American or the Cobalt hotel, a massive gold crucifix swinging from his neck, Big Tony would bellow, "The Lord has given me authority to hurt you if you lie!" Then he would demand answers from the victim, who was usually quivering in fear on some filthy, infested sofa. He would ask for the money he was owed, the drugs that were lost, the names of people he was searching for. Whatever Tony wanted, Tony threatened to get by kicking and punching the other person in the head, midsection, and legs, over and over while the victim pleaded for him to stop. Each kick and blow was delivered with shouts of "Praise the Lord!" and "The truth sets you free!" When beatings didn't appear to work, Big Tony would smear them with faeces. Most of the targets were drug addicts. Some were prostitutes.

Amazingly, Big Tony didn't perform this kind of thing quietly. Not Tony Terezakis. He actually had them filmed with the assistance of his own son, calling his movies "Bible Thumpers." In all, Tony and Junior shot almost twenty hours of these films. When Tony's ex-wife, Beverley, discovered them, she turned them over to police, who promptly charged Tony and son with assault, forced confinement, and various other criminal activities.

During Tony's trial, the films were shown to the jury as evidence. The jury, absorbing the fear and agony on the faces of Tony's victims, was horrified and aghast. Tony, however, laughed. They were only actors, he claimed in his defense, saying that he'd paid them to act as they did in the productions, which would be used to teach people the importance of always telling the truth. For all his efforts to improve the morality of Vancouverites, Tony was sentenced to eleven and a half years in prison.

For a time, those incidents in the Vancouver area involving the Angels, either directly or indirectly, became almost commonplace. It's not that people accepted them. It's just that they found it easy to ignore them, in the belief that "Oh, it's just those crazy bikers killing themselves off again."

This all ended with the Surrey Six massacre.

BEAR CREEK PARK is a pleasant place in Surrey, a suburb of Vancouver. There are lots of trees, plenty of open space, and a playground for kids with a train they can ride on. It's even nice in February, which is when I was there in 2008 with a lot of other people. We all watched a flock of doves being released and flying off into the sky. But as pleasant as Bear Creek Park is, none of us wanted to be there that day.

We were attending a public safety rally in memory of two good hard-working guys named Chris Mohan and Ed Schellenberg, both of them shot to death in a biker gang–related massacre.

If you don't know the details, you're probably thinking to yourself, "Just a couple more bikers getting mowed down by guys they tried to rip off, or something like that." Well, it was nothing like that. Ed Schellenberg was a fifty-five-year-old gas fitter from Abbotsford, B.C., with a teenage son and a wife who'd made her husband pizza for dinner. Chris Mohan was twenty-three years old and living with his parents in suite 1504 of the Balmoral Tower apartment building. Schellenberg had arrived at suite 1505 to check and repair a gas fireplace. Mohan had stepped out of his apartment to go to a basketball game. Both were shot in the head, execution style. For what?

Some people said, "For being in the wrong place at the wrong time." That's crap. They were doing what they were supposed to do in places they were supposed to be. A gas fitter, working on his own, is called to check on a fireplace and he's in the wrong place? A nice young guy opens the door of the apartment suite rented by his family to meet some buddies and watch a basketball game together and he's in the wrong place too?

There were others killed as well, of course. Four of them, all involved with the Red Scorpions biker gang, were the real targets of the execution. They included two brothers, Corey Lal and Michael Lal, along with Ryan Bartolomeo and Ed Narong. The Red Scorpions, as the names of these guys suggest, are a non-racial gang who for years ran dial-a-dope lines in and around Vancouver. Race comes second to loyalty and respect where the Scorpions are concerned, qualities that any Hells Angels member could agree to. The Scorpions have "RS" tattooed on their arms and necks in case anyone has a problem identifying them.

So six men were killed in suite 1505 in October 2007, and three Scorpion members—James Kyle Bacon, Matthew Johnston, and Cody Haevischer—were charged with murder and conspiracy. A fourth Scorpion, Dennis Karbovanec, came clean and confessed to killing Mohan, Bartolomeo, and Michael Lal, which got him a life sentence with a chance at parole after fifteen years. That was in April 2009. The court banned the release of details in order to protect the rights of the other accused, who, despite whatever Karbovanec might have said, pleaded not guilty.

Their trial finally began in October 2013, six years after the killings. Observers figured the trial could take as much as an entire year. Justice sure has a way of moving slowly. Getting this far involved more than a hundred investigators and led to the police charging four of their own members with breach of trust, obstruction of justice, and fraud. These kinds of things happen when a high-profile case and big money is involved. They shouldn't happen at all, of course, where the police are concerned.

The three Red Scorpions pleaded not guilty to charges of first-degree murder. According to the prosecution, the Scorpions had targeted twenty-one-year-old Corey Lal, who was the tenant of the apartment. Lal had been dealing drugs and taking business away from the Scorpions and Angels, so the Scorpions offered him a deal: pay them $100,000 as a means of acknowledging that the Scorpions/Angels ruled the drug trade on the lower B.C. mainland.

Lal disagreed—not about the bikers' dominance of the business but about handing over $100,000 in cash. In that case, the bikers agreed, they would have to kill him. So on October 19, 2007, they picked up a couple of guns, gathered at a local Korean restaurant, had an associate who was living at the Balmoral apartments hand over his security fob, used it to enter the building, and rode the elevator to the fifteenth floor.

Bad planning. First, they should have ensured that Lal was alone, which would have simplified things for everybody. He wasn't. The others—Lal's brother Michael, plus Narong and Bartolomeo—were watching Ed Schellenberg service the fireplace in the apartment, and just as the Scorpions barged their way into Lal's pad, Chris Mohan passed by and saw and heard everything. All were potential witnesses. So instead of shooting one guy they shot six, in two groups of three. Execution style, with a single bullet to the head. That's how biker gangs see life: if you have the guns, you make the rules, and if the rules are broken you lose your life. It's always been that way, but now and then an event like the six murders in Surrey brings it all home in a tragic and stupid manner.

THE SURREY SIX massacre launched a biker and drug war in and around Vancouver, and in fact throughout the whole province of British Columbia. Almost without exception, these were retribution or "Get off my turf" killings. Whatever the motive, look how risky it was to live in and around Greater Vancouver and be at least suspected of having a connection with bikers and drugs during the first six months of 2009:

JANUARY

20 Jamie Bacon's car is shot at while he's driving through Abbotsford. He was the brother of Jarrod Bacon, a guy so rough and scary that the local police warned that anyone dealing with him could be at risk.

22 A forty-two-year-old man is shot and wounded in a robbery at an Abbotsford marijuana grow operation.

23 Two other men are wounded by shots fired outside an Abbotsford home.

24 The occupant of a Surrey home is wounded by shots fired through his door.

27 Andrew (Drew) Cilliers is shot in a targeted attack.

FEBRUARY

2 James Ward Erickson is shot in an apartment in Surrey.

3 Brianna Helen Kinnear, twenty-two, is found shot in a truck in Coquitlam.

3 Raphael Baldini, the owner of suite 1505 of the Balmoral Tower, is shot in a parking lot in Surrey.

6 William Wayne Cloud, nineteen, is fatally stabbed in a Vancouver house.

6 Kevin LeClair, who has ties with the Hells Angels, is shot in a parking lot of a grocery store in Langley.

8 An unidentified man is shot in a west-side Vancouver parking lot.

11 Nicholas Gordon Smith, twenty-four, is shot in the basement of a Vancouver house.

12 Shots are fired at a house in Burnaby.

16 A driver is wounded by shots fired at his SUV outside a Surrey strip club; two suspects are charged with attempted murder.

16 Nicole Marie Alemy, whose husband was a friend of Raphael Baldini, is shot and killed in Surrey in a flurry of gunfire while driving her husband's car with their four-year-old son in the back seat.

26 Cory Stephen Konkin, thirty, is shot in his car in Maple Ridge.

27 An unidentified man is shot outside his Surrey home in what police call a targeted attack.

MARCH

2 Sukhwinder Singh Dhaliwal, thirty-two, is fatally shot in Vancouver.

3 A young woman is killed and a man wounded in a shooting in a Burnaby apartment.

3 Sunil Mall, twenty-seven, is shot in his car in East Vancouver.

3 Shots are fired in a drive-by shooting outside a suspected drug house in Surrey.

5 A man is shot in a drive-by shooting in Vancouver.

10 Two men are fatally shot in a Vancouver-area apartment.

15 Laura Lynn Lamoureux, thirty-six and involved in the street-level drug trade, is gunned down in a Langley gutter.

19 Marc Bontkes, thirty-three, is fatally shot in a Vancouver parking lot.

30 Sean Murphy, twenty-one, is fatally shot in his car in Vancouver.
31 Ryan Richards, nineteen, is fatally shot in a field behind a produce store.

APRIL

4 A man is fatally shot in an SUV, a targeted murder according to police.
6 Lionel Tan, twenty-four, is shot to death near his BMW at a Vancouver gas station.
15 Betty Yan, thirty-nine, is fatally shot in her Mercedes at an industrial strip mall.

MAY

1 Joseph Randay, eighteen, and Dilsher Singh Gill, seventeen, are abducted and fatally shot.
16 Christopher Roy Whitmee, thirty-four, is fatally shot in a targeted killing near Surrey.
28 Sarjbit Nagra, twenty-nine, is targeted and shot in Vancouver.

JUNE

11 Jeffrey Qi Feng Bian is fatally stabbed in a Vancouver condominium.
30 Jaswant Rai, thirty-six, is found shot to death in an SUV in Vancouver.

By mid-summer 2009 at least two dozen fatalities and forty injuries, most of which were the result of gunshots, had been recorded by police as associated with gang violence in the Greater Vancouver region.

The gang war was the result of Mexico's crackdown on its drug cartels, which supplied cocaine to B.C. biker gangs in return for marijuana. The reduced supply cut the profits of the Independent Soldiers and their allies, the United Nations gang, whose main rackets are running guns and smuggling marijuana (BC Bud) into the United States. So when the IS and UN gangs moved into the cocaine trade to expand their market and make up for lost profits, the Red Scorpions launched an all-out gang war that included the killings of the Surrey Six.

ALL OF THIS VIOLENCE stained Vancouver's growing reputation as one of the world's great cities. But things just as deadly and gruesome were happening elsewhere in British Columbia and farther afield, revealing how the Angels and their sometime allies had transformed themselves from anarchistic bikers to corporate-thinking gangsters.

Consider Prince George, a city of seventy-two thousand in the B.C. interior, about five hundred kilometers northeast of Vancouver. The drug trade in Prince George is tightly controlled by the Hells Angels, and has been for many years. But the Angels hardly touch the stuff. They want only the money, which they get through a puppet club called the Renegades.

Nothing demonstrates the Angels' new attitude more effectively than their use of puppet clubs. Remember that the Hells Angels based their appeal on hell-riding motorcycles and the loyalty of brothers. If you didn't ride a Harley-Davidson, you were dirt. And if you failed to wear and respect a Hells Angels patch, you risked getting a beating and maybe worse. But this far into the twenty-first century, you can lack both a bike and a patch and still be associated with the Angels. All you have to do is hustle your butt and make money for them. The Renegades did just that in and around Prince George, dealing cocaine.

You might think that a city deep in the heart of nowhere would have a pretty minimal demand for cocaine. Prince George, after all, got its start as a lumber and mining town where the drugs of choice tended to be beer, rye, and tobacco. Not anymore. The Renegades did so well with cocaine that they contracted with another club to deal crack exclusively. This third organization became known, naturally, as a finger-puppet club, calling itself the Crew. Maybe to impress the Angels, who remained at the top of the food chain, the Crew built a nasty reputation for chopping off the fingers of those who failed to pay their drug debts. This may have made the Crew bolder, or maybe they just wanted to get more attention from the Angels. In any case, the Crew took over the Independent Soldiers. The Soldiers were once as independent as their name suggests, until one night in a Prince George nightclub when a fully patched Angels member got himself killed by a Soldier. Soon most of the Soldiers were killed off, leaving the rest to bow and scrape and sell for the HAMC.

It gets confusing, I know, but the situation in Prince George is a perfect example of the way the Angels find their power weakening even while they're widening their influence. Around 2010, into this mix came a gang known as the GTS—the Game Tight Soldiers— all willing and able to play puppet for the Angels.

So here's the picture: four gangs—the Renegades, the Crew, the Independent Soldiers, and the GTS—control the drug trade in Prince George, and are in turn controlled by the Hells Angels. The four puppet organizations want to do more than move large quantities of drugs. They're in competition with each other for the Angels' respect, and they'll go to great lengths to earn it. Like dealing with drug deadbeats by cutting off fingers and setting up torture chambers in crack-house basements.

It's not just that the gangs in Prince George are so violent. It's that they're so brazen. In the summer of 2008, nineteen-year-old Brittany Giese, twenty-three-year-old Garrett McComb, and a nineteen-year-old male friend were sitting in a Lincoln Navigator parked on a downtown street when a passing car raked the SUV with bullets. The shooter missed Giese and McComb, but their young friend was wounded and hospitalized. Whatever Giese and McComb had done to make themselves targets would be enough for most people to either find a means of appeasing their enemy or simply get lost for a while, but the couple did neither. Instead they hung around town, failed to make things right with whoever was on the other end of the gun, and four months later were found shot to death in a home near the campus of the University of Northern British Columbia. The likely motive: punishment for not paying their drug-related debts.

Around the same time, Prince George police arrested Joey Arrance, owner of a local tattoo parlor and a member of the Game Tight Soldiers gang, on a firearms possession charge, along with Arrance's girlfriend, Kirsten Fredin, and her fifty-six-year-old mother, Linda Joyce Fredin. Arrance was a "striker," meaning a junior member, of the gang with some connections to the Renegades. The firearms consisted of a loaded Glock 10-mm automatic, a spare loaded magazine, a hand grenade, and a bulletproof vest. The two women were released from jail, but a few weeks later someone torched first the tattoo parlor and then the Fredin home. Linda Fredin, who was confined to a wheelchair and couldn't escape the smoke and flames, suffered serious burns and died later in hospital. Arrance received a three-year prison sentence and was banned from entering Prince George for eighteen months.

No one in Prince George, least of all police investigators, doubted that the fires and the woman's death were gang-related.

Just to confirm the suspicion, the province of British Columbia later announced that it planned to seize more than $270,000 in assets, including a diamond pendant worth more than $42,000, and about $25,000 in cash from Joey Arrance and Kirsten Fredin. That's a pretty impressive accumulation of goodies to be earned from a small tattoo parlor.

CLOSER TO VANCOUVER and the Pacific shore, the city of Kelowna is to all appearances a more laid-back town than Prince George.

Don't count on it. The kinds of murders that occurred in and around Kelowna in recent years, all of them linked with the Angels and their puppet clubs, are the stuff of which nightmares are made.

As elsewhere, the Angels in Kelowna sit at the top of the food chain and use puppet clubs to sell the drugs and take the risks while the Angels take the profits. Drug traffic in the Kelowna area is apparently extensive enough to justify two puppet clubs for the Angels—the Throttle Lockers and the Kingpin Crew.

You have to ask yourself what kinds of guys get involved in Angel puppet clubs. It's a little like getting a job at a big Vegas casino, with all its money, glamour, and glitz, except that your job is to clean the washrooms and sweep the floors. If you're both smart and tough, you don't do that kind of work. You're where all the excitement is and the big money flows. So what kinds of guys join puppet clubs? People with no self-respect, no ambition, and perhaps no brains. Maybe this is why for years the Hells Angels have referred to the Kingpins as Pinheads.

As I mentioned earlier, puppet club members may try to impress their Angel bosses by being as nasty as they think the Angels can be, which leads to stupid moves and dumb violence. Like the murder of Kelowna resident Dain Philips.

Philips was an easygoing kind of guy. One day in June 2011, his two sons told him that they were having a problem with a couple of other kids at Rutland high school, and that it looked like it could get violent. So Philips arranged to meet with the kids' parents, assuming that a little logic and persuasion could soothe the waters.

Well, they didn't. Whether or not Philips was aware of it, the two kids hassling his sons had connections, through their fathers, with the Throttle Lockers. Philips was met by at least seven men armed with baseball bats and hammers and beaten to death on a lonely road on a mild June evening. Seven men were eventually arrested and charged with his murder, including fifty-three-year-old Robert Cocks, president of the Throttle Lockers. The accused included his brother, Norm Cocks, and Robert Thomas, both of them full-patched Angels.

I can't say for sure, but I bet that even Sonny Barger in his meanest darkest days would say this was a bit of overkill. Or maybe even a lot of overkill. No drugs or money were involved, nobody's old lady had been fondled, no snitches were involved. Just some guy saying, in effect, "Hey, why don't we settle this thing between our kids and get on with our lives?" To which a group of guys says, in effect, "We're meaner SOBs than you'll ever be and we'll prove it!" Even their fellow prisoners shared that view: Robert Thomas and Norm Cocks were both beaten up pretty badly by other inmates. It's called jailhouse justice, and sometimes that's the only kind you can count on.

The case of Brittney Irving is no less tragic and just as illustrative of the way things are among the Angels in B.C.

Brittney was a beautiful green-eyed, freckle-faced twenty-four-year-old who should have had life by the tail. Instead, she had a problem. She was addicted to OxyContin, and paid for it by operating a marijuana grow-op in her home, almost certainly selling the grass to the Kelowna Angels. After the RCMP raided her home in early 2010, she chose to undergo treatment and beat her addiction. Which, of course, meant she'd no longer be raising marijuana plants. But first she had to close one more drug deal.

Telling a friend about the deal, she reportedly said, "I'm going to meet someone that's a really bad person, and I'm scared of what I'm going to do."

What she was about to do, apparently, was tell an Angel that she'd no longer be a source of the BC Bud they were dealing at a good profit. Pulling out of the business is not something the Angels take lightly; in their view, it's like being a buyer who doesn't pay for her purchase. Either way, the Angels are out of pocket, and nothing angers an Angel more than feeling he hasn't received money due. A little persuasion may have been applied to convince Brittney to somehow stay in the business, and when she refused, it probably got out of hand.

The details are sketchy, but the reality is clear. The day after she agreed to the meeting in a local motel, her Ford Explorer was found abandoned on a country road. Her body was located a few days later. The police arrested Joey Verma—originally from the Independent Soldiers and associated with the Kingpin Crew (either way, he's a puppet)—and charged him with her murder. Reports suggested that for the three years he awaited trial in prison, Verma, who claimed Irving's death had been a sanctioned hit, was busy recruiting for the Kingpin Crew.

Everything links up with Vancouver, one way or another. One of the accused murderers in the Surrey Six massacre, Jamie Bacon, had two brothers, Jonathan and Jarrod. The Bacon brothers. They're quite a family. Jarrod beat an attempted murder charge in 2005 when the victim had second thoughts about testifying against him. He couldn't beat a weapons and trafficking charge in May 2009, which got him twelve years in prison, less time served. By then the three brothers had taken control of the Red Scorpions gang and were planning to go head to head with the Angels for control of British Columbia's marijuana, cocaine, crack, meth, and heroin markets. Their plans were slowed down when Jamie was charged with his role in the Surrey Six case and Jonathan was gunned down outside the Delta Grand Hotel in Kelowna. Seated in the vehicle with Jonathan were Larry Amero, a full-patch Angels member, and pretty young Leah Hadden-Watts, niece of the president of the Haden, B.C., chapter of the Hells Angels. Jonathan died from the shooting, Amero was seriously wounded, and Hadden-Watts was paralyzed from the neck down. No one was arrested and charged.

The horrors continued. In December 2012 a homeless woman named Janice Shore, unable to pay a drug debt, was found chained to a tree in Surrey, savagely raped and brutally beaten, with facial fractures and several other broken bones. She clung to life for two months before finally succumbing to her injuries.

She wasn't the first. In September 2010 a woman named Ashley Machiskinic was believed to have fallen out of a window in an East Vancouver hotel—until someone reported that her shoes followed her out the window a few minutes later. Suicidal shoes? No, drug-dealer punishment for not paying her debts. Over a two-year period, as many as six women may have died in this manner.

And it spreads. The headless body of a Lloydminster man named Bob Roth was located on a country road north of Edmonton, Alberta. Roth, fifty-four, was a quiet man who drove a truck for a living but had also fostered some connection with biker gangs. His head was located sometime later in the city. Members of the White Boy Posse, another puppet club of the Hells Angels, were arrested and charged with his murder. Roth's crime? Inability to pay his drug debt.

What's the purpose of such dramatic, headline-grabbing murders? Do the killers really get a thrill out of reading about their exploits in newspapers and hearing them described on radio and TV? Perhaps, but others believe it extends beyond that, to a motive I mentioned earlier: ambition. These guys, most of them in Hells Angels puppet gangs, are trying to prove they're capable of extreme violence and able to carry out any assignment without fear. They're working themselves up the pyramid, just as your average MBA graduate shoots for being CEO. Their message to customers: "Don't mess with us." Their message to the Angels: "We're here, and we deserve a share of the same cream you're lapping up."

5

HELLS ANGELS IN THE LAND OF HIGH TEA

In many ways, the Hells Angels have become showbiz. But maybe Sonny Barger was the biker version of a song-and-dance man from the beginning.

Back in the 1960s, when he was still calling the shots and the Angels were as hot as the Rolling Stones, Barger decided to copyright the club's name and its death's head image. From that point forward, anyone who tried to cash in on the club's fame and notoriety would face the righteous wrath not of a dozen or so hairy, menacing, denim-clad bikers but—Omigod!—a bevy of heavyweight lawyers. Those who laughed at the idea of semi-literate hoodlums acting like Coca-Cola didn't laugh long. Companies from Disney on down heard from the Angels' legal representatives whenever they appeared to be using the Angels' identity without legal authority.

The message, however, may not have reached Britain by 2010. Or at least not the high-end fashion house of Alexander McQueen, who launched a line of goods that clearly ripped off the Angels' identity. They included a jacquard box dress imprinted with a design that blended the death's head with something that looked like the creature in the 1979 film *Alien,* a silk scarf that repeated the same motif, a knuckle-duster ring, and a clutch purse using the ring design as a clasp. The dress was priced at £900, or about $1500, and the ring at £300, or about $500.

In the fashion industry, this would have been called ironic and fun; after all, "old ladies" riding on the back of a Harley do not wear $1500 dresses. The Angels called it something else. They unleashed their U.K. lawyers with instructions that Alexander McQueen receive the legal equivalent of a good kicking from an Angels gang.

Apparently it worked. In what may have been the quickest settlement with the widest implication in the industry, London-based Alexander McQueen* practically threw itself under the Angels' bus while pleading for mercy.

In most settlements of this kind, the loser tends to agree to cease and desist. The Angels' legal beagles went further. Not only did the Alexander McQueen label agree to stop using the symbol immediately and destroy any products it had in inventory and in retail stores like Saks Fifth Avenue, it also agreed to track down merchandise that had already been sold. In other words, every customer who purchased any of these items was to be contacted and negotiations were to be conducted to recover the products. Then Alexander McQueen would destroy them.

The cost would be enormous, not just in tracking down the items one by one, but in buying them back: Alexander McQueen sold its products to wholesalers, who marked them up before passing them on to retailers, who easily doubled the price to

---

* The suicide of founder Alexander McQueen in February 2010 is not related to this incident.

customers—and the inflated price would be the one the fashion house would have to pay.

Companies dealing with retail goods encounter copyright and design issues all the time, but few cave in as quickly and totally as Alexander McQueen did. Was its case really that weak? Or did it have something to do with the way the Angels' legal advisers stated their position? "This isn't just about money," the Angels' lawyer explained, "it's about membership. If you've got one of those rings on, a member might get really upset that you're an imposter."* Evidently, the idea of upsetting a Hells Angel member anywhere in the world was enough.

THE FIRST REACTION people have when they hear about Hells Angels roaring through the streets of London or villages in Cornwall or the Cotswolds is "Really?" Britain may have changed as much as the rest of the world has, but it's still viewed as the home of the Royal Family and a place where it's important to know how to properly pour tea.

On the surface, you could almost believe that the British-based Angels have been influenced by the society around them. They don't have tea parties, but in 2002, along with other cycle clubs, at least one Angel rode his Harley-Davidson in a royal pageant marking Queen Elizabeth II's Golden Jubilee. Julian Sher, who's written about the Angels in the past, thinks that "England is one of the few countries where the myth of the Hells Angels as lovable rascals endures."† He suggests that bikers in England benefit not

---

* Joe Fay, "Hells Angels Slap London Dressmakers with Trademark Suit," *The Register,* October 28, 2010 (www.theregister.co.uk).
† Paul Stokes, "Hells Angels Movement," *The Telegraph,* August 14, 2007.

only from slick PR operations but also the disbanding of English police squads that might have infiltrated them.

Do England-based Angels and other MC gangs really get by with a stiff upper lip and a belief that all they have to do is Stay Calm and Carry On? Not bloody likely.

Not based on what happened to Gerry Tobin in 2008. Tobin, a fully patched Angel (of an estimated 250 in all of Britain at the time), attended the annual Angels-sponsored Bulldog Bash near Stratford-on-Avon. Yeah, that's the same place associated with William Shakespeare, who might have written a couple of new plays if he'd attended one of these bashes with the other fifty thousand people there.

The format is the same every year. Bikers and their buddies, along with thousands of wannabes and the curious, get together to hear rock bands perform, hang out in beer tents, attend drag races, and watch stunt-riding demonstrations. To this good clean fun the Angels add wet T-shirt contests, erotic dance shows, and a topless bike wash. Despite all this fooling around, over the years the Bulldog Bashes caused little trouble for the local police. Lately, however, their position has changed. This is not a charity function, after all. To attend the Bulldog Bash, you need to lay out a fair chunk of cash for every event, money that goes directly into the Angels' coffers, and they don't share the profits with anyone. As Warwickshire's Assistant Chief Constable Bill Holland said in early 2013, "The Hells Angels are an organized crime group recognized by five forces in the UK and by many police services and some countries internationally. We have intelligence that shows the Bulldog Bash event is used to fundraise for activities that cause harm to the public regionally, nationally and internationally."* In

---

* http://news.bbc.co.uk/2/hi/uk_news/england/coventry_warwickshire/8119365.stm.

response to a police request, officials declined to issue a permit for the 2013 Bash, which was cancelled. The Angels vowed to revive it the following year.

But back in 2008, things were rolling along nicely when Gerry Tobin attended the Bash. According to those who met him there, he had a good time, and to the extent that a fully patched Angel can qualify as such, he was considered "a good guy." In fact, his buddies called him Gentleman Gerry. He was a qualified mechanic who maintained a steady relationship with his fiancée in South London, which is where he headed at the end of the August 12 Bash. Getting to London meant riding through Warwickshire, home of a British chapter of the Outlaws, who tended to refer to all Hells Angels as maggots.

The Angels' Bulldog Bash was considered an affront to the Outlaws; in previous years they'd even threatened to bomb the event. Nothing happened, but in 2001 an Angel riding through Outlaws territory on the M40, a superhighway leading to London, was shot three times in the leg from a passing car. Everyone, including the victim, knew it had been an Outlaws hit, but the Angel refused to testify and the case remained unsolved. Things were different seven years later.

Riding alone, sporting his Hells Angels patch, Tobin was unaware of three cars positioned behind him. On cue, the leading car, a green Rover, sped up to ninety mph to pull up beside him. The Rover was driven by Dane Garside, vice president of the Outlaws chapter. Beside him was the president, Sean Creighton, and in the back seat was Simon Turner, the sergeant-at-arms. Their windows were lowered, and when Creighton gave the order, he and Turner fired two shots at Tobin. One hit him in the head, killing him instantly, although crashing his bike at ninety mph would have produced the same result.

The whole exercise had been set up with all the precision and planning of a military operation. Behind the Rover were four other Outlaws in two cars as backup and spotter. All three vehicles sped away from Tobin's wrecked body and equally wrecked Harley. At a prearranged destination the men torched the Rover and visited a pub to share a few beers in celebration.

Everyone knew who was involved and why, but no one on either side was talking. The Angels, perhaps, decided they would settle things in their own manner. But before they could, English detectives began making arrests based on clues found in the burned-out Rover and statements from witnesses. All seven men were arrested and charged. Creighton submitted a guilty plea and offered to take full responsibility for the murder, letting his buddies off the hook. Nothing like a martyr to generate hero worship, I suppose, even if it's sampled from behind bars for the rest of your life.

The judge was having none of it. He sentenced them all to life in prison, with no parole eligibility for twenty-five to thirty years.

These Outlaws were an interesting batch, according to their police records. Turner had been convicted and jailed for stabbing a stranger before tossing gasoline on him and threatening to throw a lighted match. Dane Garside had been involved in an ax attack on another man. His brother Karl, riding in one of the following cars, sported a list of convictions, including the wearing of brass knuckles as a spectator in a courtroom, one of the less serious if more blatant offenses on his record. Others had been caught with sawed-off shotguns and various other paraphernalia.

Another thing that garnered media attention was a detective's suggestion that the Warwickshire Outlaws hadn't acted on their own. They may have proposed the hit on an Angel passing through their territory, but they would have sought approval from the top before making such a move.

THE BIKER WAR may look like a mere skirmish compared with North American clashes, but it shone a light on the U.K.'s bike culture, where everything ties to the Angels in one way or another. Their first U.K. chapter sprouted in the late 1960s. The Outlaws have been battling them since at least the mid-90s, although the Outlaws' strongest base remains in the Birmingham area. The Angels were the only one percenters who really mattered, but since 2010 things have been changing: other clubs now want to play in the same sandbox.

- **The Blue Angels** began in Glasgow, taking the "blue" in their name from the Scottish flag. (Others say it stands for Bastards, Lunatics, Undesirables, and Eccentrics.) They've ventured into the Leeds and Sheffield area, and are unique in one measure at least: they tend to favor British bikes like Triumphs and Nortons over American Harley-Davidsons.

- **Road Tramps**, formerly known as the Reapers, are an Irish-based gang dating back to 1987. They appear to have a small British following.

- **The Bandidos** are present in Britain on a small scale, and, next to the Outlaws, are considered the Angels' strongest opponents.

- **Mongols**, allies of the Outlaws and considered the most violent of the gangs, have reportedly been spotted in Britain setting up either drug trafficking networks or money-laundering operations. Probably both.

- **The Vagos** were launched when Hispanic members of the Psychos out of San Bernardino broke away from the original club. They wear green, and their club insignia shows the Norse god Loki riding a motorcycle. The Vagos have five official chapters in Scandinavia and could be looking to Britain for their next move.

• **The Rebels** are an Australia-based MC, but some of its members have been seen in England. They may or may not be welcome. New Zealand banned the club and deported any Rebels who arrived there with plans to organize a chapter. They bring a different flavor to the business. Police who raided an Australian chapter of the Rebels discovered narcotics, firearms … and a live crocodile.

6

SIZING UP THE COMPETITION

From the beginning, the Hells Angels have been at war with other clubs. Let's recall that while they virtually defined what a one-percenter motorcycle club is and does, they weren't the first on the scene. That honor belongs to the Outlaws, whose identity was established not only as a motorcycle club/gang but as one involved in criminal activity. They began in 1935, almost twenty years before the Angels.

In 2013 I wrote *Charlie and the Angels,* which focused on the open hostility between the Outlaws and Sonny Barger's crew. The book was well received by readers, but not, initially, by the media. Why? Because too many crime reporters felt that a club so large and powerful couldn't exist without getting the same ink and attention bestowed on the Angels. "If these guys are so bad," went the usual comment, "how come I haven't heard about them?" Some of these reporters could spin a thousand words about the Hells Angels off the top of their head but almost nothing about the Outlaws, and they resented anyone—including me—covering a story they'd missed for, oh, about fifty years or so. I felt like something of a voice in the wilderness. But it's important that people understand the gangs' scope and support the law enforcement agencies attempting to control them, if not shut them down; otherwise, the wars between the Angels, the Outlaws, the Pagans, and other MCs will continue to spread.

"Why bother?" you may be thinking. "Let 'em all kill each other off."

But there's always collateral damage. The gang wars don't happen on far-off battlefields or inside gang clubhouses. More often than not, they happen in the middle of other people's lives. When a bomb goes off in a bar or a car parked on your street or a gang rakes a house with automatic-rifle fire in a drive-by shooting, you'd better hope you and your family aren't within range. And when one explosion or another occurs between two clubs, don't assume that'll end the war. The conflict continues, ebbing and flowing according to the combatants' strategies and leadership.

The feud between the Angels and the Outlaws grew out of roots that have continued to fuel it for more than fifty years. Talk about holding a grudge! It began when the Outlaws, the original in-your-face MC, noticed the fun the Angels were having out in California and sent a delegation from Chicago to suggest an alliance. It was meant as a friendly gesture, but the Angels responded by beating up the Outlaws, ripping off their patches, and sending them limping back to Chicago. When the Outlaws' leadership asked for an explanation, about the only response from the Angels was a simple "Fuck you!"

Okay, brawls between motorcycle clubs are not uncommon, and are often settled by a sit-down between the club leaders. But such a snub could not and would not be ignored by Outlaws past, present, and future. They make certain of this with two of their most often quoted mottos: AHAMD—All Hells Angels Must Die, and ADIOS—not just Spanish for "goodbye" but the acronym for Angels Die in Outlaw States.

The Outlaws are allied with the Bandidos, which gives them the strength they need in the West. They battle from time to time with the Pagans and Warlocks. But no other group gets their backs up and the bullets flying like the Angels.

The Outlaws like to brag that they started at a place called Matilda's Bar on old Route 66 in McCook, Illinois, smack in the middle of the Great Depression. In other words, they're the real thing: guys who love to ride sitting in a bar with nothing to do and nothing to lose, drinking beer and deciding they'll function outside the law. So they choose a name that defines them and a lifestyle that rejects all the values others are trying to follow. On that basis, all the other MCs are copycats.

The Outlaws originated the whole idea of one percenters, although when it came time to choose a patch design, they basically lifted the skull and crossed pistons worn on the back of Marlon Brando's jacket in the 1953 movie *The Wild One*. They call the skull "Charlie." The fact that they haven't achieved the same level of notoriety as the Angels, Mongols, Bandidos, and other MCs may be a tribute to their style. As the Outlaws see it, if you're tough enough, you don't have to strut around to prove it to the people who should know. Their lack of notoriety may also be a reason why the Outlaws haven't grown as large as most other clubs in the United States, although they do well in other countries.

When they're not riding their Harleys, the Outlaws make money in traditional one-percenter fashion—through drugs, prostitution, strip clubs, extortion, and whatever else puts some coin in their pockets. This leads to prison terms from time to time, and the Outlaws, unlike most of their rivals, not only accept the risk but glorify it. Spending time in jail earns an Outlaw the right to sport an LL tattoo, meaning Lounge Lizard. All chapters maintain lists of incarcerated Outlaws and encourage the prisoners' old ladies and club brothers to write to them regularly, assuring the men that they aren't forgotten and are even honored by those on the outside.

Just as the Angels built much of their persona around Sonny Barger, the Outlaws trace a lot of their style and attitude to Harry "Taco" Bowman.

Taco Bowman was the Donald Trump of one-percenter clubs. Forget about hanging in roadhouses and sleeping in tenements or dull suburbs. Taco came out of Detroit and soon established himself as a first-rate administrator. With a different goal he might have risen to CEO of General Motors, he was that good. And that ruthless. Instead he came up through the ranks of the Outlaws in the late 70s, becoming first regional president, then national vice president, and in 1984 international president. Bowman took charge of the Outlaws with an iron hand, ruling that any chapter must get his approval before taking action against a rival club.

He also had a policy of spreading the word among Outlaw chapters whenever something went down right. If Bowman approved a hit on another club member or an Outlaw who broke the code, he made a point of sending newspaper clippings to all Outlaw chapters.

Being a good administrator did not mean being soft-hearted. At an Outlaw meeting in Fort Lauderdale on New Year's Eve 1993, Bowman announced that all chapters were not to tolerate any disrespectful action by the Hells Angels or the Warlocks. The first act was to bomb and then torch the clubhouse of a Chicago chapter of the Angels, followed by similar action against the clubhouse of the Warlocks' Orlando chapter.

Through all this and more, Taco Bowman lived another kind of life. He and his family occupied a luxury house in an affluent suburb of Detroit. He sent his children to private schools and drove a Cadillac more often than he rode his Harley, although it should be mentioned that the Cadillac was heavily armor-plated.

In the end, Taco overreached. He directed the murders of Outlaws he suspected of being snitches, and approved the attempted assassination of both Sonny Barger and Angels Ventura chapter president George Christie. It all caught up to him in 1997 when he was indicted for charges under the RICO Act, including murder, kidnapping, assault, trafficking in narcotics, and other infractions. Placed on the FBI's Ten Most Wanted list, he successfully evaded arrest until June 1999, when he was arrested while visiting his family's home in Sterling Heights, Michigan. Found guilty, he received three sentences of life imprisonment.

The club hasn't had a man like Taco Bowman running things since, but they have achieved a fair rate of success in the United States and around the world just by doing what they've always done. Although they have changed their strategy somewhat: they've set things up so that the Bandidos take the limelight (and most of the flak from law enforcement), leaving the Outlaws in the background to handle money and strategy. There's been talk of a possible similar arrangement with the Mongols. If that happens, the three clubs' alliance would create an organization outnumbering the Angels three to one, with members who are younger, hungrier, more determined, and more violent.

And they all hate the Angels.

THE ANGELS' TACTIC in dealing with rival gangs is to seek either annihilation or assimilation. Their only interest is in wiping smaller and weaker rivals off the face of the earth—unless the smaller gangs prove as tough or tougher, in which case the Angels extend an offer to join forces. As Angels, of course. If the clubs are substantial in size and tough enough to stand up to the Angels, deals can be struck.

The merger of the Angels with the Dirty Dozen MC is a classic example.

The Dozen were an Arizona-based club as territorial as any pack of wild animals. They wanted to own Arizona, and did whatever it took. Back in the 1980s an out-of-state club riding through Arizona stopped at a bar in Mesa, parking their dozen or so bikes outside while they went in for a drink. When a group of DD riders spotted the bikes, one of them pulled a pair of pliers out of his tool kit and went down the line of Harleys, cutting every fuel line in turn. Then they lit one end, setting off a spectacular display of exploding fuel tanks. The Dirty Dozen members just sat back and watched, laughing and drinking beer.

Then, in the early 1990s, the Vagos launched a chapter in Phoenix and set off a territorial war. The Dozen started with threats, which led to some beatings, which led in turn to a few shooting incidents. When Vagos president Arizona Don Halterman found a pipe bomb strong enough to flatten a city block on his doorstep, he decided that Arizona may be a pretty state but he'd be better off in a safer one. The Vagos moved along.

This kind of thing impressed Sonny Barger, who served out his four-year term for conspiracy in Arizona State Prison. Maybe the location gave him a special appreciation for the state and for the Dirty Dozen. In fact, after his release Sonny moved to Cave Creek, north of Phoenix, which may have softened the Dozen's attitude toward him enough to take his offer of a friendly merger seriously.

So in 1997 members of both clubs met at the HAMC clubhouse (a former Arthur Murray Dance Studio) in Oakland.

To the surprise of many, it worked. The DD patched over to the Angels without even a bout of arm wrestling to settle things.

There was something in it for both sides. The Angels had recognized that they couldn't annihilate the Dozen without bloodshed. A lot of bloodshed. Moving into Arizona would give them a big state with lots of wide-open roads and, thanks to the Dirty Dozen's past efforts, no serious rivals. In return, the Dozen got instant worldwide respect from the death's head patch. Or, in the words of Robert "Chico" Mora, "We got ourselves a bigger playground." And that new and bigger playground, Mora reminded other Dozen members, provided access to the organizational structure the Angels had built up over the years, including a team of high-powered lawyers on retainer and a string of legal businesses that included rental properties, movie houses, and other operations generating an impressive cash flow.

Like it or not, the Dirty Dozen also picked up the Angels' reputation as meth-dealing brawlers, recklessly hostile to anything and anyone who appeared to disagree with them, a reputation that Mora claimed was overblown. "I have a three-part gospel for staying out of prison," he said. "One: Don't commit senseless, needless violence against the citizenry. Two: Don't sling dope. And three: Don't print the government's money."* Follow those rules, Mora suggested, and law enforcement will leave you alone.

THE TRUTH IS, the Angels prefer assimilation over annihilation these days. Why? Because they're getting old and soft? Maybe a little. But the big reason is that gang wars are bad for business, and that's what

---

* Craig Outhier, "Hells Angels Shootout," *Phoenix* magazine, October 2011, p. 108.

the Angels are all about now: business. Wars and playing King of the Hill attract attention from the law and take up time that the club's movers and shakers can put to more profitable use. Ask a top-level Angel to choose between taking a tire iron to a rival gang member in a roadhouse or doing a deal to move a kilo of meth, and he'll choose the drug deal every time. And if the roadhouse brawl threatens future deals, he'll tend to avoid it.

But the Angels can't avoid these brawls. They haven't been hungry for years, while the other gangs want their turn at the trough—and the only way to get it is by challenging the Angels physically, not economically. Look, if Budweiser wants a piece of the beer market that Miller controls, they'll take the gloves off by cutting prices, introducing new brands, featuring good-looking girls in their ads, or doing whatever else it takes to wipe out the competition. When bikers want to wipe out competition, that's what they do, too. Literally.

This is happening all over the world, because that's the kind of organization the major biker gangs are. They may be driven by different incentives—fear, greed, jealousy—but their ultimate goal is the same: destroy the Angels.

And the picture keeps shifting. Just when the Angels think they know who represents their biggest threat, some new alliance joins two or more clubs together, or some club that was barely on the map last year is now ready to elbow in on their territory and can't be ignored anymore.

So how do the war-avoiding Angels deal with this? It depends on the competitor, the location, and the chapter—and I can't think of a better example than the Dago chapter. (It's located in San Diego, but the Angels always like to rename things and places according to their own style, and if it has a racial or ethnic kick to it, all the better.)

The Dago Angels had a lot of things going for them and one big thing going against them. Among the good things was their location. I don't know of nicer weather in North America than the weather you enjoy in San Diego, especially if you like to spend time on a motorcycle. And things were just as good economically. San Diego is the major Pacific port for the U.S. Navy, with thousands of other military personnel nearby, especially at the army's base in Camp Pendleton. It all adds up to a large and constantly revolving market for drugs and girls, especially strippers and hookers. It also provides an opportunity to acquire military-grade weapons and ammunition.

So all in all, the Dago Angels have it as good as any chapter in the country and a hell of a lot better than most. Which is one reason I arrived in San Diego to infiltrate them for the FBI and the DEA.

I'd been there in early 2000, running a small photography studio that the Angels used to take pictures of themselves, their tattoos, their bikes, and their women. I made a few contacts, but then got sidelined helping to bring down a major Russian-based heroin operation. A year later I was back, this time in El Cajon, a suburb of San Diego and the site of the Dago chapter clubhouse. I spent a lot of time with the Dago Angels, and was present at a DEA ambush that took two hundred pounds of coke from the Angels when the DEA agents posed as Mongols. And I was around during the famous shoot-out between the Mongols and Angels at the 2002 Laughlin River Run when three bikers died and thirteen others were injured.

Only the Mongols would take on the Angels like that, shooting across a crowded casino floor with hundreds of bystanders running and ducking for cover. So who are these guys anyway?

NO GROUP IN CALIFORNIA during the late 60s and early 70s was riding higher than the Angels. Hunter S. Thompson's book transformed their image from lazy, greasy bums to clever, ruthless outlaws living a life that spoke to middle-class Americans' fantasies. Soon they were as much a part of popular culture as movie stars and sports heroes. Eric Burdon and the Animals sang about them ("San Francisco Night"), and Willie Nelson's "Angel Flying Too Close to the Ground" was reportedly written for a friend who belonged to the Hells Angels.

So around 1970 if you were a serious biker, especially in California, you naturally wanted to join the Angels, which is what a group of Hispanics tried to do. They either didn't know or didn't care that the Angels maintained a strict whites-only policy (and do to this day: more about this in Chapter 15). Chicanos—and anyone with black, brown, yellow, or any color of skin besides white—are never welcomed.

The Hispanics and Mexicans weren't just snubbed by the Angels; they were ridiculed and mocked for even asking. With nowhere else to go, they formed their own MC, vowing to make it powerful enough to kick ass wherever and whenever they felt it was necessary. Powered by the vicious lifestyle commonly found on the streets of East Los Angeles, the Mongols were driven as much by revenge against the Angels as by the joy and camaraderie of club membership. So while the Angels were intimidating most of California and much of the rest of the world, the Mongols became bent on exceeding them in violence and brutality.

It took a while for the Angels to notice. Only when the Mongols added a "California" bottom rocker to their patch and began calling their San Diego club the Dago chapter—the name the HAMC had already given their own San Diego chapter—did the Angels strike. In September 1977 two Mongols, Emerson Morris and Raymond

Smith, were shot and killed as they rode their motorcycles on Interstate 15 near Santee, north of El Cajon. In case the Mongols didn't get the message, two Angels drove to the funeral, placed some red and white carnations (HA colors) on the coffins, and walked away, leaving their car at the curb. The car soon exploded, severely injuring three Mongols. Hells Angels Dago chapter president Guy Castiglione was eventually convicted of the bombing and sentenced to life in prison. Later, when drive-by shootings and gift bombs hadn't seemed to make the necessary impression, the Angels sent a tire to a Mongols-run Los Angeles bike shop, asking that it be repaired. It wasn't just a tire; it was another bomb. It killed the owner's brother.

This was enough to spur the Mongols into action. When they began hitting back, they chose their targets carefully. They weren't going to settle for picking off riders on an interstate or whoever happened to be in the vicinity of a bomb; they chose high-ranking Angels to make their point. The best way to kill a snake, they figured, is to cut off its head, and the best way to get an army's attention is to start killing the generals. Leaders, after all, are quick to send grunts into battle to die but a lot more careful about charging the enemy's guns themselves.

The Mongols began by shooting Raymond "Fat Ray" Piltz at a biker bar in Lemon Grove, California. Then they drove into El Cajon to take out a high-ranking Angel at Dumont's Bar, two blocks from the Dago chapter clubhouse. Another killing of an Angels chapter president finally persuaded the leadership to start taking the Mongols seriously. In the mid-1980s the Angels and Mongols came to an agreement: Barger and his Angels would run things in Northern California, and the Mongols would take charge in Southern California.

No one really believed the truce would last, and when it ended everyone suspected the Mongols would start riding against the Angels as harshly as ever. In fact, many believe that one reason Sonny Barger moved from Oakland to Cave Creek, Arizona, after he was released from prison in 1992 was to escape the Mongols.

The Mongols didn't just raise the bar for inter-gang brutality. They raised it for animalistic behavior, too. At club functions, members were expected to engage in sex acts, including "wing parties" where badges were awarded for specific acts. The color of the badge, or "wing," identified the act. Green wings, for example, were awarded for having sex with a woman carrying a venereal disease; purple wings for having sex with a female corpse.*

When the Mongols chose to open a chapter in San Jose, the truce ended with the 2002 River Run in Laughlin. That's when the Mongols pulled out all the stops, and the battle was on.

In December 2005, a group of Angels in Norco, California, was trying to play the good-guy role by supporting a Toys for Tots drive: nothing like a gang of Harley-Davidson-riding Santa Clauses to build community support. After the drive, a bunch of Angels got together in a local steakhouse, seated with an innocent off-duty fireman who'd been helping out. When a group of Mongols spotted the Angels in the restaurant the encounter led first to taunts, then to fists, and finally to guns after the Mongols pulled theirs and wounded three Angels along with the fireman. The following year, when the Mongols' Jorge "Solo" Viramontes sold a gas grenade to a guy he'd met, he bragged about having other weapons for sale, including hand grenades and rocket launchers. He could sell 'em all, except for one of the rocket launchers, which they planned to use to blow up a courthouse

---

* United States District Court for the Central District of California, February 2008 Grand Jury Indictment, "Black Rain" investigation.

where a brother Mongol was about to go on trial. Unfortunately for Solo, he'd made the sale and bragged about his plans to an undercover police officer.*

All of this became known after the U.S. Bureau of Alcohol, Tobacco and Firearms launched Operation Black Rain following the Laughlin shoot-out. The operation resulted in eighty-six counts against the club and its members—and that's when things fell apart for the Mongols. What the Angels couldn't accomplish with guns and bombs, the cops did with grand jury indictments and trials. To the disbelief of many in the biker fraternity, the Mongols began turning against each other, giving state's evidence to save their own butts. At one point they even lost the use of their logo and patches when a court ruling declared them illegal, although this was eventually overturned.

By the summer of 2013, the number of Mongols in Southern California was estimated by some people at between five and six hundred, but I doubt if there are much more than four hundred Mongols all across the United States.

The Mongols were and are minor players in the MCs' biggest profit producer: narcotics, especially cocaine and heroin. The Operation Black Rain indictment listed numerous transactions, but most consisted of small amounts, usually involving possession of no more than five grams or so. No club, however, exceeds the Mongols in violence, a tradition that today's smaller, tighter organization seems intent on continuing. And that's why both the cops and the Angels still fear them.

---

* "Black Rain" investigation.

THE PAGANS never got very far from their home base in and around Philadelphia, and maybe that's a good thing. Especially for the Angels.

The Pagans grew out of the region around Annapolis, Maryland, in the late 1950s, and for years their most distinguishing feature was their motorcycles: rather than Harley-Davidsons, they rode British Triumph bikes. Maybe that choice (Marlon Brando rode a Triumph in *The Wild One,* the movie loosely based on the Hollister "riot") made them quieter and more benign, in their early years at least, than the other MCs. They were basically a cycle-riding group of buddies, more interested in the open road than in open wallets.

All this changed around 1965 when Fred "Dutch" Barrows climbed into the club president's saddle and decided that what the Pagans needed was more members, more organization, and more money. Especially more money. He took the first two steps by expanding the club into six chapters in Maryland, Virginia, New Jersey, and Pennsylvania, and by creating a club constitution to lay down the law about membership and duties.

The money came from the club's entry into the business of producing and selling crystal meth. They learned the recipe from a Mob-connected guy known only as "Rock and Roll," but since some of their earnings had to go back to the Mafia bosses, they ditched R and R to cook their own meth, free of any royalties. Their chef, Jimmy "Jimmy D" DeGregorio, started his own meth kitchen, and all his product went to the Pagans' "mother chapter" in Philadelphia. The Philly chapter sold it to other Pagan chapter presidents, who sold it to members, who distributed it to retail customers—a pretty standard distribution system for outfits like Procter & Gamble and Coca-Cola, but considering how tightly controlled it was, almost unique among motorcycle clubs.

Jimmy D was apparently a good cook. He added purple food coloring to his meth to identify it, although by the time it was "stepped on"—diluted with Manitol, a baby laxative—it was almost back to its original white.

Things went along well, even after Dutch Barrows was shot and killed in Virginia. When the Pagans absorbed the Sons of Satan, a badass club in Philadelphia, they boasted almost a thousand members in more than forty chapters, all under the watchful eye of the Philly home chapter.

The situation changed when Little Nicky Scarfo rose to the top of the Lucchese family, who ran the Mafia's operations in Philadelphia. One of Scarfo's first moves was to institute a street tax on anyone who was unconnected and running deals on the streets of Philly. This included every bookie, tattoo artist, strip club operator, pizza maker, chop-shop operator, and drug dealer without a direct link with the Luccheses. Especially every drug dealer. Scarfo, an honest-to-goodness psychopath involved in at least a dozen murders, got everyone's attention with this new order. Everyone, that is, except the Pagans, who refused to have anything to do with him and his buddies. When Scarfo sent one of his Mob guys to tell the Pagans to shape up and start paying their dues, the Pagans laughed at him and threw him out of their clubhouse.

This enraged Scarfo, who wasn't used to being ignored, let alone insulted. His response was to have a Pagans dealer kidnapped and beaten up before dumping the victim practically on the doorstep of the Philly chapter's clubhouse.

From that point forward, it was the Pagans against the Mafia. Most people would have put their money on the Mob. If so, they would have lost. In the kind of no-holds-barred combat that broke out soon afterward, it wasn't size or power or money that determined the winner. It was attitude. And determination. And maybe a little sadism as well.

For almost a year, beatings, killings, and kidnappings in and around Philadelphia took their toll on both sides, generating wide coverage in the local media. And one thing the Mafia doesn't like (with the exception, of course, of the late John Gotti) is a lot of publicity. Soon everyone in the region knew that the big bad Mob was going up against the fun-loving motorcycle riders, and the Mob wasn't getting the best of things, whether in the press or in the streets.

Everything came to a head on the day Jimmy D and another Pagan grabbed a Mob dealer off a Philadelphia corner, hustled him into the dealer's car, and told him to drive to a spot that the Mob member knew was their killing zone. Passing a police precinct, the Mob dealer swung the car toward the cop shop, jumped out of the car, and ran screaming past the surprised cops toward the precinct door, assuming he'd be safe inside the station.

He wasn't. Jimmy D followed him, drew his gun, and right in front of the cops, emptied his bullets into the dealer. Then he threw the gun to the ground and raised his hands while the dealer lay dying at his feet.

Thanks to the Pagans' connections, the Mob's reputation, and the money the Pagans could hand over to the best lawyers in Philadelphia, Jimmy D was back on the street within days. At his trial he pleaded guilty to a manslaughter charge, and served less than two years in prison. Manslaughter? Shooting someone in the back, in front of a half-dozen cops who were too surprised to draw their own weapons? How's that for beating a rap? It was enough to persuade Little Nicky that maybe his plan to include the Pagans in his street tax was a trifle premature. He announced their exemption from the tax, much to the relief of the other capos in the Lucchese family and the joy of the Pagans.

The Pagans had been as tough as any one-percent gang and far tougher than most, and their successful action with Scarfo and the Mob only added to their glory. They soon expanded their base of operations, shifting power to a new mother chapter in Rocky Point, Long Island, and venturing into other money-making businesses that included arson, extortion, car theft, and weapons trafficking.

So when the Hells Angels decided to strengthen their operations in and around the New York/New Jersey/Philadelphia area, they ran up against a determined bunch of Pagans who said, "Hell no!"

One tactic the Pagans used against the Angels was to absorb other MCs that wanted to share in the action. It was the fastest, most efficient method of gaining power through numbers and seemed to work. Most of the time.

In July 1994, eight Pagans showed up at a charity fundraiser picnic held by the Tri-County MC in Hackettstown, New Jersey, prepared to persuade the Tri-County members to improve their prospects by trading their identity for a Pagans patch. The members didn't think this was such a good idea and expressed it directly, which led to fistfights, which led to knives and guns, which led to two Pagans, Glenn Ritchie and Diego Vega, shot dead and a Pagan and a Tri-County biker wounded. Another Tri-County member had his throat cut.

A few years later, seventy-three Pagans arrived at the Hellraiser Ball, an indoor motorcycle and tattoo show on Long Island that a number of Angels attended. The Pagans rushed the doors, the Angels held their ground, a dozen or so people were wounded, and a Pagan rider was shot to death by an Angel. The firebombing of a South Philadelphia Pagan-owned tattoo parlor soon followed.

Much of the Pagans' tough attitude stemmed from its president, Steven "Gorilla" Mondevergine, a former Philadelphia police officer. After just three years as a Philly cop, Mondevergine was fired for allegedly accepting bribes from an illegal gambling operation. He denied the charges, which were eventually dropped, but Gorilla had had enough of the law enforcement side of things and began a career as a carpenter, riding his motorcycle on weekends. Eventually he set his saw and hammer aside and teamed up with both the Pagans and the new Philadelphia Mob boss Joseph "Skinny Joey" Merlino.

Skinny Joey and the burly biker got along well—so well that they began to patch things up after the war over Little Nicky's street-tax edict. He didn't get along so well with others, however. In August 1999, walking home from a neighborhood Philadelphia bar, Gorilla Mondevergine was ambushed and shot nine times at close range. Miraculously, he survived, and like a good one percenter, refused to identify the shooter. Within a few months, however, a Philadelphia tattoo parlor known to be favored by Hells Angels was firebombed, and in November 2000 Mondevergine took two shots at the leader of a street gang that might have been contracted by the Angels to take out Mondevergine in 1999. The other guy had better aim; Mondevergine missed with both shots. The attempt got him twenty-seven months in prison on a racketeering charge.

In 2005, shortly after Mondevergine's release, Hells Angels vice president Thomas Wood left Cheerleaders, a South Philly topless bar, climbed into his gray pickup truck, and headed home via the Schuylkill Expressway at one-thirty a.m. Witnesses said a white Chevy Suburban van pulled alongside the pickup and fired a volley of shots at Wood, killing him instantly.

This may have done it for the Angels. Later that year they closed their Philadelphia chapter.

AMERICA IS STUDDED with wannabe clubs whose members watched the Angels grow in reputation and power and decided they'd like some of the action themselves. In several cases, riders tried to join the Angels and were repulsed for one reason or another, leaving them with less than warm feelings. Sometimes this led to an "Angels are pussies compared to us" attitude, and actions to prove it.

Here are some of the most prominent of these wannabe clubs.

The Free Souls were based in Oregon in the late 1960s. Their name sounds like a folk singing group. Even their patch design—an ankh, the ancient Egyptian symbol for eternal life, inside a motorcycle wheel—looks friendly compared with the death's head Angels symbol and the Outlaws' "Charlie" skull. They haven't grown much beyond Oregon, with just one chapter outside that state, but members have been arrested and charged with various crimes that include drug trafficking, weapons possession, and vehicle theft.

The Highwaymen came out of Detroit in the mid-1950s sporting a black-and-silver patch that featured a winged skull wearing a motorcycle cap inspired by Brando's in *The Wild One*. They've since spread out of Michigan south as far as Florida. For some reason, the club has held a special allure for military veterans suffering post-traumatic stress disorder. Law enforcement agencies have charged Highwaymen members with the usual litany of offenses, including racketeering, murder for hire, assault, police corruption, cocaine trafficking, vehicle theft, and mortgage and insurance fraud. The police corruption charges were laid on four Detroit officers involved in drug trafficking as part of the Highwaymen operation. FBI agents who raided the Highwaymen clubhouse in 2007 seized a large cache of illegal firearms that included assault rifles, shotguns, and handguns. Their investigation lasted two years and involved wiretaps and informants, one of whom was eventually murdered.

The raid illustrated a new facet of Detroit's downfall in recent years. When evidence revealed that the clubhouse had been used as a drug den, the court ruled that it was to be forfeited to state law enforcement agencies. The eviction caused some consternation among neighbors—the clubhouse had been by far the best-maintained building in that part of the city.

The Warlocks, which originated in Philadelphia in 1967, counts a large number of Vietnam War veterans among its members. They're also solidly and unashamedly racist, many of them adding white supremacy symbols to their insignia. The Warlocks' colors are red and white, and their patch is a Harpy, a winged woman from Greek mythology who constantly stole food from the king. They maintain chapters in the eastern United States as well as in England and Germany. Most of the Warlocks' troubles with the law involve widespread trafficking in methamphetamines. The 2008 arrest of a Bucks County chapter president revealed that that one chapter had moved more than five hundred pounds of methamphetamines.

Sons of Silence Motorcycle Club (SOSMC) is another 60s-era group whose founders were probably inspired by the Angels' success around that time. They got started in Niwot, Colorado, a small town about a hundred kilometers north of Denver. Despite their low-key status, the SOSMC has established chapters in fourteen states as well as a handful in Germany.

A major 1999 raid by agents of the Bureau of Alcohol, Tobacco and Firearms resulted in the arrest of thirty-seven members on charges of illegally possessing weapons (including four hand grenades) plus twenty pounds (nine kilograms) of methamphetamines. A later raid in an Iowa chapter produced more drugs, more weapons, and more arrests.

The SOSMC may be striving for a little more class and honesty than similar clubs. For example, their motto is written in

Latin—and how many bikers know Latin? It's *Donec Mors Non Separat,* or Until Death Separates Us. And their patch consists of an eagle superimposed on an uppercase letter A that looks familiar. It should: it was lifted from the logo of the Anheuser-Busch beer company, presumably the producer of the club's favorite beverage.

AND YET THE ANGELS' most recent challenge hasn't come from other motorcycle clubs. It's come from the streets, and it may be the most devastating of all and ultimately fatal.

Let's remember that most MC members come from middle or working class backgrounds. At the very least they own their bikes, they have a place to sleep, and they may have families. Their anger at the rest of society may be real, but it's a little contrived. Most one percenters would be busy doing something else if it wasn't for the "brotherhood" that gives them strength, courage, and security.

Out on the streets, it's different. When you lack most or all of those assets, your anger and outrage are real. Mix in some racial discrimination and a generally dismissive attitude from the rest of the world, and that anger becomes even more sharp-edged. So when an opportunity comes not only to lift yourself up out of the gutter into real wealth but to do it while giving the finger to the rest of society, especially the guys riding by on their $15,000 Harley-Davidsons, you become driven in a manner that few one percenters will ever match or understand.

Those were the forces driving the street gangs that rose out of California in the late 1960s, especially the neighborhoods of southeast San Diego. And just like the motorcycle clubs, once they'd established their power and influence, more chapters began appearing in other regions of the United States and down into

Mexico. Communities as far afield as Minneapolis and Denver are home to gangs with San Diego roots, most notably the Logan Heights gang and its affiliates.

The Logan Heights gang, born during the turbulent 60s in the region around Memorial Park and Oceanview Boulevard, was the first to gain national prominence. Nothing much distinguished the gang from other groups in and around San Diego until November 1992, when David "D" Barron helped rescue the Arellano-Felix brothers from a shoot-out in a Puerto Vallarta disco. The brothers, who ran the Tijuana cartel that supplied much of the cocaine and other drugs entering California, bonded with Barron and his fellow gang members, opening the door to enormous profit opportunities.

Things did not get off to a good start, however. A few months later, in May 1993, the Logan Heights gang and the Tijuana cartel tried to set up a hit on drug lord "Chapo" Guzman at the Guadalajara airport. The San Diego gang supplied the hit men, who were told to watch for Guzman arriving in a white Mercury Grand Marquis town car. When a car matching this description arrived at the airport, the gunmen opened fire, killing six civilians—among them Roman Catholic cardinal Juan Jesus Posados Ocampo.

Was it a case of mistaken identity? Perhaps, but the cardinal, who was shot almost point-blank, emerged from the car wearing a long black cassock and large pectoral cross. It would be difficult to confuse him with drug baron Guzman. What's more, the cardinal had recently condemned the illicit drug trade and all who engaged in it.

Whatever the cause of the cardinal's death, the reputation of the Logan Heights gang was established. So was the close working relationship between the gang, the Tijuana cartel, and the Mexican

Mafia. One way or another, whenever the Angels choose to deal in drugs coming across the border into California, they have to tap into some connection involving the Logan Heights gang.

But as intimidating as the gang may be, they're not the top of the pyramid when it comes to menacing street gangs flowing out of Southern California. That honor goes to the MS-13, aka Mara Salvatrucha 13.* They're not only the largest criminal gang in the United States, with membership estimated by some law enforcement organizations as surpassing thirty-six thousand, but the most ferocious. And they're not interested in merely eliminating any individual or organization that represents a serious threat; they want to use their actions as a means of warning others. That's why the bodies of MS-13 victims are frequently dismembered after death. The usual technique involves decapitation, with the head sometimes left with the body, sometimes deposited in a prominent location, and sometimes disposed of separately.

They also engage in activities that even the Hells Angels consider disgusting, including running prostitution rings involving girls as young as fourteen. In late 2012, Anthony "Critico" Pineda-Penado became the eleventh MS-13 gang member that year to be convicted of trafficking in underage females for the purpose of prostitution. He pled guilty to the charge in Montgomery County, Maryland, and was sentenced to eighteen years in prison. Among the revelations was the discovery that young girls, often lured from middle and high schools, were required to have sex with a minimum of ten men each day or face beatings.

---

* No one appears certain of the origin of the gang's name. The best guess suggests that *Mara* is Salvadoran slang for gang, and *Salvatrucha* is a blend of Salvador and *trucha*, meaning to be alert. The numeral 13 may be an intentional effort to defy fortune by choosing an unlucky number.

MS-13 operates on the thin line between severe intimidation and angry psychopathy. How else would you explain the following incidents, which represent just a small taste of their activities?

On December 23, 2004—two days before Christmas—six MS-13 members sprayed an intercity bus near Chamelecon, Honduras, killing twenty-eight civilians, most of them women and children. When the others ceased firing, one of the gang members boarded the bus and walked down the aisle methodically executing survivors. The massacre had been organized as a means of protesting the Honduran government's efforts to restore the death penalty. The MS-13 members were all eventually caught and tried. Four were convicted and two were released.

On June 22, 2008, a father and his two sons were shot to death by Edwin Ramos, an MS-13 member, after the father's car briefly blocked Ramos's car from making a left-hand turn.

In June 2009 three men were killed by MS-13 members in three separate incidents on Long Island, New York. One victim was a thirteen-year-old boy shot in the head while playing basketball. The boy, Wilson Batista, was African-American, and MS-13 was at war with the Bloods, a predominantly black gang. On that basis alone, the young boy was shot. In another instance, three MS-13 gang members went looking for the Latin Kings, another Hispanic gang "at war" with MS-13. Encountering twenty-eight-year-old Edgar Villalobos, they questioned his gang affiliation. Villalobos, who belonged to no gang, tried to defend himself by claiming to be a member of MS-13. The three MS-13 members attacked him with a gun, a knife, and a machete.

Later that year, two MS-13 members on Long Island were convicted of shooting a nineteen-year-old woman who gang members felt had "disrespected" another MS-13 member. When the woman's two-year-old son began crying at the sight of his dead mother, he was shot in the head as well.

The list goes on and on. These are not some street toughs out of control. They're members of a gang as disciplined and driven in its goals as any criminal organization, including the Angels and other MCs. And while many may think street-gang members tend to wipe each other out—a claim applied to biker gangs as well—that's neither true nor reassuring. Members of MS-13 have also been convicted of attempting to murder a U.S. federal agent because he was, in the gang's opinion, too successful at cracking down on their activities.

The gang's first goal in that operation was to obtain a high-powered assault rifle, like an M-16, that would penetrate the agent's bulletproof vest. This is disturbing in itself, but the planning behind the plot is even more unsettling. The order for the hit was issued by an MS-13 clique (the gang's word for chapter) in El Salvador and passed on to leaders in Virginia, who were to make arrangements for the assassination to be carried out by the Flushing, New York, clique. Anyone who considers MS-13 to be a bunch of wild street kids running around with weapons in their hands is not dealing with reality. They are strong, they are mean, they are organized, and they go head to head with the Angels and other clubs in pursuit of the same criminal activities: drug dealing, prostitution, money laundering, and extortion. And to that list you can add MS-13's people-smuggling, illegal immigration, and a sackful of other crimes.

FOR MUCH of the twentieth century the Italian Mafia represented the most feared and efficient criminal organization in North America, a position it maintained even with the rise of the Angels and their various MC-related competitors. The Italian organization's response to the bike clubs, especially the Angels, was to recruit them and engage their services to the Mafia's benefit, usually as drug distributors.

While the Mafia continues to play a major role in organized crime, it's generally agreed that its power is waning. There are a number of reasons for this decline. One is the assimilation of Italian immigrants into American society, making it more difficult to recruit inner-city Italian youths than in the past. Another is the law enforcement agencies' concerted efforts in investigating and prosecuting members, especially via RICO. The fall of high-profile leaders like John Gotti eliminated more than the mystique associated with the Mafia; it eliminated much of the experienced management as well.

By the end of the twentieth century it appeared that the Angels and their cohort gangs were capable of filling the Mafia's role, and for a time they were. But too many challengers arrived on the scene, including Mafia-styled organizations rooted in Russia and China. And even they pale by comparison with the more violent one percenters like the Pagans and the Mongols. Toss MS-13 and their cronies into the mix, and the Angels may begin to look like a fraternal organization rather than a widely feared bunch of toughs.

7

ALL IN A NIGHT'S WORK

You have to hand one thing to the Angels: they know how to adapt when it comes to making money illegally. I'm not suggesting they're into computer programming or any kind of sophisticated black magic, but they've moved from things that take little more than muscle and nerve into white-collar crime, where a little muscle always helps but the game is really about deception and lies.

So here's a rundown of the ways the Angels have generated big bucks for themselves in the past and how they've set their sights on the future, especially in the face of such competitors as vicious street gangs and better-equipped law enforcement.

NARCOTICS

It's six a.m. on August 26, 2012, a balmy Sunday morning, and George M* is crouching behind a shrub, waiting for the signal. A

---

* Name withheld for security reasons.

three-year veteran of the Emergency Response Team (ERT) with the RCMP, he feels cold despite the warm air. There's six minutes to go before they enter the house and he's felt this chill before. Your teeth chatter, your organs feel frozen, and you wish to hell you can get this over with soon.

It's not just the pre-dawn timing that's getting to George. It's the knowledge that he and the rest of the team will be busting down doors of a biker clubhouse. Bikers are always dangerous and unpredictable. Hell, they wear badges of honor for battling cops. They may be heavily armed and have booby-trapped the place for all George knows.

The raid has been set up by a "friendly," who George knows is inside, along with nearly a dozen genuine bikers. The friendly has been told to drop to the floor and stay still when the raid begins. Bullets could be flying and in the heat of things anyone could become a target.

Time's up—let's go.

Two minutes later, the excitement is fading and George is no longer chattering from the cold or anything else. He's almost as high as the customers for some of the club's product they've seized. When raids go this well, the team talks like a bunch of baseball players: no hits, no runs, no errors, and nobody left on base. High fives all around, and then the work begins. The suspects are cuffed and sent downtown and the evidence is assessed. Plenty of drugs, lots of weapons, and piles of cash—many piles of cash. A quick count estimates $4 million. All that money in a beat-up clubhouse full of greasy bikers in torn jeans and leather boots.

Where did the money come from? George M and the other RCMP members, who'd spent months planning the raid, said it originated with Kevin Van Kalkeren from Osoyoos, British Columbia, right on the American border. Van Kalkeren, forty-four, had flirted around drug dealing for years, much of it associated with the Hells Angels. In this case he was acting as broker on a deal to import two hundred kilograms of cocaine. The police said it was also a family affair, claiming that a bunch of Van Kalkeren's relatives not only knew about his involvement in drugs but helped him out in various passive ways, such as holding some of his properties in their name. On that basis, the police sought to seize not just Van Kalkeren's assets but those of some family members as well.

Two Angels, including vice president David Giles and sergeant-at-arms Bryan Oldham, were also charged.

Just another day in the life of a narcotics cop? Maybe, but consider this: Osoyoos is a pretty little town of fewer than five thousand permanent residents, most of whom are involved in fruit orchards or the tourist industry. This is not a gritty, down-at-the-heels place in the Rust Belt, nor a big city of high-rollers who snort coke the way the rest of the world uses salt. Yet one dealer was able to gather $4 million and funnel it through a single chapter of the Hells Angels on a coke deal. How many other small-town deals of this size are going on each week in the biker empire?

DRUGS HAVE BEEN bread and butter for the Angels since Sonny Barger rode a tricycle. It can be argued, of course, that the Angels and their cohorts in the drug business are simply playing one side of the supply-and-demand equation. If people in America, Europe, and elsewhere demand drugs, the Angels and others will supply it.

It's the extent of the Angels' involvement in the drug scene that blows the minds of many, along with the careful attention they pay to maximizing profit and minimizing risk. In many ways, the Angels could be used as a case study in an MBA course demonstrating those two skills. Maybe they have been.

Here's an example.

Back in the 1950s and 60s the Angels focused on marijuana sales. But compared with other drugs, growing, harvesting, and distributing dope is a labour-intensive, low-profit business. So the Angels remain involved almost entirely on an arm's-length basis. They'll make contacts with grow-ops to produce the stuff and get puppet gangs to do the risky distribution side of things. They involve people like Rob Shannon, a cool-looking guy from Abbotsford who lived the high life for a time, including owning a large cigarette boat—painted in garish green and black and capable of doing close to a hundred kilometers an hour—and a matching customized truck to haul it around. His high living ended in 2008 when he was arrested by U.S. authorities as he entered the country to talk over a deal with a large American dealer. Shannon had managed the B.C. side of an operation that smuggled high-potency B.C. marijuana into Washington State in things like hollowed-out logs, PVC pipes, and propane tankers, sometimes as much as two tons per shipment.

His connection with the Hells Angels was never in doubt, despite protestations to the contrary by him and others rounded up in the same operation. The Angels who shared in the $3.5 million deal over the years stayed out of prison, and Shannon was not prepared to testify against them. He got a twenty-year sentence. At least he didn't get a bullet behind the ear.

Hey, it's business, and business always involves taking chances. The idea is to maximize the profit and minimize the risk. Every businessman knows that. And so do the Angels. Which is why they tend toward methamphetamines. And which is why it's sometimes referred to as "biker's coffee."

OF ALL THE RECREATIONAL DRUGS available in America and Europe, it's difficult to think of one more destructive than methamphetamine, usually produced as crystal meth for sale on the street. We know about codeine and heroin, but I'm told that getting off these is child's play compared with dropping a serious meth habit. Many people have maintained a heroin addiction over much of their lives without suffering serious health effects. Jazz musicians like pianist Bill Evans and singer Anita O'Day used heroin on a regular basis. I don't recommend it. Nobody would. But they and other people managed to function pretty normally and create a lot of great stuff while both handling and concealing their addiction from most of the world. When Anita O'Day died at age eighty-seven it was pneumonia that killed her, not drugs.

You can't do this with meth. Two years of regular meth use will age you twenty years at least. The kinds of things you'll suffer from are the stuff of nightmares. You'll lose your teeth, break out in acne, and suffer from insomnia, diarrhea, constipation, and a host of other disgusting effects. In the end it will kill you. You won't give a damn about these effects for a while because you'll be enjoying the euphoria and sense of self-confidence that meth delivers before the paranoia and psychosis kick in. By that time you're half dead and don't care about the other half. Some of the saddest sights you'll ever see are before and after pictures of attractive young women who become hooked on meth and turn tricks to support their habit. In the beginning, this is easy. But after a year or two the tricks don't come so readily. The girls are toothless, their skin is covered in sores, and they're emaciated and paranoid. The tricks aren't there anymore, but the addiction is.

Here's where the Angels' business sense kicks in. Unlike heroin and cocaine, which has to be brought in from other countries at great risk and expense, the Angels can produce meth from scratch.

Recipes are everywhere. The ingredients aren't difficult to obtain, but not everyone can operate a successful meth kitchen from day one. Make a mistake in handling some of the inflammable and corrosive ingredients and you'll find yourself in the middle of a fiery explosion.

Once an Angel chapter appoints a meth chef, they've achieved what's known in the straight business world as vertical integration: you make the stuff, you market it, you distribute it, and you sell it to the end user—all without having to share the profits.

The Angels haven't sewn up the market for meth or any other drug in the United States and Europe, nor are they likely to do so. The legalization of marijuana may be just around the corner, which will eliminate that product from the shopping list. Meanwhile, competition for harder drugs will grow more intense and will likely originate with street gangs and others whom the Angels would prefer to avoid—not just because they match or exceed the Angels in viciousness but because there's more money to be made more easily by other means, and the Angels are always interested in easy money.

ONE OF THE MORE disturbing developments where the Angels are concerned has been their spreading association with other well-established criminal organizations, each able to add one important element to the mix. It's a little like picking an All-Star team, except there's nothing starry about these guys. There *is* something frightening about them, however. Especially a recent case involving Alessandro Taloni.

Taloni was associated with the Montreal Mafia clan led by Vito Rizzuto. On one level, Taloni had a pretty good life. Ensconced in a fancy home in Beverly Hills and tooling around Los Angeles in luxury cars, living the California dream, who wouldn't admire the good-looking thirty-nine-year-old? Why, his only duties appeared to involve meeting a chartered jet at L.A. airport now and then and visiting places like the star-favored Beverly Hills Hotel, where he'd meet other men, wait for them to utter a code word, answer with another, and accept a briefcase.

We all know what's going on when we hear this kind of description. It was borne out when Taloni was arrested and charged with trafficking in narcotics.

The drugs and money traveled in both directions. High-grade marijuana arrived on chartered jets from Canada, and massive quantities of cocaine flew back to Montreal in a similar fashion. When U.S. drug agents intercepted one of the planes in October 2010, they found $5.5 million in cash on board. They also located $2.6 million in cash and eighty-three kilograms of cocaine in Taloni's Mercedes-Benz sedan. Taloni eventually pleaded guilty and received a ten-year prison sentence and a $10 million fine.

The investigation revealed that this was not a Mafia-exclusive operation. It involved, in addition to members of the Rizzuto clan, the Akwesasne Mohawk First Nation reserve on the border with Quebec and New York State, Mexico's Sinaloa drug cartel doing an estimated $1 billion annually in narcotics, and the Hells Angels.

The Montreal end of things was directed by Jimmy Cournoyer, a modest guy who gave himself the nicknames Cosmo and Superman. Cournoyer, from Laval, Quebec, acted as the broker between the mob and the Angels, who provided transportation and security services to move tens of thousands of kilograms of high-grade grass from B.C., plus large amounts of hydroponic marijuana and ecstasy from the Montreal area.

There may or may not be honor among thieves, but with big money to be made from cocaine and other drugs, there's a lot of cooperation. Whether this kind of partnership between drug cartels, First Nations gangsters, the Mafia, and the Angels will survive or not, we all pay, one way or another, for every large-scale success they score together.

PROSTITUTION

Some middle-class people like to think they operate on a different planet from the Angels and other biker gangs. Some do. Most don't, whether they acknowledge it or not.

Consider a middle-class guy from any community in America sitting downstairs in his recreation room at two in the morning. He's a decent guy, holds down a well-paying job, plays a little golf, does a little fishing, attends his kids' soccer games, has a beer with his buddies now and then, and never fails to pay his taxes. His wife and kids are upstairs, sound asleep. He turns on his computer and logs onto a porn site. The site charges him a few bucks every month to watch women being sexually degraded. The fees are charged to his credit card and show up with some innocuous name like "Sporting News Index" or "ChampionBassFishing.com," so his wife never knows what he's watching or what it's costing him. Maybe she already knows and doesn't care. But she should. And he should as well. Because chances are he's feeding money to the Hells Angels via the internet.

Sometimes he's feeding them something more valuable than money. Like his identity.

Whether he's buying access to a porn channel or chatting with some woman online and on-camera (who may well be controlled by the Angels), he'll be asked to provide a wealth of information for the momentary pleasure he's seeking. This includes his name, address, credit card number, card expiry date, and card security code. With this in hand, plus other data from the internet connection, whoever's on the other end of the line is well on the way to stealing his complete identity. They can sell it to big-volume operators in Europe or Asia, or they can use it to create a complete set of ID to fall back on in the event of police takedowns and warrants. Imagine how much more secure an Angel feels if he can "prove" he's not the man the cops are looking for.

Even if the guy in the basement at two in the morning manages to escape having his credit card information used illegally, he's still not involved in a "victimless" crime. Payments to access porn sites are often handled by an e-transfer company, which can—and does—move money around instantly and clandestinely, hiding the funds both from the country in which it's spent and the country in which the porn company is located. So no taxes are paid, coming or going. Interpol estimates that the tax revenue lost by Canadian and American economies alone totals in the billions of dollars each year.

You may think it's cool to avoid paying taxes. But like them or not, taxes are used to cover costs that everyone in the country shares. You're not short-changing the government; you're short-changing your neighbors and family. And who benefits? Usually it's a bunch of hairy, Harley-riding gangsters who'll use the taxes you avoided in order to buy, among other things, narcotics. And let's not forget the other losers: the young women ensnared in the Angels-run prostitution rackets.

THE INTERESTING THING to me is that the Angels are always insulted whenever they're accused of making money from prostitutes, as though it were beneath them. You can almost hear them saying, "Hey, we deal drugs and steal cars and beat people up, but we don't run no prostitutes!"

Which is a lie. They have long been involved in prostitution in Las Vegas and Amsterdam. "Okay, yeah," they'll say. "But it's legal in them places!"

Their denials are a crock. Anytime you encounter a situation involving women, sex, and money, you risk bumping up against a Hells Angel.

PROSTITUTION NO LONGER INVOLVES putting women on a street corner and forcing them to have sex with strangers. Not on the scale that the Angels and other biker gangs have practiced it for years. For one thing, that kind of racket involved a lot of transportation and supervision, and all bikers are basically lazy and impatient when it comes to making money.

Since the 1990s, two developments have changed the way biker gangs operate in the sex industry. One was the spread of the internet. The other was the collapse of the Soviet Union.

The internet brought pornography into every living room and virtually everywhere a customer could be found. All that's needed is a camera, a location, and participants, willing and unwilling, to perform. Which is where the collapse of the Soviet Union comes in.

Organized crime rose out of the ashes of Communism in Russia. It also removed any kind of cushion for people in need of assistance, including young women either disenchanted with their home life or addicted to narcotics or both. Usually both. The Russian Mafia was quick to spot the opportunity, and soon corraled hundreds of young women to perform in pornography videos at studios in and around Moscow. Their connections with Western crime organizations, including biker gangs, provided an entry first to DVD sales and later to internet downloading.

The scale of this kind of business grew enormously, which led to a need for money laundering to hide the profits from tax authorities. But it also led to other, more tragic developments.

"Shooting them having sex in those videos, it breaks their spirit," Bobby Perez of the Dago Hells Angels told me. "You get 'em doing what they're told to do in front of the camera and that's it. They're done. They're not gonna marry some lawyer and live in the suburbs when they're finished that stuff. They do what they're told, go where they're told to go."

Perez was among the most vicious of the Dago Angels, tuned in to everything they did. He knew about the business, even as far off as Moscow. He knew that the "film stars," the girls with dreams of something besides a life of prostitution, would be caught in a trap they could never escape. After enough appearances in porn videos, they'd be shipped to brothels in Germany, the Netherlands, and elsewhere as "fresh meat." Then, after a year or two in these almost respectable businesses, they would in turn be moved along to make room for younger, newer "fresh meat" and shipped to brothels in Asia and Tel Aviv, which maintains more than 250 brothels in a city of barely 400,000 people.

If your idea of a brothel involves velvet walls, music, and big comfy beds, forget it. They are for the most part disgusting places, as disgusting as the Furmis brothel in Tel Aviv, where police charged through iron gates guarded by armed men and through iron doors leading to the elevator. Inside, they climbed to the third floor, finding a narrow, dimly lit corridor furnished with only a suspicious wooden cupboard. Behind the cupboard they met other bodyguards and yet another door, which opened onto a filthy two-room brothel holding ten frightened and miserable young women. The only furnishings were stained, foul-smelling mattresses.

When young women from Eastern Europe are ready to be replaced with "fresh meat," many are sent to North America as tourists or as domestic workers. Whatever the explanation, they're in the hands of the Angels or the Bandidos or some other gang and put to work in strip clubs, massage parlors, escort agencies, or porn movies and shows. Now they're bound three ways: threatened with beatings and death if they try to escape; told they'll be sentenced by authorities to long prison terms as illegal immigrants; and addicted to drugs, including cocaine, heroin, and methamphetamines.

Biker gangs are deeply involved in this racket. Their tentacles extend almost everywhere illicit sex is produced, distributed, and sold. Prostitution on this scale involves far more than pimping the women. It involves human trafficking, often across international borders, and control over victims that amounts to the same kind of slavery as employed in the American Deep South prior to the Civil War. This includes the buying and selling of human beings as though they were cattle, and life-and-death control over each individual.

It also includes treating the women involved in the sex trade like animals. No, worse than animals. Every farmer and every animal trainer knows that a good animal represents an asset worth caring for. You don't whip a thoroughbred racehorse until it's bleeding to make a point, or starve a herd of dairy cows to make them produce more milk, or expose a flock of egg-laying hens to a family of foxes.

But that's the way most sex workers are treated by motorcycle gang members or the people they assign to the job. Like a woman named Stacy* in the generally quiet and very middle-class city of London, Ontario, who became involved with a local businessman who also happened to be a high-ranking member in the local Hells

---

* Not her real name.

Angels chapter. They launched a legitimate (she thought) business together. When the operation began losing money, he persuaded her to become a stripper at a local club, then applied physical and emotional abuse, eventually setting her up as a prostitute in a local motel. Stacy remained in this "relationship" for years—at one point her boyfriend broke all her toes in retaliation for her attempts to escape. Eventually, a motel resident saw the couple fighting in front of her room at the motel and called the police.

The boyfriend was charged with various offenses but served little time in prison because Stacy refused to cooperate fully with police. Why? Because, despite the assurances of police protection, she knew that the boyfriend and his biker friends would eventually hunt her down and kill her.

It all goes on under our noses, and much of it involves the Angels and other biker gangs. It's a vortex, a whirlpool that prevents victims from escaping. Anyone who thinks someone involved in the sex trade, as either a stripper or a prostitute, can simply walk away from the business and her pimp is delusional or blind, and maybe both.

You need proof? Consider Margo Compton. She's not the only example of the power that the Angels hold over their victims. She may not even be the most dramatic and pathetic. She's simply one of the best known.

Margo became involved with the San Francisco Angels, working for them under the direction of Otis "Buck" Garrett in the Love Nest, a city brothel. (Which, by the way, puts the lie to the Angels' claim that they're not involved in this racket.) Garrett was a classic Angels case, a guy who pursued every avenue available to make a buck for himself and the Angels. Past president of the Angels' Vallejo chapter, he was involved in money laundering, ran a large-scale meth operation with "kitchens" in San Bernardino and Modoc

County, and was facing charges of distributing methamphetamine through the Angels chapter in Winston-Salem, North Carolina.

Trying to escape her life in the brothel and be a good mother to her six-year-old twin daughters Sandra and Sylvia, twenty-four-year-old Margo agreed to testify at Garrett's trial for pimping and human trafficking. She entered the witness protection system and was moved, with her girls, to Laurelwood, Oregon, about forty kilometers from Portland.

The Angels have eyes everywhere.

Late one summery afternoon, Bonnie Sleeper arrived at Margo's two-bedroom bungalow in Laurelwood, bringing a bouquet of flowers for her friend and the twin girls. No one answered the door, yet someone appeared to be home because loud rock music blared from inside the house. The front door was locked, but when Bonnie went to the back of the house, the rear door pushed open easily.

Inside the house, Bonnie encountered a nightmare. Two bodies were sprawled on the living room floor. One was Margo Compton, obviously dead. Next to her lay Margo's fiancé, Gary Seslar. Shot twice in the head, Seslar was nevertheless alive, unconscious in a pool of blood from him and from Margo. He died soon afterward.

The horror was just beginning. When police arrived in response to Bonnie's hysterical telephone call they discovered the bodies of the two little girls in one of the bedrooms, both wearing matching swimsuits and each clutching a teddy bear. The bed was soaked in their blood. Both had been shot behind the left ear. Later, in testimony that finally brought Garrett and his accomplices to justice, it was revealed that Margo had been forced to watch as her daughters were shot.

There was no doubt that the killings were connected with Margo's agreement to testify against Garrett. And there was no doubt that Garrett, who was in San Francisco when the horror unfolded, had put out a contract on Compton. The shooting of Sandra and Sylvia was obviously premeditated and just as obviously ordered as a means of terrorizing any potential witnesses against the Angels. Without the shooter, however, the police did not have a case. They needed to find whoever was inhuman enough to carry off a crime that was so cruel, so outrageous that (as it became known later) even the Aryan Brotherhood had turned down the job when approached by the Angels' leadership. Killing the two adults for the right price would have been acceptable, said Mike Thompson, a former council member of the Aryan Brotherhood. But not the two little girls. "It might sound strange," Thompson was quoted about the killings, "but we do have some ethics."

Robert "Bug-Eye Bob" McClure didn't suffer from that particular handicap. He was an Angels prospect, a hanger-on waiting to earn his patch and be fully accepted within the gang. He was also in debt to Garrett for some meth he'd consumed at Garrett's expense.

Every Angel knows that "snitches wind up in ditches." Garrett made an offer to Bug-Eye: if he would travel to Oregon, enter the Compton house at night, and kill the little girls in front of Margo before killing Margo herself, Garrett would erase Bug-Eye's debt, recommend that he move from prospect to fully patched Angel, and score two pounds of meth to sweeten the deal. It was an offer McClure simply could not refuse. He first shot Seslar to eliminate a witness, then marched Compton into the bedroom to witness the execution of her daughters, and finally shot Compton herself before fleeing.

All of this came out years later when McClure, now a fully patched Angel, was sent to prison on a trafficking charge. It's a mark of McClure's psyche that he couldn't avoid bragging about the murders while behind bars. Angels and convicts generally despise snitches, but they despise child killers even more, and some of them passed the word on to authorities.

Garrett's and McClure's trials took place in the Washington County courthouse in Hillsboro, a small town near Laurelwood, where the prosecution built its case almost entirely on the testimony of prison informants and bikers who said the two had talked behind bars about the killings. Between the roster of incorrigibles in the dock and the infamy of the crime, it was the biggest spectacle in memory for a quiet area given more to deer hunts and sidewalk bazaars.

Streams of outlaw bikers, including Sonny Barger of Oakland, roared into town to watch the trial. They made it clear, however (or tried to), that Garrett and McClure were renegades who committed the murders without the sanction of their biker clubs. The death's head emblem and the rest of the patch they wore? Didn't mean a thing. The Angels don't kill little children.

A parade of witnesses was flown in from California prisons, all of them wearing orange jumpsuits and bound in chains. Most had quit, or "rolled out," of prison gangs to turn informant. Some were already in the federal witness protection system.

Both sides used snitches to try to prove their case. The prison snitches were the most fascinating and revealing to civilians whose only exposure to hard time behind bars had been through bad Hollywood movies. In their testimonies, the inmates spoke of ruthless men with nicknames like "Dirty Dick," "Booger," "Bulldog," and "Doug the Thug." Being behind bars did not weaken the power of these guys. It just meant the targets of their wrath were other prisoners.

The prosecution's string of informants included "Iron Mike" Thompson, a convicted murderer who'd rolled out of the Aryan Brotherhood prison gang. Thompson contended that he'd been so sickened by McClure's and Garrett's confessions about killing the little girls that he'd almost ordered the two men executed by prisoners he controlled. Even the toughest inmates don't respect people who kill children, whatever the motive. "Child molesters, child killers, they don't stay on the mainline in the prison," Thompson testified. "If they're not locked up, they're killed. That's the way it is."

Josef Casal, another inmate, said McClure bragged of pumping bullets into children's "little heads," saying the smaller .22-caliber ammunition was more effective on children because it wouldn't make them "blow up." An ex–Hells Angels Oakland chapter president swore that McClure admitted killing the girls in an Oakland bar while they were arguing over a woman.

McClure never took the witness stand. He was being railroaded, he declared through his lawyer. Garrett gave his own attorney advice throughout the trial, shouting "Hearsay!" at some testimony. It was all b.s. McClure and Garrett were convicted and each received four consecutive life sentences.

The sentences may not be enough to balance the brutal murders of four people, including two innocent children. But they may not be the entire punishment either. Convicts have their own set of ethics and their own means of dishing out retribution. McClure, and possibly Garrett, may either serve their lives out in solitary or spend every day looking over their shoulder for some fellow prisoner with a shiv who dreams of becoming a hero.

Garrett at least can enjoy, if that's the word, some notoriety. Sonny Barger and his boys in Las Vegas run a website called Sin City's Baddest with an attached site titled Big House Crew. Garrett's picture is there along with several dozen other Angels serving long and well-deserved prison sentences, all of them displayed with great pride.

YOU WANT MORE HORROR? Nothing in recent years beats the story behind Robert Pickton and the pig farm he maintained near Port Coquitlam, B.C., where he abused and murdered as many as fifty women, most of them sex workers and drug users from Vancouver's Downtown Eastside. Many of the women, it was revealed at Pickton's trial, were first taken to an after-hours nightclub called Piggy's Palace located on a rural road literally around the corner from the Pickton farm. The women were given drugs at the Palace, then sexually used and abused before being taken to the farm and murdered.

Only at a formal government inquiry into the case was it learned that Piggy's Palace was a favorite hangout for Vancouver-area Angels and that Pickton's brother David was suspected of dealing in drugs, although no charges were ever laid in that offense. (No charges were laid against him in the disappearances and murders of all those women, either, even though David was a co-owner of the property and was considered the stronger—and brighter—of the two brothers.)

RCMP and other law enforcement agencies remain convinced that a good deal of drugs were distributed at Piggy's Palace. And everyone on the B.C. mainland believes that where drugs and Angels are involved, the Angels will have their hands in the cash register one way or another. Whether they also had their hands in the gruesome activities that went on at the pig farm, where very few of the women's remains were ever located, is another story.

STOLEN BIKES, BOATS, AND CARS

Car theft is among the most basic street crimes available, a step or two up from shoplifting, yet some Angels still practice it as an easy way to make a buck. Or, in the case of John Newcombe and his Angel associates, $750,000 in the small B.C. community of Peachland.

Newcombe ran Cycle Logic, a Kelowna-based business selling motorcycle accessories and servicing Harley-Davidsons. It also employed some local Hells Angels and members of the Kingpin Crew, which made it a logical place for local police to keep an eye on. In August 2012 they launched raids on Cycle Logic and on Newcombe's Peachland home, recovering a treasure trove of stolen vehicles that included pickup trucks, cars, boats, trailers, ATVs, motorcycles, and a key-cutting machine. They also located guns, ammunition, and $270,000 in cash tucked away in the ceiling.

Newcombe explained the cash by claiming to be a high-stakes gambler. He had a little more trouble explaining the stolen cars and trucks, whose Vehicle Identification Number (VIN) had been changed, making them difficult to trace as stolen property.

Stealing motorcycles has always been an appealing sideline for the Angels, and not always for the profit motive. Bike gangs may declare their undying love for their Harley-Davidsons, but they rarely express their affection by looking after their bikes. The next time you encounter a long "run" by the Angels or any other gang, watch for at least one of them with serious mechanical trouble. They don't need the stolen bikes for money. They're more likely to need them for parts to repair their own broken-down machines.

In the event that their Harleys are well cared for, and if the Angels chapter is a little more sophisticated, they may look for a daily double. This involves insuring a bike for its maximum value, reporting it stolen after a reasonable period of time, and collecting the insurance coverage. Meanwhile the bike gets a new paint job and a new serial number and is sold to a new buyer who may or may not suspect its origins.

ONLINE GAMBLING

I'll say this for the Angels: most of them may not know how to turn on a computer, but they sure know how to make money from it. Or at least find people around the world to do it for them.

The explosive growth of online gambling beginning in 2000 did not escape the Angels' attention, and by August 2008 a number of video poker pros began complaining of extortion plots, armed robbery, and murder. It began in Sweden in 2003 when a man named Andreas Oscarsson decided to start an online gambling site that he fully expected to provide a lot of enjoyment for participants and, incidentally, a lot of profit for him and his partners.

Unfortunately for Oscarsson, his partners were some European chapters of the Hells Angels who'd advanced him $250,000 to launch PokerListings, an umbrella site for several poker-playing options. Whether Oscarsson didn't know or knew and didn't care, the Angels' money came from their drug-dealing and the transaction was "black-bagged." You'd think he might know and care that the deal included paying $2 million back to the Angels within a fixed period of time, which meant an annual interest rate measured at *30 percent per month,* far beyond the level that the law allows.

By one measure, PokerListings was a success in that it quickly acquired a large number of fans eager to play online poker. But almost no business can generate enough profits to cover such high borrowing costs, especially when those lending the money have their own methods of calculating the unpaid balance. Three years after starting PokerListings, and having paid his creditors about $5 million in exchange for the original $250,000 loan, Oscarsson sold the company and moved to the United States.

Yet, unbelievably, the Angels declared that Oscarsson owed them an additional $2 million. Thomas Möller, the Swedish Hells Angels' president during the Nordic biker war of the mid-90s,* showed up at a meeting of PokerListings financial agents claiming he was operating as a debt collector on behalf of a company owned by Stefan Bengtsson, the nephew of the richest man in Sweden. One of the agents rejected Möller's claim, complaining about the loan and threatening to call the police. The next evening, in front of his own house, the agent was shot in the leg. When questioned by police he claimed he didn't see the shooter and couldn't imagine why it had happened.

In August 2008, after two years of living in New York, Oscarsson decided it was safe to travel back to Sweden for a family visit. Well, it wasn't. While asleep in his father's home in Trollhättan, he was shot twice in the head by a contract killer who'd entered the room through an open window. The killing remains unsolved (as do 95 percent of murders in Sweden), but high-ranking Swedish officials, investigative reporters, and much of the Swedish public are convinced that the Hells Angels had wreaked revenge on a man who dared to reject the idea that the Angels could justify $7 million interest on a $250,000 loan over three years.

THE SPECTACULAR GROWTH of online gambling provided a dilemma for American banks and a golden opportunity for the Angels.

The banks and credit-card issuers were reluctant to process payments between the gambling sites and the players. This was in response to pressure from the federal government, which wanted to outlaw the gambling operation. A lot of money was to be made from online gambling, but the banks preferred to avoid creating enemies in the Treasury Department and elsewhere, which hampered the business severely. Or might have.

---

* Details covered in Chapter 12.

There are always other ways to score a win, in poker and in processing money, and the poker companies found a few. One was to disguise winning poker players as online merchants selling everything from jewelry to golf balls. A guy in Illinois who wins $10,000 on a full house isn't paid for the full house; he's paid for ten thousand golf balls that one of the poker companies sold for him. How can the banks object to that? Of course, a portion of that ten grand went into the coffers of PokerStars and others—as much as one-third of all the money spent by the gamblers was raked off this way—but this didn't matter to the banks. As far as they were concerned, they were participating in a legal retail operation.

When billions of dollars began moving between gamblers, online gambling sites, and money handlers, the temptation became too much for the more aware and alert Hells Angels leaders. They wanted to get their hands into the flood of cash, and here's how they did it.

The poker companies needed a third level between themselves and the banks to make the banks feel comfortable. These became "payment processors" who "processed" payments on behalf of phony corporations, moving the cash handed over by the gambling operations to the winners. PokerStars acknowledged that it received money from American gamblers through company names that, in the words of a U.S. Attorney's Office release, "strongly imply the transaction has nothing to do with PokerStars," and that it used whatever company names "the processor can get approved by the bank."*

---

* Press Release, U.S. Attorney's Office, Southern District of New York, "Manhattan U.S. Attorney Announces $731 Million Settlement of Money Laundering and Forfeiture Complaint with PokerStars and Full Tilt Poker," July 31, 2012.

The Hells Angels were suspected of being involved in setting up these processors, giving them the opportunity to skim millions in fees, charges, expenses, or any other means they could successfully sell to the players.

PokerStars wasn't the only outfit busted at the time. Full Tilt Poker also came under suspicion of misrepresenting player funds deposited in online gambling accounts as safe, secure, and available for withdrawal at any time. Gamblers charged that the company did not maintain funds sufficient to repay players and distributed more than $400 million of the money to its owners. By March 31, 2011, Full Tilt Poker owed approximately $390 million to players around the world, including $160 million in the United States, yet it had only about $60 million on deposit in its bank accounts. No one seemed to know where the rest of the money went. It was simply gone, and no one was talking. Least of all the Angels.

In January 2014, Full Tilt Poker announced that it would release $82 million to about thirty thousand players in the U.S. who claimed they'd been waiting three years for their money. If this proved to be true, it still represented barely half of the amount claimed by Full Tilt players.

NOT ALL ANGELS' gambling activities involve such grand schemes. In some places they're content to swim with smaller fish.

In March 2013 police raided a swank banquet hall north of Toronto where several hundred "guests" were enjoying a Super Bowl party that involved betting on everything from the coin toss to the final score. The party, with an estimated two thousand attendees, had been sponsored by Platinum Sports, headquartered in Costa

Rica but managed by a collection of gangsters including Angels Robert Barletta and Billy Miller, president of the London, Ontario, chapter of the Angels, plus two other Hells Angels associates. A number of other men were charged with engaging in bookmaking, keeping a common gaming house, and conspiracy to commit an indictable offense. Almost $2.5 million in cash was confiscated by police, proving this wasn't just a group of neighborhood guys getting together to share chicken wings and beer while watching a football game.

Nor was it the first time Platinum Sports had been in the news. In April 2004 a woman named Louise Russo entered a sandwich shop to buy a meal for herself and her disabled daughter. While waiting for her order she was shot in the back when Antonio Borrelli, a Platinum Sports debt collector, and Paris Christoforou, a full-patch Hells Angel, jumped out of a vehicle and began firing into the shop. They were attempting to take out Mob member Michele Modica, who owed money to Platinum Sports, and didn't give a damn about anything other than getting revenge for an unpaid debt. Russo was caught in the line of fire. She is paralyzed from the waist down and forever confined to a wheelchair. Welcome to the world of the Angels.

Others were implicated in the tragedy, and Platinum Sports eventually paid $2 million to Ms. Russo (in twenty-dollar bills). Does this make up for what she suffered and continues to suffer to this day? Not a chance.

Such dramatic and appalling incidents draw attention to the violence that illegal gambling can generate, but its effects extend well beyond this, especially where the Angels are concerned. Profits are used to trade in narcotics, support prostitution and other sex-trade activities, and hire heavyweight legal advisers to minimize the risk of severe penalties. Some even suggest that the money is spent on local, regional, and even national politicians to buy their favor. If that's the case, you can add graft and bribery to the list.

So these are not just hairy, beer-swilling men raising a little hell. They are, or can be, numbered among society's most sophisticated criminals.

8

WHITE COLLARS AND GREASY FINGERS

Even the Angels keep business records, although they have nothing to do with either taxes or accountants. It's all a matter of who gets what share of the huge profits being made, usually from drug deals.

In July 2000, while Montreal police had a Hells Angels chapter under surveillance, they discovered that the club maintained two apartments in the same building, and that members' visits to the apartments coincided with drug deals. The cops had keys made and entered the apartments whenever the Angels weren't around. They discovered that money was brought to one apartment equipped with counting machines. The amount of money counted by the machines was recorded on a computer disk and stored in a safe in the apartment. The cash itself was transferred to the second apartment for storage.

In a six-month period, the police estimated that more than $5 million had moved through this one location, and suspected that other locations may have been maintained around the city.

Multiply that figure by locations around the world moving large quantities of Angel drugs, and the amount becomes staggering. In fact, it's so large that the Angels have to give a lot of thought to the problem of keeping the cash away from authorities.

The best way is to invest the money in what appear to be legitimate businesses, which is something the Angels in British Columbia have done on a grand scale.

Well past the drug haven near the Gastown area of Vancouver, East Hastings Street becomes something of a mecca for students from nearby Simon Fraser University and elsewhere. Block after block of stores in the 4000-address area attract the kids with latte cafés, hip-hop clothing, and other retail operations catering to the well-under-thirty crowd.

In 2004, *The Vancouver Sun* printed a list of businesses and properties along that stretch that were owned by the Hells Angels. From tanning salons and tattoo parlors to a clothing store and a coffee bar, all served as a means to conceal the Angels' stash of cash from investigators.

Among the most intriguing was a SuperValu store, part of a massive grocery chain. The franchise operation, on which hundreds of local families depended for their food items, was owned by a man named Ross McLellan, a full-patch member of the Haney Angels chapter. Before he became an Angel he was an honest-to-goodness millionaire, having made his fortune in the real estate and supermarket businesses. In December 2006, while on a flight to Maui for a vacation with several other Angels (which should tell you a lot about Angel taste in resorts and Angel access to money for things like winter vacations), McLellan died of a sudden heart attack.

McLellan's estate was valued at more than $5 million, and included $4.2 million in real estate; a Rolls-Royce, a Ferrari

Testarossa, a Hummer H2, and other luxury vehicles; autographed photos of Mickey Mantle, Roger Maris, and Joe DiMaggio; and a Bengal tiger rug.

Most of his estate was left to his seven children, born of three different women. To his fellow Angels he left only his Angel jewelry and a request that he be given "a traditional Hells Angels funeral service" with fellow Haney-chapter Angels as pallbearers.

By tracking Hastings Street alone, *The Vancouver Sun* revealed that local Angels chapters have included other wealthy entrepreneurs [*sic*] in recent years. Werner Giovani Gonzalez, a Haney chapter member, was both a director of a Hastings Street boutique and a real estate agent. Convicted cocaine dealer Francisco (Chico) Pires was a director of Big Shots Café, and Damiano Dipopolo owned Digstown, a hip-hop clothing store with a tanning salon and tattoo shop attached. Dipopolo also held the business license for Caffe Napoli, a coffee bar on Commercial Drive. Back on East Hastings, Kensington Travel listed Nomads Angel Nicodemo (Nick) Manno, forty-five, as president and secretary.

The president of the Angels East End chapter, John Bryce, was the longtime owner of Hi-Way Choppers located just off Hastings in the same general neighborhood. Bryce also had a numbered company that listed the same address as the Drake Hotel and strip club, plus at least four properties in Burnaby and North Vancouver. Where did he get all the cash for these investments? For many years, he listed his occupation as "longshoreman." Later he changed it to "businessman."

The Vancouver Hells Angels just may be the shrewdest cycling gang in North America, if not the world. They're surely among the wealthiest, in part because their canny business minds are good at connecting dots to link one business opportunity with another. Here's an example.

Vancouver is known as Hollywood North, with a thriving movie industry that attracts rich and sometimes flaky people on the lookout for drugs, sex, and almost any other vice you can think of. So the Angels invest in trucking and limousine companies to service these people, operating alongside and in competition with legitimate independent owners.

When an actor comes to town, the Angels know who and where he or she is. If it's a guy who asks where the action is, the Angels take him to strip clubs they own and, if necessary, hook him up with prostitutes they control. Everything stretches out from the movie racket, which is basically show business. So are rock bands and concert venues, especially those that encourage paying cash at the door. How much of the cash that Angels-controlled businesses collect from star-struck kids finds its way into legitimate places where it can be accounted for and taxed the way that money you make is recorded and taxed? Damn little.

Angels are naturally drawn to cash. Forget investments like bonds or equity shares. Flash a handful of hard cash in front of them and they're definitely interested—and no one deals exclusively in more cash than foreign currency exchange businesses. Here's the best part: because the cash originates in countries all over the world, various Angels chapters can get in on the action, move huge amounts of money around, and never raise concerns by law enforcement agencies unaware of the bikers' involvement.

Currency exchange operations can also set their own price. Say you hear about a money-exchange company offering 3.75 to one if you exchange your dollar for that currency—Czech, Russian, whatever. So you hand them your hundred dollars, and instead of getting 375 of the foreign currency back you receive maybe 280 or so. If you complain that this is far lower than the advertised rate, you're told that the advertised rate is only for very large transactions.

If you complain to law enforcement, you're told that the currency exchanges can charge any rate they want because they treat money as a commodity. And if you complain too loudly and too long … well, you find yourself facing some angry Angels who persuade you to accept their deal and go away.

Here's the beauty, so to speak, of the deal for the Angels: the money they use to exchange currency is drug money. Once they've done business with it, the money is laundered—meaning it's tax-free, untraceable, and no longer evidence of criminal activity. *And they make even more money from it.*

THE GREAT RECESSION of 2007–2008 was the biggest financial disaster for the U.S. economy since the Great Depression of the 1930s. Tens of thousands of homes were foreclosed and abandoned, creating heartbreak for an untold number of American families. But as everyone on Wall Street knows, one person's economic disaster is another person's economic windfall. And when the Hells Angels become involved it's more than a windfall—it's a dyed-in-the-wool sure thing. So when the disastrous collapse of the American housing market triggered an international credit crisis and launched the Great Recession, scavengers everywhere saw an opportunity. Including the Angels. Anyone with large amounts of cash on hand—especially dirty cash that needed to be laundered before it could be safely spent—faced the biggest potential windfall in recent history.

It worked like this: buy the houses for as little as half their actual value, and rent them out. You've now hidden the dirty money and generated a flow of clean cash from rental payments. (By the way, how effective do you think the Angels might be in collecting any outstanding back rental payments?)

And that's just the beginning. Buying all those houses creates a sense of demand that lifts their market prices, meaning money can be borrowed against the now higher equity value. Make phony improvements to the houses, submit counterfeit invoices for them, and write off huge amounts of tax as a result. And hey—any houses you can't rent to "real" people you rent to fictitious tenants and use the place as a grow-op. If the house is ever raided the tenants will have "disappeared," leaving the police with no one to charge and a very weak case against the Angels.

MEANWHILE, back in British Columbia, things kept getting stranger and stranger.

Vancouver once had its own stock exchange, launched back in 1906. Almost all the companies listed on the VSE were small manufacturing or venture/start-up firms, or mining exploration stocks. The exploration stocks were basically a form of high-stakes gambling. Someone would incorporate a mining firm, obtain (or claim to have obtained) mining rights in a promising area, and sell shares to the public as a means of generating cash to look for the gold or silver or whatever. If they struck gold, so did the shareholders. If no gold or silver or whatever was found, well, the company management gave it a good try, right?

The idea of finding gold and mining it for a profit was at least marginally realistic, unlike some other deals available from companies listed on the VSE. Like Cross Pacific Pearls, which planned to grow a fifteen-pound pearl in a giant clam and set it up as a tourist attraction at a Hawaiian shopping center. Or companies that planned to develop and market a cure for baldness. Or the firm that sold shares to manufacture a chlorine-free pool cleaner. Step right up folks, and hand over your cash.

The VSE listed shares in about twenty-three hundred companies and did an estimated $4 billion in trading during 1999. In the opinion of many in the investment industry, most of the companies on the exchange were either total failures or total frauds. The report of a 1994 investigation into the VSE referred to "shams, swindles, and market manipulations" within the exchange. In 1999 the VSE vanished, merged into the Canadian Venture Exchange.

The exchange may have effectively disappeared, but some observers believe that the people who pulled multimillion-dollar scams on it are still around, along with schemes that don't need a VSE or any other stock exchange to draw in the suckers. And a few of them appear to involve full-fledged Hells Angels, dealing with unlisted and rarely traded operations known as "pink slip" companies.*

Consider De Beira Goldfields Inc., an exploration company that owns the rights to land that can be charitably described as an insignificant piece of moose pasture. De Beira went public as an OTC (Over the Counter) or "pink sheet" stock in April 2006, naming a Vancouver man, Mike Fronzo, as its founder and CEO. According to the company, Fronzo's previous occupation was longshoreman (as was John Bryce's, mentioned earlier), which makes you wonder how a guy who spends his day hauling cargo on and off ships knows anything about launching and running a gold exploration company. Fronzo passed the company on to some Australian promoters who'd been active in the adult porn and internet gambling industries. Without drilling a single hole or disturbing a single moose, within weeks the Australians had built the company's valuation from zero to US$600 million.

---

* "Bulletin Board Firm Linked to Hells Angels," *The Vancouver Sun*, July 1, 2006.

As soon as I hear about a guy who claims to be a longshoreman and who does a deal with guys in the pornography and gambling rackets, my antennae start vibrating; I figure there has to be a connection with the Hells Angels. I found one.

The Australian guys were introduced to Fronzo by Ralph Biggar, who was once a broker with Georgia Pacific Securities in Vancouver. In 2003 Biggar created Tora Technologies Ltd., which, aside from Biggar's name at the top of the organization chart, had just one thing going for it: an agreement with L.A. Embroidery Inc. to market L.A.'s custom embroidery services on the internet.

Not much to build a business on, but Biggar gave the owner of L.A. Embroidery 250,000 shares in Tora in exchange for the rights. The owner of L.A. Embroidery is Tony Pires, who also happens to be a full-patch member of the Hells Angels Nomads.*

Tora managed to get itself listed as an OTC stock in the United States, where it began trading in May 2005 at five cents per share. Over the next few months a series of purchases, all for the same amount—$125,000—were made in Panama and England. One year later the five-cent stock was selling at more than a dollar. Those who purchased shares when the stock was first issued saw their investment grow twenty times within a year. Do you know of any investment that grew that fast while having no sales and only one full-time employee on its staff list?

This wasn't the first investment deal involving Fronzo and Pires. In 1999, they and a few other investors sank money into an American company, Value Software Inc., and International En-R-Tech Inc., listed on the VSE in its last days. Other members

---

* "There's More Here Than a Two-Bit Miner and a Golf Cap," *The Vancouver Sun,* November 18, 2006.

of the investment group included Ronald Lising, a full-patch member of the East End chapter of the Hells Angels.

Two years later, Lising and Pires's brother, Chico, were convicted of trafficking drugs through a Vancouver-area strip club and a local hotel. Each received a four-and-a-half-year prison sentence. Also in on the deals was John Punko, another full-patch member of the East End chapter. In 2001 Punko joined his buddies in prison after being convicted of threatening the Crown counsel who was prosecuting Lising and Chico Pires on drug trafficking charges.

FORMER *VANCOUVER SUN* COLUMNIST David Baines, who used to write on financial and investment matters, looked into a firm called Ialta Industries Ltd. One of its major shareholders was Glen Jonathan Hehn, another member of the Hells Angels Nomads. In January 2007 the B.C. Securities Commission issued a cease-trade order against Ialta for failure to file necessary financial statements.

Baines also looked into a guy named Marcel Rada, who became president of Montrose Exploration Ltd. Guess who was Montrose's largest shareholder? The same Glen Jonathan Hehn. Whenever Montrose held a shareholders' meeting, Hehn could look forward to seeing Ralph Biggar and Tony Pires.

If you don't know a whole lot about penny stock trading, OTC markets, or pink sheet companies, that's okay. Neither do I. And neither, I'm betting, does anyone in the Hells Angels. They likely could not have entered this (mostly) con game without fair-weather friends—friends that include brokers and lawyers who want to help the Angels deal with large piles of cash, whose existence becomes more a risk than an asset with every passing day.

Meanwhile, the Angels at the top make the most of their money: guys like Francesco Amoretto, Vancouver's Nomad president, who owns a million-dollar house with his lawyer friend Kim Marie Heath. Good for them, but how many guys belonging to "outlaw" motorcycle clubs live in million-dollar-plus houses? It's further proof that the Angels haven't been strictly a motorcycle club for several years. They are first and foremost guys who are at least associated with people convicted of dealing drugs and human beings, along with various assaults and murders. Damiano Dipopolo, the East Vancouver Angel member mentioned earlier who runs Digstown Clothing with branches in Vancouver and Kelowna, owns a huge house in Vancouver and two more in Kelowna. And after Ronald Lising (more about him later) was released from prison for threatening a Crown attorney, he bought a half-million-dollar house and an expensive new SUV. Did he earn that much behind bars?

With the help of those ready to share in the cash stash, even if it means rubbing shoulders with bikers, the Angels can always find a new way to make money—illegally, of course. When the Goods and Services Tax (GST) was introduced to Canada it had loopholes, as every new system does. The Angels, no doubt with a little help from bookkeepers and accountants, jumped on them.

Angel members in Vancouver would send big-ticket items like house furnishings to an Angels chapter in Ontario, charging a high price and adding the GST to the bill. The Ontario chapter would claim to have purchased the stuff to sell to an American Angels chapter. The GST doesn't get added to U.S. sales, so the Ontario chapter would apply to the Canadian tax authorities for a reimbursement. In six to eight weeks, a check would arrive in the mail. Of course, neither the furnishings nor the sale ever existed. Talk about found money!

It also worked the other way around as a means for the Ontario boys to return the favor. The nonexistent furniture (or whatever) would be shipped to an Angels chapter in B.C., who would pass it on to a member in Washington State. Since the applicants had different GST account numbers, it took a long time for the tax people to realize that something wasn't right and start demanding the money back. By that time the numbered company would have vanished, to be replaced by a new one, and the scheme would start all over again.

It's almost a prerequisite that Hells Angels members be greedy far beyond the average person and even beyond the average crook. Case in point: Raymond Foakes, forty-eight, of Rohnert Park, California, who was sentenced to seventy months in prison and ordered to pay $1,085,000 in restitution for his role in a multi-million-dollar mortgage fraud scheme. Foakes, a former president of the Hells Angels Sonoma chapter, pleaded guilty in October 2011 to conspiring to commit bank and wire fraud, wire fraud, and money laundering. In his plea agreement, Foakes admitted his involvement in a scheme to fraudulently obtain mortgage loans for parcels of real estate in Northern California.

Foakes got his hands on mortgage money he didn't deserve by submitting virtually fictional mortgage loan applications and drastically altered bank statements. Many of his loan applications stated that he'd been self-employed for ten years as the owner of "Foakes Concrete" with a monthly income of about $24,000; his bank statements would reflect balances and deposits confirming this level of earnings. No one seemed to seriously question these documents. He got his hands on enough money to buy buildings that he'd immediately convert to grow-op houses and then reap the rewards. Think of it: a free house and a steady income from illegal plants. Know any legal businesses that enjoy those kinds of advantages?

The Angels' business activities are more than just "shady." They cost every one of us in many ways, especially when they involve narcotics and prostitution. Moreover, they often elbow legiti-mate businesses out of the market by competing in a manner that no honest business ever would. Who knows how many of these businesses have been told to close up and clear out so that the Angels have things to themselves? And while many of us may complain about the treatment we get from phone and cable companies, to my knowledge no phone or cable company has yet threatened to blow up or burn down your house if you don't play along.

ONE FINAL observation:

Remember the guy named Ronald Lising who made some investments with fellow Hells Angels members before getting a prison term for threatening a Crown attorney ... then bought himself a house and new car as soon as he was released?

In May 2013 the same Ronald Lising got himself hired as a seasonal trash collector for the City of Vancouver. He managed to keep the job for a couple of months before the city's sanitation managers learned about his past and sent him packing.

So what's a big-time Hells Angel doing collecting garbage? Is he that down and out? Or is it possible that the Angels have spotted a new way to make, hide, and launder money through the trash collection business?

9

FRENCH CONNECTIONS

In the 1970s, when the Hells Angels first realized the power and influence they'd established by being big, bad, loud, and aggressive, they began to think like a business corporation. After all, they shared that corporate hunger for profits—big, fat profits, preferably made with little effort and no risk.

Corporations also have structure, so the Angels tightened up the rules about who does what and for whom and why. And you can't have a big successful company without things like legal advice and trademark protection, so although these took a little longer to fall into place, the Angels began to acquire them as well.

But the biggest lesson the Angels absorbed from Corporate America was the axiom that everyone from Henry Ford to Martha Stewart has lived by every day: business corporations either grow or they die. The Angels had no interest in dying. But they would arrange, if necessary, to have their competition die in their place. And nowhere in the world were they more successful at this than in the province of Quebec.

SURPRISINGLY, the first excursion the Angels made beyond the United States was not to Canada but to New Zealand. Still, that journey to the other side of the world didn't represent a major move for them, being more significant for the distance covered and the Berdoo–Auckland lifestyle gap than anything else. Canada remained the obvious choice for any initial expansion of the Angels, and they did it by moving into Quebec in the mid-1970s. The process, however, was circuitous.

The plan was to patch over existing MCs, but it was slow going, and succeeded only in absorbing Popeyes in Laval and Sherbrooke. The Angels had better luck in British Columbia, where they patched over Satan's Angels in 1983. From there they began moving east, absorbing the Grim Reapers in Alberta, the Rebels in Saskatchewan, and Los Bravos in Manitoba.

During this period, a loose alliance of well-established Ontario clubs—the Outlaws, Satan's Choice, and Para-Dice Riders among them—resisted patching over to the Angels. The largest of these was Satan's Choice. (Some have remarked that they might be a rung or so up the IQ ladder from the Angels because at least they know how to use an apostrophe, but never mind.) Satan's Choice was relatively strong but had only seven chapters, all of them in Ontario. Still, Ontario was the place to be if you were looking to expand your drug, prostitution, and other rackets, and so in 2000 two Angels flew up to Toronto to negotiate a patch-over. Everything was amiable. They talked over the deal and agreed to disagree. No insults, no punches, no threats, and especially no patch-over. And yet when the Outlaws arrived with similar intent a short while later, the Choice thought it was a fine idea, and most Satan's Choice chapters became Outlaws.

The Angels weren't giving up. If the English-speaking bikers in Ontario wouldn't side with them, maybe French riders beyond

Laval and Sherbrooke would. Quebec had spawned several roughly organized biker clubs, most of them in rural areas. As comparatively disorganized as they were, the clubs had a reputation for riding harder and living tougher than others in Canada, which to the Angels sounded like a better fit than the Anglo gangs.

By far the most dominant gang in Quebec were the Popeyes—and since Ontario and Quebec were geographically adjacent, there was certain to be competition and bad feelings between the Popeyes and Satan's Choice. So when Satan's Choice patched over to the Outlaws, creating a true coast-to-coast operation, the Popeyes outside Laval and Sherbrooke, who'd patched over years earlier, began looking for a Big Brother of their own. They found it in—surprise!—the Hells Angels. Or, as the francophones call them, Les Hells.

The Angels were overjoyed to absorb the rest of the Popeyes. The move would give Les Hells a foothold in Canada, and from there they could expand west all the way to British Columbia and east to the Atlantic Ocean. Most of the Quebec bikers spoke French more than they spoke English, if they spoke English at all, but this wouldn't be a major problem in the eyes of the Angels. It was all a matter of translation. Beyond that, they'd all be brothers under the skin, right?

Wrong. Neither the Angels nor any of the other large American clubs understood the Quebec psyche. Quebec bikers had their own vision of themselves in—or out—of society and it didn't match the Angels', especially when it came to giving and taking orders.

The first Canadian Angels patches, on the backs of former Popeyes members, hit the streets in early December 1977. The first body hit the pavement less than two months later.

THE POPEYES had been founded by an amazing guy named Yves "Apache" Trudeau, also known as "The Mad Bumper." Trudeau was maybe five-six and 150 pounds. Whether it was that or something in his childhood, he carried a chip on his shoulder as big as Mount Royal itself. In different circumstances his combination of intelligence and drive might have made him a CEO of a Fortune 500 company or the most successful battlefield commander in any army that would have him. Instead, it made him a natural-born killer.

By the time his Popeyes had patched over to the Angels, Trudeau had already murdered four other bikers. Whether or not the Angels knew about this and believed it made the gang more attractive, Trudeau was not prepared to change just because he carried a different patch on his back. Within two months of becoming a Hells Angel, he heard about an Outlaw member being spotted in a bar in downtown Montreal, now declared Angels territory. Trudeau saw an opportunity to make a point.

The Outlaw was Robert Coté, a young biker who'd apparently gone into the bar just to have a beer or two. On Trudeau's orders, someone picked a fight with Coté, who was asked to leave the bar. When he stepped out onto the street a car pulled up and Trudeau, from the back seat, shot Coté in the head. The Outlaw biker died in hospital a few days later. Whether from fear or opportunity, membership in Les Hells grew massively from that point.

Trudeau became a killing machine, sometimes as a hired gun and sometimes entirely on his own. He eventually admitted to killing forty-three people, although the total may have been even higher. He was indiscriminate in choosing his victims. Young, old, biker, ordinary citizen—if Trudeau believed you didn't deserve to live, he felt justified in killing you by whatever means.

His victims included Jeanne Desjardins, who tried to help her grandson, an ex-Angel named André Desjardins, avoid Trudeau's wrath. Trudeau beat her to death, shot her grandson and his girlfriend, and dumped all three bodies in the St. Lawrence River. A few months later he attached a bomb to the Harley-Davidson belonging to Outlaw member Donald McLean. When the bomb exploded it killed both McLean and his girlfriend, Carmen Piche. Trudeau's style even caught the attention of the Montreal Mafia, who hired him to gun down Michel Desormiers, a brother-in-law of Mob boss Frank Cotroni.

By the 1980s the Angels were a force in the Montreal area, with several powerful chapters in competition with each other to become top dog. The original Montreal chapter grew so large that it split into multiple chapters, including Laval in the north, Sorel down the river to the northeast, and Lennoxville, about eighty kilometers east of the city. All three chapters represented the thinking and attitude of the "new" Angels, the bikers who saw the organization not as a bunch of guys interested only in raising hell but as a business structure with an opportunity to generate a lot of money for its members. They didn't mind building the perception that Les Hells were not to be fooled with. Hey, intimidation was part of their business plan: if you do a deal with the Angels, you better live up to your end of the bargain. It made things easier in negotiations and in collecting profits.

Most of these business guys watched other Angels' antics with a mixture of tolerance and annoyance. It was the wilder, basically stupid actions by some Quebec Angels that got under their skin. Like those of L'Apache Trudeau, and the idiocy of Denis "Le Curé" ("The Priest") Kennedy, so named for his dark, gaunt appearance.

Kennedy, a member of the Laval chapter and a buddy of Trudeau, had a heavy drug addiction, especially with cocaine, and got himself seriously in debt with his major connection, Frank "Dunie" Ryan. Ryan was a leader of the West End Gang, which traced its origins back almost a hundred years. Mostly Irish, the West End Gang were busy with an even wider assortment of criminal activity than the Angels. They'd begun with truck hijackings, kidnapping, armed robbery, and extortion, later moving on to home invasions and protection rackets and ultimately drug trafficking. Just as effectively as Les Hells, the West End Gang forged allegiances with other criminal organizations within and well beyond Canada. They imported hashish and cocaine from the United States, South America, and Europe, working in partnership with local Mafia families and Hells Angel chapters.

Because of these connections, Ryan had cut Kennedy a lot of slack. But by early 1982 Kennedy's drug debt to Ryan and the West End Irish boys, estimated at $150,000, was too much to ignore. Ryan cut off Kennedy's supply until the account was settled. Kennedy now feared that Ryan could order a beating or even a hit on him if he didn't come up with the tens of thousands of dollars his connection was demanding. And so, whether it was Kennedy's drug-addled state or a measure of his basement-level IQ, he concocted a zany plan: he would kidnap one of Ryan's children, hold the kid for ransom, and when the West End Gang leader paid up, he'd settle the account with Ryan's own money. Hey, was that brilliant or what?

No, it was stupid beyond belief. The only thing even stupider than that would be to brag about his plan to a lot of people. Which, of course, he did. Repeatedly.

Big surprise: Ryan got word of the plan and was naturally more than a little upset. He was, in fact, outraged, and insisted that the Angels take care of Kennedy in the only appropriate way: fire bullets into the Priest's brain.

At first glance, this sounds a little far-fetched. Okay, Kennedy was a dope freak and broke a few rules by planning to kidnap

Ryan's children. But killing him would mean bumping off another brother. The Angels didn't have a beef with Kennedy, beyond his being a nitwit. Should they really dispose of a biker brother on the say-so of someone who wasn't an Angel himself?

Yes, they should. Wiping out "Le Curé" would both weaken the overly violent Laval chapter of Les Hells and please the head of their biggest drug-trading partner. The Angels chose business over brotherhood. It wasn't the first time, and it certainly wouldn't be the last.

Four Angels, including Kennedy, were shot, bundled in sleeping bags and wrapped in chains and weights, and thrown into the St. Lawrence. The killing of "The Priest" not only weakened the Laval chapter of Les Hells but strengthened others, especially the Sorel Angels. Accordingly, they voted in a law declaring that Angels could sell cocaine but were prohibited from using it themselves—a law obviously directed at the Laval chapter, who were notorious coke addicts. The bikers from the north were infuriated. Laval, they declared when word of the new law reached them, was not going to take orders from anyone, including another Hells Angels chapter. Who did those guys in Sorel think they were, telling other Angels what they could and couldn't shove up their noses? They'd see about *that*. So the boys in Laval passed their own law: every Angel was free to do as much of any drug as he wanted, and no one had a right to stop him.

No one was happier about that than Yves Trudeau himself, who had acquired a major addiction to cocaine. Fuelled by drug-induced paranoia as well as his own sociopathic tendencies, Trudeau went on a killing spree over the next three years, committing at least eighteen murders. Most of the victims were bikers.

SO IN MID-NOVEMBER 1984, when Dunie Ryan was murdered, suspicion naturally fell on Trudeau. In this case, however, L'Apache wasn't involved. Dunie was whacked by one of his own people, a West End Gang member named Paul April.

Dunie was the kingpin of hashish and cocaine trafficking across much of La Belle Province. Distrusting banks, he was rumored to have between $50 million and $100 million in cash hidden somewhere handy, perhaps at Nittolo's Garden Motel, a garish restaurant and sleepover palace on Montreal's St. James Street West. Ryan's power and rumored wealth generated greed and resentment among his own gang—and especially in Ryan's buddy Paul April.

April, like the slow-witted "Le Curé" Kennedy, was deeply in debt to Ryan, a fact that you might expect Ryan to take into account when April informed him that a sexy young woman drawn to criminal bosses was waiting to meet him in room 40 as soon as he was free. Ryan duly headed toward room 40, opened the door, and walked into a trap. April and four other associates of Ryan, including Bob Lelièvre and Eddie Philips, Ryan's own errand boy, were waiting. Their plan was to restrain Ryan and force him to tell them the whereabouts of his cash. Ryan, however, fought back so violently that he had to be subdued with a 12-gauge shotgun blast to the chest and a .45-caliber pistol shot to the head.

Ryan's death understandably wreaked havoc on April and his cohorts' plan. They quickly exited room 40, leaving Ryan's body on the floor, complete with $6500 cash in his pocket.

Emulating Kennedy's stupidity once more, April and the others began to brag about how they'd wiped out Montreal's undisputed drug lord. They must have thought it would win them respect, but all it did was attract attention—especially from Allan "The Weasel" Ross, who quickly stepped into Ryan's shoes. The killing of his predecessor may have made him the boss, but the Weasel was clever enough to know it hadn't made him safe as long as April and his gang were around. And Ross knew precisely who could solve the problem.

Within two weeks of Dunie Ryan's murder, two workmen delivered gifts to the apartment shared by April, Lelièvre, and two associates in recognition of April's new leadership position, official or not, as head of the West End Gang. The gifts included a VCR copy of *Hells Angels Forever*, a VCR player, and a brand-new television set on which to view it. April and his friends told the guys to thank the Angels for the gesture. The delivery men left, April and his friends hooked up the VCR, turned on the TV set, and were blown to pieces. Eight others were injured by the bomb, which also destroyed part of the apartment block itself.

Yves L'Apache Trudeau was the mastermind behind the hit, one that further cemented his reputation. And yet Ross refused to be intimidated by Trudeau. Ross had offered the biker $200,000 to carry out the hit, paying him $25,000 up front. When Trudeau arrived to collect the balance of his money, Ross and other West End Gang members told him that certain Hells Angels chapters owed the Irish boys almost $300,000 in unpaid drug debts, and that Trudeau should collect from them.

Surprisingly, Trudeau agreed. But when he went to the Sorel chapter and asked them to pay up, they laughed at him. The Halifax chapter, who'd just received their Hells Angels charter, agreed to pay him $100,000, but they weren't happy about the deal. The Laval chapter refused to even acknowledge their debt to the West End Gang. Their refusal typified the north chapter's attitude toward business, an attitude that the cooler, more practical chapters resented. The guys in Laval used drugs heavily but sometimes outright refused to pay for quantities bought from the West End Gang and other suppliers, who were beginning to mistrust all Angels. Laval was also overly prone to violence, refused to acknowledge other chapters' concerns, and were generally a major pain in the ass.

All of which was enough to launch the Lennoxville massacre.

BY MARCH 1985 the Angels in Lennoxville and elsewhere came to the conclusion that the Laval chapter had to be either eliminated or at least taught a brutal lesson. Otherwise, Les Hells in Laval would continue to cramp the style of every Angels chapter in the province and maybe beyond. Angels who were at least as interested in making money as in raising hell proposed drastic action.

As you might expect with a bunch of guys who can calculate profit margins and work out complex business deals, a lot of preparation went into the plan. The Lennoxville chapter would announce a party with all the usual temptations—sex, drugs, rock 'n' roll, and whatever else would attract their brothers. Of the ten members of the Laval chapter, it was decided that six would be killed, two would be told to retire or face the same fate, and the remaining two would be transferred to the Sorel chapter.

On the night of the party, initially only three Laval members appeared. They were quickly murdered by the thirty-five Lennoxville Angels. Two more of the targeted six were enticed to the party and suffered the same fate. Three months later the five decomposing bodies were located at the bottom of the St. Lawrence River, bearing the Angels trademark: they'd been wrapped in sleeping bags and chains and weighted down with concrete blocks.

So who was the sixth targeted Angel from Laval, the one guy who managed to avoid the fate of his brothers? None other than L'Apache himself. Yves Trudeau had checked himself into a detox center near Oka just before the party invitations arrived. A member of the Montreal chapter visited Trudeau there and told him he was out of Les Hells and would have to remove his gang tattoos. There was no room for negotiation.

When he returned home from the detox center, Trudeau discovered that the Angels had taken his Harley-Davidson and $46,000 in cash. "If you want your bike back," he was told, "you've got to make two hits for us." Trudeau was given their names. He succeeded in killing one, a man named Jean-Marc Deniger. When he was unable to locate the second targeted victim he was given back his motorcycle, which was little comfort when he learned that the Angels had put a $50,000 contract on his head.

Yves Trudeau had a decision to make: stand up and be a man or survive. He chose survival.

He approached law enforcement officials with a deal. He would provide intimate details on the killings of forty-three people and general information on another forty murders and fifteen attempts. He would also become a full-fledged police informant, spilling the beans on all the Hells Angels actions they needed to know about and testifying in court against his former brothers. In return, he wanted entry into the witness protection program, including a new identity, police guards, and an income. Oh, and one more thing. About those first forty-three murders? Yves committed them, and he wanted a special deal on any charges laid against him.

He got it. After Trudeau confessed to shooting twenty-nine people to death, blowing up another ten, beating three until they died, and strangling one, the police charged him not with first-degree or even second-degree murder but with manslaughter, meaning that even though these forty-three people died at the hands of L'Apache, he didn't really mean to kill them. For this he received seven years' jail time. Largely based on his testimony, four Lennoxville gang members were convicted of killing the five Laval

Angels and received life sentences. In the early 1990s, Trudeau, who managed to survive his seven years behind bars, was released with a new identity and received several thousand dollars from the government, including a weekly $35 allowance for cigarettes.

Was this a deal with the devil? Without a doubt, and on both sides. When one of the country's most vicious serial killers, a guy with no evident compassion for anyone or anything except his own survival, is essentially forgiven for murdering more than forty people, you sure can't call it justice. Meanwhile, the Angels see one of their own confess to killing several of his brothers, get away with a light sentence, and help convict a few more brothers by naming names and pointing fingers. So much for trust and loyalty.

Incidentally, the trial involving the Lennoxville murders was something of a lesson in itself. Five Angels were tried for first-degree murder—Jacques Pelletier, Luc "Sam" Michaud, Réjean "Zig-zag" Lessard, Robert "Snake" Tremblay, and Robert Richard. The trial was as raucous as you might expect. Near the end, one of the twelve jurors even confessed that he'd accepted a $25,000 bribe with more money promised if the bikers won a full acquittal.

Richard was the only member to be acquitted. On December 3, 1986, the others were sentenced to life in prison, which usually means no parole eligibility for twenty-five years. Not in this case, however. Michaud, who'd quarreled with other gang members in prison, was released after just seventeen years and retired from the biker life to live with his daughters. Pelletier was paroled in 2008, but not for long; he was soon brought back behind bars for various parole violations.

The most interesting of the original four was Lessard, whose role in the massacre was described as "master of ceremonies," the guy who ordered the deaths and supervised the beating and shooting of the victims. He admitted to leading the event, but claimed that, based on the Angels' values, it had been the only solution, and anyway he didn't pull any trigger. Lessard had come from a wealthy family, growing up amid comfort and culture. Freed from both prison and the biker life, he became a Buddhist.

The Lennoxville massacre was virtually inevitable, given that the entire Laval chapter was composed of hotheads whose vision rarely extended further than the next party, while the Lennoxville boys' moneymaking emphasis meant devising plans, setting goals, and exerting discipline. And although other Angels and other clubs bemoaned the idea of brothers turning against brothers as they had in Lennoxville, some things began to change. The Angels lost their enthusiasm for war and started to think like businessmen. Other biker gangs, meanwhile, saw this as a sign of weakness and an opportunity for them to muscle in on the Angels' turf.

Each side misjudged the other. Which inevitably led to La Guerre des Motards, the biker war that made the Lennoxville massacre look like a schoolyard skirmish.

TWO MONTREAL-AREA ONE PERCENTERS had watched the violence and double-crossing among the Angels with interest. Salvatore Cazzetta and Maurice Boucher had been members of a white supremacist gang calling themselves the SS, and planned to join the Angels soon after Les Hells landed in Quebec. Almost from the beginning, however, Cazzetta had second thoughts. A good motorcycle club had to demand discipline and honor from its members, and Cazzetta didn't see much of either with the Angels. In fact, when no MC measured up to Cazzetta's standards, and when he learned about the shocking events at the Lennoxville massacre, he and his brother Giovanni launched their own club. They called it the Rock

Machine, and chose to avoid some of the Angel elements that other clubs had adopted.

Rock Machine members, for example, would not wear greasy denim vests with their death's head or any other symbol on the back, the kind of thing that identified them to police and turned the public against them. Instead of patches they wore rings bearing the image of an eagle and their motto, *À La Vie À La Mort*—In the Life and the Death. As well, they soon forged an agreement, based in part on the founding Cazzetta brothers' Italian heritage, with the Quebec Mafia. Cazzetta also found a way to work amiably with the West End Gang and the French-Canadian DuBois gang. Whatever his other qualities, he was a shrewd and ambitious businessman, more interested in creating profits for himself and his gang members than in joining them for a three-day run to nowhere.

Boucher wasn't as turned off by the Angels as his friend Cazzetta had been. As a matter of fact, he intended to join Les Hells—as soon as he completed the little matter of a forty-month prison sentence for committing armed sexual assault on a nine-year-old girl, an act that typified his interests and morality.

The rape of a child did not appear to lower Boucher's standing among the Angels. Hey, what's a little pederasty among brothers? Boucher wore his prison time as a badge of honor, a stand-up guy who could take everything the law handed him and come out laughing.

Apparently it worked. Boucher rose all the way through the ranks of the Angels' Montreal chapter, right alongside his old buddy from the SS. As he gained power he also gained a reputation for being something of a nag, the guy who kept asking members if they'd done the things he'd told them and if they'd done them the way they should. This constant nattering earned him the ironic nickname "Mom."

Unfortunately for Sal Cazzetta, the Rock Machine leader began sliding off his perch just as Boucher was mounting his. In 1994 Sal was arrested and charged with attempting to import eleven tons (11,175 kilograms) of cocaine into the country, leaving the Rock Machine in the hands of Giovanni, who lacked the drive and finesse of his brother.

Mom Boucher may or may not have regretted the fate of his buddy Sal, but regrets had nothing to do with his next move. The combination of his friendship with Cazzetta and Cazzetta's close relationship with the Quebec Mafia had eased the way for the two clubs to get along with each other. The peaceful coexistence began to crumble when Cazzetta was out of the picture and into prison. That's when the competition between the two clubs for street-level drug sales in Montreal and the rest of the province began to grow edgy, driven almost entirely by Boucher.

Boucher's goal was simple: complete control of the street-level drug trade in Montreal. Nothing less would satisfy him. Standing between him and success was the Rock Machine, his old friend Cazzetta's club. Well, too bad. On July 14, 1994, two members of an Angels puppet club entered a downtown Montreal motorcycle shop and shot its Rock Machine owner dead.

The war was on. By the time it ended, over eight years later, more than 150 people had died violent deaths, including a large number of innocent bystanders. And less than a year into the war, one incident marked the viciousness and basic stupidity of the gangs, a tragedy that resonates with law enforcement and the general public to this day.

Around noon on August 9, 1995, two young boys were playing in front of Saint Nom de Jesus school in a quiet residential section of east Montreal. Nearby, a Jeep was parked at the curb with a Hells Angels associate named Marc Dubé sitting behind the wheel.

Suddenly the vehicle vanished in an explosion of smoke and flame, instantly killing Dubé. When the debris settled, one of the boys—eleven-year-old Daniel Desrochers—lay on the ground, a piece of shrapnel from the Jeep buried in his head. The boy died in hospital a few days later.

Until that point, the public's reaction to biker-gang battles had essentially been "Let them kill each other off—who cares?" But the violent death of an innocent young boy playing near a school on summer vacation, bolstered by images of his mourning mother and tearful schoolmates, shifted opinion dramatically.

Most people believed that the bomb had been planted and detonated by Les Hells, despite the fact that one of their own, an albeit small-time drug dealer, was the victim. Were the Angels back to bumping off their own people? It may well have been so. Later, an informant claimed that Mom Boucher had been complaining about the Angels' lack of enthusiasm for the biker war. They were being too passive, too easygoing in dealing with the Rock Machine and others. They needed a call to arms, something to raise the anger of every Angel and drive him to seek out and kill every Rock Machine member he could find. The informant further reported that an Angel named Scott Steinert, a guy known for his psychopathic tendencies and his efforts to please Boucher, had bragged about owning remote-control devices ideal for use with bombs.*

The concept of blowing up a low-level comrade as a means of inciting the rest of the group to take action against their enemies may seem far-fetched, but most people within and outside law enforcement considered it true. And if you can't conceive of performing such an act, you don't share the same mindset as Mom

---

* Julian Sher and William Marsden, *The Road to Hell: How the Biker Gangs Are Conquering Canada* (Random House, 2010), pp. 68–71.

Boucher. Few people do. Remember, this is a man who, following his imprisonment for raping a young girl at the point of a gun, won the leadership of an organization that is presumably as disgusted with such an act as the rest of society. Anyone who even attempts to rise to the leadership of a motorcycle gang, let alone succeeds, possesses unstoppable ambition and a severe deficit of scruples.

When police bomb experts concluded that the bomb that killed Daniel Desrochers had been set off by remote control, indicating that whoever pushed the button must have known that two children were playing nearby, public anger seriously escalated. The Angels denied any involvement, claiming they'd never kill one of their own let alone an innocent child, but they didn't help their case when they offered Daniel's mother cash as a means of easing her loss.

Public outrage was too intense to be focused on the bikers alone; an equal measure of anger was directed toward the police. With much justification (and a little hypocrisy, in light of the public's belief that bikers "were just killing themselves off"), people felt the police hadn't taken the biker war seriously enough.

Law enforcement agencies responded by launching l'Escouade Carcajou, the Wolverine Squad, a province-wide response to the biker war that drew upon the Sûreté du Québec (or SQ, Quebec's provincial police), the RCMP, and local forces. They were handed practically a blank check by the provincial government with orders to halt the war and shut down the bike gangs. Various levels of Carcajou would obtain information on the gangs via wiretaps, informers, and general observations, and would share their findings in order to build a solid case that would lead to convictions and long jail terms.

It was a total disaster. Infighting and jealousy among the various levels accomplished little over the next few months, and the entire program imploded. I almost became collateral damage myself when I agreed to infiltrate the Angels' Sherbrooke chapter and report back directly to the RCMP, who were financing and handling me. I made some progress, befriending some key Angel contacts by posing as an outsider assigned to "take care of" a woman whom I identified as a rat and asking around for assistance in finding her. She'd been a stripper and was now a snitch. The Angels, of course, hate informers, and naturally assumed that "take care of" meant whacking or at least giving her a damn good beating.

All was going well until, during a press conference, an SQ guy—who might have been looking to raise his public profile or to come across as someone close to the decision-makers or maybe was just dumber than a tree stump—bragged that he and his colleagues were getting ready to bring the hammer down on the Hells Angels. In case anyone doubted him, he said, "And we've recently inserted an agent in place for that very purpose," meaning, of course, me.

I couldn't believe it. I was laying my life on the line to get vital information that would make this guy look good, and he'd just blown my cover completely. I couldn't leave town fast enough. I told the Mounties that as long as l'Escouade Carcajou was relying on fools like him, the Angels were safe.

IN 1997 l'Escouade Carcajou was replaced with Carcajou II, mandated to go after a wider group of targets than just biker gangs. It would seek evidence against all drug dealing and gang-related criminal acts in Montreal and Quebec City and, it was hoped, not make the same mistakes as the Wolverine Squad had.

But it did. When the infighting rose again, forces began dropping out and the entire operation collapsed.

They finally got it right in 2005 with six regional joint-force squads, or ERMs (Escouades régionales mixtes), composed of the RCMP, the SQ, and municipal forces communicating through six bases across the province.

By that time, much damage had been done. Some of it consisted of bar fights and scraps. A lot more involved cold-blooded executions committed by the Angels and members of the Rock Machine, streetwise toughs slugging it out with guns and bombs and not caring at all about the damage they were doing to others around them. And some of the attacks were so blatant, so in-your-face, that it seemed only a spaced-out Hollywood scriptwriter could have thought of them, let alone carried them out.

Like the murders of Diane Lavigne and Pierre Rondeau.

Mom Boucher grew obsessed with the thought that any one of his brothers, if arrested, could become a police informant. It had happened before. It could happen again. Some guy Boucher trusted might be picked up on a trafficking charge, face ten years in prison, and decide to save his own hide by making a deal with the newly aggressive cops to testify against the Angels. What could Boucher do to stave off such a risk?

He had an idea. What if the most likely guys, the ones who were closest to him and knew the score and might become turncoats, what if they committed crimes so extreme that they'd never even be allowed to become informants? And what if their actions intimidated the police themselves, persuading them to back off a little on the Angels, take a kind of live-and-let-live attitude? Something like killing a few prison guards at random, just because of who they were. The notion that unarmed guards would be virtually as innocent as young Daniel Desrochers never appeared to enter Boucher's mind.

He chose three Angels to do his bidding: Stéphane "Godasse"

Gagné, Paul "Fon Fon" Fontaine, and André "Toots" Tousignant. Apparently none of the three had any second thoughts about the assignment. If Mom ordered it done, it was done.

So on a June afternoon in 1997, Gagné and Tousignant drove alongside a minivan that had just exited Montreal's Bordeaux prison. Without knowing or caring who was behind the wheel, they fired twice through the driver's window, striking correctional officer Diane Lavigne in the arm and the head. She died instantly. In September it was Fontaine's turn to join Gagné. They followed a converted schoolbus used to transfer prisoners between jail and the courthouse. When the bus stopped for a red light in the suburb of Rivière des Prairies, Fontaine stepped in front of the vehicle, rested his arms on the hood to steady his aim, and fatally shot the driver, corrections officer Pierre Rondeau. Next he aimed at Rondeau's partner in the passenger's seat, fired twice, but missed.

Boucher's plan was not only amoral. It was stupid. Rather than intimidating law enforcement officers it enraged them, along with the public. It also failed to silence the shooters Boucher had chosen: Gagné eventually testified against Mom.

But Boucher, incredibly, almost had the last laugh.

Based on wiretaps, video surveillance, documents seized from the Angels clubhouse, and, most effectively, testimony from Godasse Gagné himself, Boucher was arrested and went on trial for the murders of the two prison guards in the autumn of 1998. Thanks to an aggressive defense launched by Boucher's lawyers against Gagné, portraying him as a man who'd say anything against anyone to save his own skin, the jury declared Boucher not guilty. They may not have had much choice. Each day of the trial a group of Angels had gathered outside the courthouse to buy themselves a place in line. Then, once inside the courtroom, they'd sat glaring at the jury members, almost daring them to convict their leader.

The Hells Angels leader swaggered out of the courtroom. That very evening, when he appeared at a boxing match in downtown Montreal's Molson Centre, accompanied by a retinue of bodyguards, many of the eighteen thousand fight fans gave him a standing ovation.

Reloaded with arrogance, Boucher met a couple of years later with Fred Faucher, then leader of the Rock Machine, in a downtown restaurant to negotiate a peace settlement between the two clubs. A photograph appeared in local newspapers showing the two bikers smiling and shaking hands, the best of buddies prepared to forgive and forget. It lasted about two months. When the Rock Machine patched over to become Bandidos, the killings resumed.

By then, Boucher had other things to worry about. Just two days after his peace banquet with Faucher, the Quebec Court of Appeals overturned his acquittal and Boucher was arrested to await a second trial. Held in an isolated cell in Tanguay's women's prison, where he could have no contact with other bikers or, for that matter, other prison inmates, Boucher was charged with thirteen additional murders as well as drug trafficking and gangsterism.

No trial before or since has been more tightly secured than the one that began in May 2002. The Quebec government reportedly spent $16.5 million to build and equip a courthouse especially to try Boucher. The jury of eight men and four women were never seen by Boucher or the general public; they were placed behind an opaque screen. It took them eleven days to reach a verdict. On May 5, 2002, they found Mom Boucher guilty on all charges. Boucher, forty-eight years old, stood grinning as the verdict was read aloud. He received the maximum sentence: life in prison with no parole eligibility for twenty-five years.

If Boucher believed he could yet again beat the system or at least enjoy a comfortable respite behind bars, he was mistaken.

Housed in the maximum security facility at Sainte-Anne-des-Plaines penitentiary, he has little contact with other inmates. On several occasions, however, the contact has led to assaults by other prisoners, including one in October 2010 that saw Boucher receive deep stab wounds to the stomach and elsewhere. Reportedly, this was only the latest of a number of attempts on his life. His respite is obviously not as comfortable as he might have hoped.

Some on both sides of the law have remarked on Maurice Boucher's charm and charisma, qualities he used to rise to the top of the Angels during the biker war. I don't doubt that he could be charming and persuasive, or that he dominated every room he walked into. People use these things to succeed in politics, in show business, in sports—why not in biker gangs?

I just wonder how valuable his charm and charisma are every time he walks into his two-by-three-meter cell, where he'll remain until at least 2027 and, if justice is really to be served, many years beyond.

10

THE GUYS WHO SPILL THE BEANS

Here's what it's like.

He finally got his move approved; they were letting him
go from the main block to the G Unit where the cells
were much bigger. G3 and G4 blocks were reserved
for kitchen staff and so he signed up for the early shift,
washing trays and working the line at breakfast. That
way he could quit early, after the trays came back from
lunch. Then he could either go out into the Yard or just
kick back and take a snooze. He'd like to keep busy,
not to have too much alone time. He was just starting
a life sentence with a twenty-five-year minimum, and
that knowledge was going to follow him like a shadow.
Anytime he stopped to think about it, the weight of it
caught up with him and hung on his back, making it hard
to breathe. The worst was after Lights Out. That's when
there was no escape.

Being in the Yard was the only way he could keep in touch with who he was. Sitting around on the grassy hill leading up to the double fence was their spot, his and the brothers'. Their little turf. That's where they could talk and trade the stories that kept their identity alive. That's where they could discuss the cars and the bikes, the girls and the drugs, adding some comedy where it fit and a lot of exaggerated enthusiasm. He'd been here only three months and already the stories were being rehashed, over and over. Whenever someone new arrived, everybody had questions. What happened to so-and-so? Have you seen my old lady? Did she ask about me? Stuff like that, it was important. You reached for it and clung to it.

It takes a while, but eventually everyone understands their situation. They were in a warehouse where broken fragments of shattered lives are kept. They were in the "Pen." The world and the club were moving on without them. He'd joined the club so that he wouldn't be alone. Now loyalty to the club had gotten him here, forever alone. All he ever wanted to do was ride a motorcycle and be the Fonz in his neighborhood. Be a member of the most famous MC in the world, the Hells Angels. Someone had once warned him, "Be careful what you wish for." Those words could have been written for all the brothers now spread across the federal prison system.

He wanted things to be over with the club, but they weren't. They'd never be. He realized this yesterday when one of the heavy guys, one of the club officers, took him aside and said "Walk with me," which meant he wanted to talk privately. So they walked. They walked past the weights pit and the tennis courts, over to the other side where you had as much privacy as you were ever going to get. When they got there the other guy took out a packet of tobacco and rolled himself a smoke, then passed the pouch to him. He rolled a smoke for himself and put the rest in his pocket.

He'd just been given something but didn't know what or why. He never asked. He would in good time. They didn't speak. They didn't have to. Back in his cell he opened the pouch and pushed the tobacco aside. Under it, at the bottom of the bag, was a key, the kind used to open handcuffs. This was serious contraband. Get caught with it and it meant thirty days in the hole on reduced rations.

The next day he was back in the Yard, making himself visible and accessible. No one came to him, no one threw him any secret looks, nothing. When the bell rang and everyone started heading back to their units, the guy who'd been the sergeant-at-arms for his chapter slipped in beside him. That's when he got the message: there's a guy on "special diet" up in seg. He was to put the key in the guy's tray, under the food. It had to be done at breakfast or it would be too late.

What the hell! He was on trays, he had nothing to do with food. What if there were two "special diets"? Which one was he supposed to choose? He needed help in figuring it out. And he had to do it right away. He'd have to ask one of the line cooks. There were four of them, but only one who he figured he could trust. The guy, the solid cook, wasn't a brother, hadn't been a biker, but he'd have to ask him anyway. So he approached him and the cook agreed to help.

He put the key in the omelette, and the tray on the cart. The guard used a kitchen knife to lift the eggs and peek under them. Everybody held their breath. He didn't find it and the tray was sent upstairs. Who was big enough, influential enough to get a handcuff key smuggled in for him? Mom Boucher himself? He never learned, but his status in the prison rose.

It didn't help. The routine set in again and the hopelessness of his situation returned like a dark blanket, wrapping him in it. He had to find a way out. He wasn't sure when the idea slipped into his head, but once it arrived it wouldn't leave him alone. Christmas came and went without a visit from anyone. By New Year's his mind was made up. On a cold and miserable January morning he asked for and was granted a phone call. He called Carcajou, the special anti-biker squad.

In a few minutes he changed from dangerous biker to collaborator, to snitch, to rat, and his life was never the same. Some won't take that step; their loyalty, their twisted morality, won't let them. Others can't take it because they have nothing to offer.

But when you can't take that dark blanket, when sitting on the grass with the other guys and living for a word, just one good word from the outside about you and the life you used to lead, isn't enough anymore, you grab for whatever little reward you can get. Even if it's only a sense that you might have done one thing, one small thing, to make all the terrible things you did, the stuff that got you where you are, to make some of it right.

That's when you turn. That's when you say, "Here's what I'll do for you. What'll you do for me?"

MAURICE BOUCHER'S FATE had been sealed by two elements. One was the impact of the various law enforcement organizations when they finally set their collective egos aside and got themselves together to tackle the biker gangs. The other was the effect of informants, guys inside the organization who provided all the evidence the police needed.

Informants who are turncoats do it, obviously, to reduce the time they have to serve for their crimes. No one was better at this than Yves L'Apache Trudeau, but a few others were in the same league.

Informants who aren't turncoats are a different breed, of course. They get into the gangs not to share in the booty and the so-called glamour of being a patched member or even a hang-around. They're a tool of law enforcement, not much different from a pair of handcuffs or a recording machine, and sometimes not much better managed, either. I know because I've played that role on various occasions.

I'm proud of what I did, but I don't consider myself a hero. In many ways it was a job, a contract to be fulfilled. I won the trust of the bikers I targeted, and when I had what I needed for whatever law enforcement group retained me—including the RCMP, FBI, and DEA—I showed up to testify against them at their trials.

The term often used by bikers and others to describe people like me is *rat*. There's probably no worse epithet that a biker or any criminal can hang on someone. But what did these same people call Otis Garrett, who ordered the six-year-old twin daughters of Margo Compton to be shot in the head in front of their mother? Or Mom Boucher, who raped a young girl at gunpoint and went on to become the much-loved leader of the Montreal Angels?

Agent K, who maintains a tell-it-like-it-is anti-gangster blog, keeps making the point that the real rats aren't the ones alerting the police to the actions of biker gangs. It's the members of the gangs themselves who exploit the community around them with narcotics, prostitution, extortion, gambling, and other actions. You are a rat to do these things; you are not a rat to try to stop them. I hope everyone gets the message.

TURNCOATS ARE another matter. Some regret what they've done and try to make amends. But most are simply interested in saving their own skin, even when it means dropping all their former friends, staying away from family members, erasing their entire past, and living inside the rules and regulations of a witness protection program. Does this make you free? Somewhat. But it's also a different kind of prison. You're not behind iron bars, but you never can, and probably never will, be as free as you once were.

Is the list of those who've turned against their buddies a Wall of Fame or a Wall of Shame? I guess it depends on your outlook, but the witness protection program is definitely not the picnic some believe it to be. I've never been part of the program, but I know several people who are. And to learn how they feel about it, I've also talked to police officers who act as witness handlers. Again, the reaction is mixed.

People in witness protection programs who are there to be protected from the criminals they once associated with (and once were) are not considered heroes by law enforcement types. The word most often used by police to describe these people is *creep*. After all, we're talking about people who rejected much of the rest of society for years just to be with and support other individuals whom they considered their brothers by every measure except genetic. They supported each other, they defended each other, and they joined each other in doing things that were both highly illegal and deadly dangerous. Then, when the chips were down, they chose to help put away their buddies for doing the same things they themselves had done ... Is that a hero? I don't know for sure.

I will say this with certainty: as creepy as some of those informants are, things would be a lot different without them. None of the major biker gang takedowns, including Quebec's Springtime 2001 (more about this in Chapter 11), would have happened if the guys who chose to cross their brothers hadn't agreed to deliver their testimony. Their motives were usually clear and straightforward. They were caught in a crime and decided to talk their way out of trouble by talking their friends into the slammer. Other times the motive was more mysterious, which meant an informant was much harder to control in the field. When a guy trades information for freedom, you can pretty well predict his actions. When he has something else driving him, you have a harder time controlling him because you're never quite sure what he's up to.

The situation depends on the individual's status. Is he happily married? Does he have kids? Was he looked after in jail? What kind of treatment does he expect when in the witness protection program?

It amazes me, and the law enforcement types I've talked with about it, that some people believe traveling to a strange new home and starting their lives over is going to be an exciting adventure, the thrill of a lifetime. Well, it's not. They get this idea when they're helping the police, who treat them as a valuable resource, a buddy who needs friendship and support. It's as if they're living two lives, like a character in a detective thriller. These witnesses/informants are popular with the police, who treat them like family, and there is little or no concern about money.

Things change when the arrests are made and the trial is over. That's when the informants become used goods to be quietly disposed of. They're transported to some dull town in the middle of nowhere. Given a minimum-wage job and a rental house or apartment, they're on their own. They're warned not to call family members or make any contact with them at all. If a loved relative dies, they don't attend the funeral or even acknowledge it. They have neither work history nor credit rating, good or bad. In these days of Facebook, Twitter, and texting, no one can participate. Their children are told to forget everything they knew and believed about their previous life. They have no old or previous friends or schools—only current ones.

The tension this creates among families is immense. Any expectations of matrimonial bliss need to be set aside for a long while. The odds are that their families are innocent, but they'll suffer anyway. In cases where the protected witness is the father, the wife moves away and takes the children with her. Now the abandoned dad needs a new identity in case the wife says the wrong thing to the wrong person, and now the loneliness grows even more oppressive.

The informants' future is intended to be dull, uneventful, and empty of any sense of achievement or outside appreciation. They are a nobody in a place that is nowhere, and they have no hope of changing things for the better.

Is it what they deserve? Maybe, maybe not. I leave it to you to decide how this might apply to the gang below.

DANY KANE

It made sense for J.P. Levesque to be skeptical of a telephone call he received one evening. The caller identified himself as a fully patched Angel who had some information for Levesque and his partners.

Levesque was the biker expert with the CISC (Criminal

Intelligence Service Canada). He was the best man—maybe the only man—to accurately decide whether the caller was a wannabe hero, a really dumb prankster, or a new twist launched by somebody like Mom Boucher to throw a monkey wrench into the works. The odds were against it being the real thing—an Angel turning against his brothers and prepared to deal goods to the RCMP and other law enforcement agencies.

Levesque listened to the caller's words, took them with a grain of salt, and assumed a wait-and-see attitude. From the little he'd heard, though, the guy was cagey and seemed to know the score. But would he come through? Tips and information often come from those upset with someone else at that moment. After hanging up, they run up against hard reality—*Omigod, what have I done?*—and never call again.

Levesque and the caller had agreed to meet on the outdoor patio of a fast food outlet. The caller would be carrying a folded newspaper. It all sounded like a spy novel, a John le Carré story, but Levesque agreed because he believed he knew the caller's identity. The caller, Levesque was certain, was Dany Kane.

Dany Kane and another Angel, Aimé Simard, had just been acquitted of a murder charge in the shooting death of a Halifax drug dealer named Robert McFarlane. McFarlane's crime? Simple. He owed the Angels money for drugs and had ignored warnings to pay up.

So why would Kane, after beating the law, decide to join them? One story had it that Kane and Simard were lovers, another that he was bisexual. The Angels, for all their brotherhood, are famously homophobic. Being a gay Angel may not get you killed, but it doesn't get you anywhere special with the rest of Les Hells, either. Besides, Simard soon hightailed it to the police with information, and Dany Kane might have decided to join him.

Levesque knew he'd been correct about Kane's identity as soon as he saw the soon-to-be-ex-Angel waiting nervously for him. The meeting went well—so well that it forged the first building block of Operation Springtime 2001, a successful attack on Les Hells by law enforcement. In time, Dany Kane became an example of everything that was both right and wrong about the power of the Hells Angels and the ability of law enforcement to deal with them.

Kane was a criminal with vengeance in his heart and more baggage in his past than Grand Central Station. Along with his sexual persuasion, various other questions remain unanswered regarding Kane and his relationship with both bikers and the law. Had the police actually offered him $1.7 million in return for his testimony? And how closely had he been associated with Dave "Wolf" Carrol, one of the Angels present during the Lennoxville massacre?

At the time he called Levesque, Kane had been convicted of trafficking drugs through a pseudo-puppet bike gang called the Demon Keepers. Strange name, even for bikers? It was a strange gang. Its name was derived from Dany's initials. The Demon Keepers were to set up shop in key markets like Toronto, Ottawa, and Cornwall, the latter being an important border-crossing point into the United States. The Demons (or Keepers) would flood the market with high-quality drugs at prices lower than those being sold by other biker gangs, eventually putting their competitors out of business. Then the Angels would walk in and have the market to themselves.

Not a bad plan on paper. In practice, it was a total disaster. The guys recruited to do the street work were chosen for their toughness and physique, not for their intellect. What's more, the majority were francophones with little command of the English language. Most of the people they approached, with a total lack of finesse, either laughed at or avoided them—usually both.

When Toronto police discovered that the plan had been hatched by Quebec-based Angels, they arrested eleven of the eighteen Keepers, charged them with minor offenses, and gave them a deal: go back to Quebec and stay there and we'll drop all the charges. The DKs took it, to a man.

When Kane entered Ontario a few weeks later, determined to resurrect the operation in Toronto, he was arrested for drug trafficking and other charges and faced four months in jail. It wasn't such a big deal. With regular time off, all he'd do was ninety days. But Kane told police that, owing to his sexual orientation, he feared the treatment he'd receive from the Angels. At first, the police weren't convinced. But they eventually came to believe that Kane was telling the truth, and that his fear would be enough motive for him to become an effective and valuable informer.

Despite the Demon Keepers fiasco—the idea was quickly dropped after Kane's arrest—he still cut a broad swath in the Angels. Maybe if he'd been a lower-key member the Angels could have used the "don't ask, don't tell" approach. Whichever way you measure it, Dany's days as an Angel were doomed. And so, perhaps, was he. Regardless of his motivation, he was the break the police needed, and much of what he revealed to them resulted in the first major takedown of the Angels and their support crews.

Dany didn't survive to see his revenge. One day in August 2000 he wheeled his Harley-Davidson into his garage, closed the door, kick-started the bike, and sat while the engine filled the space with carbon monoxide fumes.

GÉRALD GALLANT

Gallant had two things in common with Yves L'Apache Trudeau. The men were about the same size—about five-six, maybe

150 pounds—and neither gave much thought to putting a bullet in the brain of whoever they either chose or were paid to kill. If you measure the number of bodies left in their wake, Trudeau was the "winner" with forty-three; Gallant's total was twenty-nine.

But the comparison ends there. Trudeau was a high-profile, swaggering addict and a heavyweight in the Angels, a guy everybody either admired or feared, sometimes both. Gallant was quiet and low-key, living in the village of Donnacona on the north shore of the St. Lawrence River. Most of his neighbors knew him as a guy who liked to pedal his bicycle from his tiny little house on a quiet street in the village, riding as far as Trois-Rivières and back, a total of 170 kilometers, in a single day. They were, naturally, flabbergasted to learn that for twenty-five years he'd been a hired killer for both the Angels and the Rock Machine, earning between $5000 and $20,000 for every hit he made.

During the biker war, both sides hired him. He remained neutral, favoring neither Les Hells nor the Rock Machine, which had formed a loose alliance with Montreal crime families as a defensive move against attacks from the Angels. He was a strict professional, in many ways like a good criminal lawyer who would defend anyone against anything if he was paid the right price.

And it gets stranger. Gallant's home was near the famous Cathedral of Sainte-Anne de Beaupré, a popular tourist center and mecca for Catholic pilgrims in search of a miracle. One wall of the great church is covered with hundreds of crutches that once belonged to people who claimed to have been healed, helped by the spirits within the church.

Gallant was hardly in the healing business. Yet on the first Sunday of every month he was seated in a church pew prepared for ten o'clock mass. Anyone who wanted to hire him and his murder weapon had to show up at the same service. If they didn't appear they'd have to wait another month. If they did show up, they would hand him an envelope containing a name, a photograph, and any other information they could provide. This would be the last direct contact they would have on the matter. He'd take it from there. His fee for the job would be deposited electronically in his bank account. Sometime during the next month he'd travel the three hundred kilometers to Montreal and fulfill the contract on his own timeline and using his own method.

Police knew nothing of Gallant's existence until 2001, and even then the story remained sketchy. A quiet killer insisting on doing business during Sunday mass in one of the most beloved cathedrals in all of Quebec? It sounded like an urban legend, a tale told by bikers with too much time and too much beer, like kids swapping ghost stories around a campground bonfire.

Eventually the stories began to stick. All the claims, all the anecdotes proved to have a basis in reality. The guy wasn't a myth. He was real—the police convinced themselves of it after identifying him in church one Sunday and tracking him from there.

In 2005 they followed him to a coffee shop and seized the paper cup he'd used. They pulled his DNA from the cup, compared it with samples found at some unsolved murders associated with biker gangs, and got a match. By the time arrest warrants were issued, Gallant had gotten word of their success and was gone. Disappeared.

The following year the police received a call from Swiss cops who had arrested a man for credit card fraud and found he was wanted in Quebec. It was Gallant. He didn't fight extradition and was brought back to face a murder charge.

Here's where it gets strange. When Gallant arrived back in Canada, he announced that he was ready to talk. About everything. He began by talking about ten murders committed by others, which led to the arrest of ten people and the closing of the same number of cold cases. He was just getting started. Next he admitted to twenty-seven murders he had committed himself and twelve others he had attempted. He also admitted that he'd killed some innocent bystanders, including a private detective who'd just moved into an apartment once occupied by Gallant's target, and wounded others, including Hélène Brunet, a waitress, when she was being used as a human shield by Robert Savard, a close associate of Mom Boucher and the guy Gallant had been paid to kill.

Imagine the cops' reaction to these revelations. All the time, the money, and the energy they'd put into solving twenty-seven murders and twelve more attempts, and this quiet little guy, who was so far under the radar they were practically unaware of his existence, dumps everything into their laps. "Is he looking for special treatment?" they asked themselves. "Something to cut his prison time maybe?" remembering the deal Yves Trudeau had cut, serving just seven years for all the hits he'd made.

To their surprise, Gallant didn't ask for either special treatment or reduced jail time. He did request protective custody—understandable considering the information he'd provided—and fifty bucks a month to cover coffee and maybe a cigarette or two. Also, enough funds to pay university tuition for his three children. The cops couldn't believe it. They had the agreement drawn up within hours. Gallant agreed to testify and was sentenced to life with a minimum of twenty-five years to be served before parole eligibility. At his trial he said, "I agreed to cooperate with police in order to repair the damage I caused and to seek forgiveness."

He was fifty-eight years old when the sentence was handed down, meaning he is not likely to see life beyond bars again.

JEFF LYNDS

Once the highest-ranking Hells Angel in Nova Scotia, Lynds joined the Nomads out of Halifax as an enforcer. In January 2009 he traveled to Montreal, where he took out a target and an innocent bystander outside a McDonald's restaurant. Then he returned to Nova Scotia, where he was arrested in May 2010 and charged with two counts of first-degree murder. He was also suspected of killing Angel Randy Mersereau, who vanished sometime in October 1999 and was long suspected to be a casualty of the Quebec biker gang war.

The tough guy decided to save his own butt, which probably doomed his fate. After filling the police in on a lot of biker details, but before his trial could begin, he was found dead in his prison cell. Suicide? Revenge? No one seemed ready to talk about it.

DAYLE FREDETTE

Sometimes I think prison makes you smart. Or smarter than you used to be when you were out on the street. That's what I think happened to Dayle Fredette. Fredette was a wannabe biker who worked his way into an Angels puppet gang called the Mercenaries. He did the usual running around for full-patch Angels, but found a way to get elevated into a real Angels chapter. How? By gathering "intelligence" and plotting the murder of anyone the chapter wanted to see dead.

It must have been pretty glamorous for a greaseball like Fredette to do what real cops do, tracking down "suspects" and figuring out how to get them killed—then being paid for it by the same guys he'd worshiped all those years. The Angels liked the idea, too. Fredette was a drug trafficker in the Beauce region of Quebec, northeast of Montreal. The Angels guaranteed him the area for his sales and in return he kicked 10 percent back, which was used by the Angels to pay for the hits Fredette made for them.

Just your normal business deal—"You scratch my back and I'll scratch yours"—until the day Fredette scratched the wrong guy.

Two years after making full-patch Angel, Fredette was told to take out a guy who deserved killing because he owed drug money, or hadn't shown proper respect for the Angels, or some other reason, it didn't matter. If someone at the top said the guy had to go, the guy went.

Fredette tracked the target in the Beauce town of St. Frederic, taking an Angel sharpshooter with him to get the job done. Fredette decided the best chance to get him was when the guy emerged from a drug rehab center. On the appointed day, Fredette and the sharpshooter hid a good distance away from center, the shooter with his rifle at the ready and Fredette with a pair of binoculars. Dramatic as hell. If it was a movie they'd be Al Pacino and Robert De Niro.

But it was no movie, and Fredette was no movie star following a script. When the guy emerged from the center Fredette said, "That's him!" ("C'est lui!") and the sharpshooter fired off a round. When the target fell, both Angels ran up and finished him off with a couple of pistol shots. Then they roared away laughing, found their favorite bar, and congratulated each other over a beer or two.

They'd shot the wrong guy. Dany Beaudin had done nothing to deserve being killed except wander into the range of Fredette's binoculars.

It didn't take long for the police to track Fredette down, and it took even less time for him to start talking. In fact, police records indicate that he started talking about everything he knew on July 2, 2011, and didn't stop until October 11.

Early in the game, probably soon after being arrested and discovering everything the police had on him, Fredette began to get smart. He negotiated a contract that said he would plead guilty to one first-degree murder charge and conspiracy to some others, including those that he and almost everyone else knew had involved Fredette pulling the trigger. What was so clever about that? Canada's "faint hope" clause for prisoners sentenced to life without parole for twenty-five years. Lifers have an opportunity to apply for parole after just fifteen years if they've achieved a good record while behind bars and if they can convince the parole board that they're unlikely to offend again. But it doesn't work for serial killers. Murder once and you can cling to the faint hope. Murder twice and you're in for twenty-five years at least.

In exchange for a guilty plea and testimony, Fredette was immune from prosecution on five other murders, including that of Robert "Tout Tout" Léger in August 2001. Léger had been a leading member of the Bandidos in Quebec when he was killed. His murder was regarded as a major score for the rival Hells Angels.

After knocking a potential ten years off his anticipated sentence, Fredette went to work on other items, most of them monetary. He secured a deal (in conjunction with legal advice) to ensure that he'd be paid $50 a month while he serves his sentence, plus $300 each year he's behind bars, plus $500 a week for the first two years he's on parole. His two young children receive monthly payments of $150 until they reach adulthood and as much as $3500 to cover their post-secondary education. He can't be sued in civil court for his actions, either. Finally, the Sûreté du Québec are to protect Fredette and his family from any retaliatory action from the Angels he double-crossed.

This is a good deal. To a guy involved in at least half a dozen murders and who dispensed cocaine, heroin, meth, and other banned substances around the province for as long as ten years, it's either very clever or damned outrageous. Based on my quick calculations, I figure the kids will get about $50,000 from taxpayers and, assuming he manages to get sprung after fifteen years, Fredette will collect almost $65,000 in cash from the same source. How much it'll cost the SQ to provide the necessary protection is anyone's guess.

A lot of people will scream bloody murder at paying that kind of money and doing that kind of deal with an admitted drug dealer and killer. But as we'll see, it could also be considered something of a bargain. Some biker snitches have been promised more. Much, much more.

SYLVAIN BOULANGER

Have you ever held a job that paid you nearly $3 million for a single contract? Listen, not even the top lawyers working for the Angels make that much on a single case. But at least one Angel has. Of course, you could say he worked for it. He produced twenty-three videotape recordings of the debriefings he made to the police and dictated a 634-page statement, all of which led to charges against more than 150 bikers. The police figured the $2.9 million he got paid was practically a bargain. And it probably was. It was also a Get Out of Jail Free card: the deal stipulated that he wouldn't face any charges, past or present.

Sylvain Boulanger, a former full-time member and sergeant-at-arms of the Hells Angels' Sherbrooke chapter, had done his share of mayhem. His motivation for turning on the Angels wasn't money—not originally, anyway. It was revenge for not being allowed back into the club after he'd quit. He was the principal source for the revelation that, in July 1994, the Angels' entire membership in Quebec had voted to launch a war against the Rock Machine.

Boulanger was as bad as any of the guys he ratted out. He admitted, for example, committing at least one murder for the Angels: "The door was open and I come up on the side and I shoot," he said. "I hear 'Ow! Ow! Ow!,' and I see him there and in my head he's dead. So I get out of there running."*

MANY WERE UPSET when they read about Boulanger and people like him getting paid to turn on their fellow gang members. Not that those guys didn't deserve it. Murderers, pimps, drug dealers, extortionists—they're all scum to people who work hard and keep their noses clean. But a lot of those people will never earn anywhere near $3 million over their entire life—and the cops give it to some lowlife who's blown somebody's head off? Is that really justice?

No, it's not. But it's reality.

The only way to eliminate gangs like the Angels, super-secret closed societies whose members are sworn to protect each other, is by getting some of them to break that oath. Can a real cop pose as an Angel and get the job done? Sometimes, but at great risk and great cost as well. Who would the police send in to pose as a wannabe Angel? Some kid fresh out of the police academy? They'd be on to him in seconds. And even if he got lucky and kept his identity hidden, he'd have to hang around the Angels for months before anyone would talk to him. It would take a year or more to work his way into the first level of their trust, and it could end in a heartbeat.

Here's how it goes down with wannabes: one drunk biker decides he doesn't know you or like you or trust you. When that

---

* Paul Cherry, "Informant Leads to Huge Hells Angels Bust," *Montreal Gazette*, April 15, 2009.

happens you have no street cred, no friends to rely on. The drunk biker walks up and says, "Who the fuck are you?," and suddenly everything rides on the head of a pin. If you're mild, he'll drop you. If you're too cocky, he'll drop you. Either way you're going down, unless your answer is dead on. But you don't know what the right answer is yet. If he hits you, do you hit him back? Lots of luck if you do. You're in a lose-lose situation.

If you survive the process, you become "known." Then you're a "friend," and after that an "associate." If you get that far you're a "hang-around" and finally a "prospect." After a year of being a prospect you may be given serious consideration, but you'll need a unanimous vote to become a member.

The entire process may take as long as five years. That's five years of not just paying the guy posing to become a member, but five years of paying his handlers, which could involve three, four, or a dozen other guys. How much do you think that costs the government? Plus there's always the risk that the cop you put into place is found out. Do you think the Angels would hesitate to shoot a bullet into his head if that happened?

Compare this with a full-patch member who's got his own reasons for turning on his brothers. If he's intelligent and can follow directions, you can put him to work in a matter of weeks. You're not waiting years to get the goods on something that happened last week. You can get it *now*, and with some pressure you might get the goods on other murders or crimes you need to clear off the record. How much is it worth, after all, to solve a dozen or so murders and put whoever was responsible for them away for twenty-five years, to get them off the streets and out of your hair?

One more point: as distasteful as they may find it, most cops would rather do a deal with the devil than tell a young cop's wife she's now a widow.

SOME PEOPLE SEE the Angels not as a threat but as an opportunity. Hey, they're not so bad, they think. More than that, they're flush with cash and they may need something I can provide, something legal that won't get me into trouble with the law.

Listen, doing business with the Angels can be hazardous to your health. You can still be charged for associating with them, whatever your job, and end up in a jail cell next to those guys for a lot of years. Or the gangs could declare war on each other. If that happens you could be eating a bullet as an associate. During the Quebec biker war, nearly a hundred of the victims died because of their association with Les Hells.

The biggest danger to your health will always be the Angels themselves, the same people you planned to do business with. One of the most important qualities an Angel can have is to be a sociopath, somebody who doesn't give a damn and, as long as you're not a fully patched member, never will. They'll set you up and tear you down anytime it's convenient and to their advantage. Bring them a plan and they'll listen, use you while they learn, then dispose of you like yesterday's trash. Take the case of Sandra Antelo.

From Colombia, Antelo was introduced to a guy named Michel Rose through a lawyer after she told the lawyer she was looking for someone with whom to smuggle cocaine. Now, who says such a thing to a lawyer? Work it out for yourself.

Rose and Antelo agreed to bring in two hundred kilograms of cocaine from Colombia, first to Miami, then into Canada. Antelo eventually came to trust Rose, who introduced her to another Quebecer named André Chouinard. Only after her husband came on board to help transport twenty-four hundred kilos of cocaine into Canada by sea did Antelo discover she was doing business with the Hells Angels.

"My husband did not want to work with the Hells Angels," she claimed later. "He had never worked with them before, and he never wanted to. My husband knew how these people worked. He said from the beginning they were not the kind of people he wanted to work with." According to Antelo, her husband agreed to work with the Angels only because he assumed it was too late for her to back out.

By the time Antelo and her husband were working on a sixth deal with Rose and Chouinard, problems began to emerge, most of them based on who would assume certain costs. Antelo's husband believed the Angels should pay. The Angels said, in effect, "Go to hell."

In June 2000, Chouinard canceled a morning meeting and asked if they could meet the following day. Antelo agreed, and as she was driving to the meeting, someone in a passing vehicle opened fire on her car. Antelo escaped the attack, suffering cuts to her face from broken glass. When she called Chouinard about it, he listened to what she had to say, then hung up. Antelo got the message. She packed up her kids, left the country, and decided to become a witness for the U.S. Drug Enforcement Agency.

Almost three months later her husband was shot to death outside a bar in Ste. Adèle, a picturesque small town in the Laurentian Mountains north of Montreal. Maybe he thought he'd be safe there. Neither his homicide nor the attempted murder of Sandra Antelo has been solved. They reaped what they had sown.

11

THE LAW STRIKES BACK

An old Arabic proverb advises, "Choose your enemy carefully, for he is the one who you will most come to resemble." It's a warning well suited to law enforcement, whose battle against the Hells Angels hasn't always epitomized high morals and solid values. But then, how could it?

It's easy to follow the Hells Angels because everything they do publicly (and a lot of things they don't) makes the news. That's the way the Angels want it, as long as it meets their needs. They want to intimidate. They want whoever they approach to feel that they're dealing with people who can easily dominate them and take revenge if they're double-crossed. It makes it easier to deal with the public.

Law enforcement officers are somewhat different. They want to be able to make news as well, but only when they succeed at knocking a few bikers' heads and having a large number of them marched off to prison for a couple of decades.

But battling the Angels for more than twenty years has taken its toll on police. As the proverb warned, they've become what they beheld and are close to drinking from the same cup. In many ways, each side mirrors the other. Both have media spokespeople to make sure the message gets out straight. Each side does surveillance on the other, and each side maintains files and personal information on the other's members. Unfortunately, both sides use intimidation, not on each other but on almost anyone they feel they can use.

I've seen cops pull a stripper in for interrogation and threaten to take her children away if she doesn't cooperate. Then the Angels will grab the same stripper and tell her that either she works for them or they'll kill her children. Cops ride Harleys and bikers wear suits, and the ultimate winner will be decided by whoever spends the most money in the right place. Each side has had its share of victories, but in recent years the Canadian cops have made some of the biggest scores. Their victories, along with police successes and Angel setbacks in the United States, may spell the beginning of the end for Sonny Barger's boys in North America.

The rest of the world is another matter.

WITH THE FAILURE of the Carcajou operation in the 1990s, police learned their lesson. Nothing would get accomplished if the cops fought each other almost as hard as they fought the bikers. What's more, the 1995 death of eleven-year-old Daniel Desrochers haunted everybody. Something had to be done. The pressure rested squarely on law enforcement, and not just in Quebec, but right across the country. The decision to get started took place under top secrecy in 1999.

It took a while to get everything prepared. We're talking, after all, about dozens of police organizations, from the RCMP to provincial police departments and right on down to local cops.

But it all came together in the Springtime 2001 operation, when nearly eighteen hundred law enforcement personnel hit the Angels in coordinated raids in Quebec, Ontario, Manitoba, and B.C. The Angels and two of their puppet clubs were taken down almost to a man.

Many of the arrests resulted from information provided by the likes of Dany Kane, and others from spinoffs of his information—for example, suggestions about gang members who might be turned or who had connections with other crimes. In the latter case, new investigations were opened but often set aside until the big takedown happened on March 28, 2001.

The SQ, the RCMP, the Montreal Urban Community Police Department, and twenty-three municipal police departments all took part in the raids, supplemented by the Ontario Provincial Special Squad, the RCMP's E Division, special squads with the Vancouver Police Department, the Organized Crime Agency of British Columbia, and the Winnipeg Police Service. In all, almost two thousand law enforcement officers conducted simultaneous raids in seventy-seven different municipalities. It even went beyond Canada. In cooperation with Jamaican police, Mexican police, and Interpol Mexico, two suspects were arrested and deported from Jamaica and Mexico back to Quebec.

The scope was massive. The task forces had finally scored to disrupt and dismantle outlaw motorcycle gangs, and they'd scored big time, especially in Quebec. It was further proof that the killing of Daniel Desrochers had mobilized the public and inspired the cops to action. And it's a tribute to the operation's planning groups that it came off with apparently total surprise to the Angels and related gangs.

Operation Springtime 2001 was the compilation of four joint-forces operations against the Hells Angels and their puppet clubs, the Rockers and the Evil Ones Outaouais chapter, in all parts of Quebec. The regional joint-force squads, or ERMs (Escouades régionales mixtes), had been hard at work. The serious damage in La Belle Province was done in Montreal, Quebec City, and Sherbrooke, with most of the arrests involving proceeds of crime, drug trafficking, and criminal organization offenses. A few side events occurred. For example, Project Bobcat, involving ERM Outaouais, targeted the Evil Ones Outaouais for drug trafficking. The goal in Quebec was to destabilize Les Hells by targeting all Angel members, both leaders and soldiers.

The Hells Angels and the Nomads controlled the large-scale distribution of drugs, particularly cocaine and hashish, throughout Quebec. In the gang's hierarchical system, the puppet clubs and associated street gangs performed the bulk of the criminal activities, especially the more dangerous and violent, along with related steps, like selling at the retail level. The big money in Quebec was made at the top, where the Angel Nomads ran things. They were responsible for distributing hundreds of kilograms of cocaine and hashish each month.

Almost all Quebec Hells Angels chapters and their puppet clubs were required to go through the Nomads to buy cocaine. Profits on hashish were much smaller, so individual dealers could choose their own sources. This led to spinoff operations and arrests, such as the time in the autumn of 1999 when Vermont border guards found US$136,832 taped to the bodies of a Quebec couple entering the state. When one of the Quebecers talked, a new investigation was off and running. It quickly revealed the complex international system needed to move drugs from grower to buyer, and all the hands taking a share of the profits along the way.

The majority of the hashish sold in Montreal came from Pakistan. It was shipped through India before being sent on to

North America, either through countries such as the Netherlands, Switzerland, and Belgium, or via South Africa or Jamaica. The drug entered Canada through the Port of Montreal, Montreal's Pierre Trudeau Airport, or Toronto's Pearson International Airport, usually hidden in with other goods.

Three drug rings handled the hashish upon arrival, and one was operated by the Nomads. The proceeds from the drugs were converted to U.S. dollars before being transferred to Pakistan, the United Arab Emirates, and India.

Some of the most effective (and intriguing) evidence seized during the raids came from the Nomads' taped conversations, especially ones that revealed their close links with other organized crime groups—like the July 2000 announcement by Norman Robitiere, an influential Nomads member, to a group of Rockers during dinner at a Montreal South Shore restaurant. "The price of a kilo is now $50,000," he said. "I made a deal with the Italians." Among the people hearing those words was Dany Kane, who was wearing a concealed wire. As a driver and bodyguard for two Nomad members, and as a member of the Rockers, he had all the opportunity in the world to wear wires and install listening devices.

By the time the search warrants for Springtime 2001 were drawn up, five Nomad members, two Nomad prospects, and one Rocker member were already in jail. When police had come upon them, they'd been in possession of eight restricted firearms and were busy studying photos of rival Bandidos. All plea-bargained a deal to serve one year in prison under anti-gang legislation. A more important move was to lay charges against all Quebec-based Nomads: thirteen counts of first-degree murder and three counts each of attempted murder, plus other charges where applicable beyond the operation.

The mass arrests created similarly massive problems. Even with a new courthouse built solely to process the charges, logistics were a nightmare. Prison officials set up seven "offices" in the Bordeaux jail, each equipped with computers and video equipment to handle the evidence compiled on hundreds of CD-ROMs, video cassettes, audiotapes, and documents.

Operation Springtime 2001 demonstrated to the public that the motorcycle gangs were more than just "good ol' boys" out to have fun. The public had a peek behind the curtain, and it didn't like what it saw. Mass murder, extensive drug trafficking, the death of innocent bystanders—it was all too much to stomach. There was more. When the working public learned about the vast amounts of money the bikers were making, they were stunned. And in September 2000 when Michael Auger, a crime reporter with *Le Journal de Montréal* who'd been covering the story, was shot six times in the back from close range,* they took to the streets. Their anger inspired and supported a range of efforts by the law to put the Angels and others in their place.

IF LES HELLS thought Springtime 2001 was the end of their troubles with law enforcement, they were wrong. The club and its puppet gangs and buddies staggered through the next eight years, with many of their key leaders vanishing from the streets. As devastating to the Angels as these losses might have been, they were also stunned—at least most of them were—to discover that brotherhood until death

---

* Remarkably, Auger survived the shooting, although only half the bullets could be safely removed from his body. After recuperating, he resumed his coverage of motorcycle gangs and published books on criminal activities before retiring in 2006.

didn't matter to everyone, especially when a member was facing at least twenty-five years of hard time behind bars. The thought surely crossed each Angel's mind that his buddy on the next bike just might be prepared to turn on his club.

By 2009, however, many of the bikers and their gangs had recovered much of their strength. Unresolved issues from Springtime 2001 remained. It was time to break the back of the Quebec-based Angels once and for all, and so another operation was planned and executed. Operation SharQc focused on Angels in Quebec, with New Brunswick, France, and the Dominican Republic added as bonus players.

The Quebec police, who hadn't been especially subtle about previous actions against Les Hells, were even less so during Operation SharQc. When announcing details of the operation, Steven Chabot, SQ's deputy director-general, bragged that "our objectives were to prosecute nearly all the [Hell's Angels] of Quebec and their main collaborators, and to bring them to court as well as dismantle five chapters and seize their headquarters."*

The second hammer came crashing down on the Angels in April 2009 when more than twelve hundred officers from twenty municipal, provincial, and federal forces executed search warrants. The haul was once again impressive: $5 million in cash, dozens of kilograms of marijuana, hashish, and cocaine, and thousands of pills. More than 120 people, including 111 full-patch Angels, were arrested and charged with the usual offenses—including murder, attempted murder, gangsterism, and drug trafficking.

Impressive, yes, but in the end, not very productive. When it became obvious that many of the arrested Angels wouldn't be tried

---

* "Hells Angels Raids 'Dismantle' Biker Gang in Quebec: Police," CBC News Montreal, April 16, 2009.

for years, breaching their right to a speedy trial, thirty-one were released. It was outrageous but true: a full two years after the raids, the government was still debating which courtrooms would be used to try the accused. Meanwhile, most of the bikers were using high-powered (and high-priced) lawyers to plea-bargain for vastly reduced sentences. Operation SharQc had involved four years of planning, thousands of people to make it happen, and millions of dollars to see it through. And soon after the dramatic media coverage, it all began slipping away.

The toughest blow probably came in December 2010 when a Quebec court ordered police to return all personal property they'd taken from the Angels, declaring that just because something had been worn by a member or carried the club's emblem it didn't make it an absolute proceed of crime. Each item was to be examined and proven beyond doubt to have been purchased with ill-gotten funds, or else handed back.

When that decision was announced, surely a hundred or so grins and high fives were shared among the Angels.

IT WAS LIKE squeezing a balloon. You squeeze here and a bubble pops up over there. Squeeze all you want—you'll never get all the air out. So what do you do? If you're a Canadian law enforcement group, you launch another operation.

Which is what happened in late 2012, after a number of things became apparent. One was a power vacuum in Quebec as far as drugs, prostitution, and other activities were concerned. The two major operations since 2001 had not only crippled the Angels and even, to a degree, intimidated them; they'd also helped weaken the Mafia's Rizzuto family. The Rizzutos had dominated the province for years. Many of the family's problems were internal, created by the rival Catroni family. Nick Rizzuto Jr. was assassinated shortly after Christmas 2009, and other key members of the group were murdered or had disappeared. And so this, coupled with the crippling of the Angels over the previous ten years, had left the entire criminal element in Quebec and points east in disarray.

On the other side of the country, people like Larry Amero, a full-patch Angel, spotted an opportunity and created a consortium to fill the vacuum. First he recruited Shane Maloney, another B.C. Angel, who happened to be out on bail—after beating up a Montreal detective who was off duty and on vacation in Mexico. Amero then added two Mafia honchos and three guys from Montreal's Irish West End Gang. He may have liked the idea of heading east; he was one of the Angels who'd been wounded in the drive-by shooting in Kelowna that took out Jonathan Bacon of the Red Scorpions.

Other events further suggested that it was time to knock the bikers around a little, especially the 2011 raid by hooded gunmen on a blasting firm in Sainte-Sophie, Quebec. The raiders handcuffed the employees and stole almost fifteen hundred sticks of dynamite. Angels were suspected of being involved.

This was all sufficient to launch Operation Loquace, the third large-scale series of raids by various levels of law enforcement. Once again the number of arrests (120) was staggering, yet not as impressive as in the past; the public was getting used to these numbers. More important was the breakup of the consortium and the fact that none of its Angels was from Quebec, suggesting that the gang was as severely crippled in that province as the law officials had hoped.

NO ONE HONESTLY expected La Belle Province to go from battleground to nursery room as a result of the multiple police operations that had been conducted, with varying levels of success, against the bikers for at least a decade. It was clear, however, that the center of biker power had shifted away from Quebec, and that a wave of biker-linked criminal activities was beginning to crest in western Canada. But on the grand scale of things, a more serious and wide-ranging surge was beginning to rise with tidal-wave proportions in the opposite direction—east, on the other side of the Atlantic.

12

BIKER WARS IN EUROPE: THINGS GET VICIOUS

The shift in the Angels' power toward Europe not only revealed the weakness of the organization; it also highlighted the changing goals of its leaders.

Think of it: everything that had inspired the concept of the Hells Angels was uniquely American—the open road, the far-ranging desert, the rejection of traditional values. And all this expressed while astride a 100 percent American vehicle whose look and sound inspire instant intimidation. The Angels' appeal is based on riding big bulky Harleys across endless miles of blacktop, cowboys on metal monsters spewing gas fumes, the epitome of individuality and freedom.

So the idea of biker gangs becoming a threat to the peace and security of Europe is difficult to grasp. Unfettered individuality is a concept more at home in America than in Europe, where almost everyone resides within a socialist atmosphere—free health care, extended vacation times, government support programs, and great emphasis on things like recycling and environmental protection.

Okay, soccer hooligans in the U.K. and elsewhere may look and act like Angels in Doc Martens, but that's about all the two groups have in common. Open roads like those in the American southwest, where the biker-gang mentality was born, don't exist in Europe. Harley-Davidsons are laughable when compared with the finesse of European bikes like BMW and Moto Guzzi, not to mention the nicely engineered Japanese lines that Sonny Barger himself praised. And while working-class Europeans may sip a beer or two from time to time, the most popular beverage remains wine. American beer? Bland and watery concoctions suitable for feeding cattle and little else. So there was something bizarre about a bunch of Germans riding American bikes and naming themselves after Mexican bandits.

But it happened. In a big way. And it all started, of course, with the Angels who'd gone offshore many years before. Not to Europe, and not even to next-door Canada, but, as you'll recall, to New Zealand.

In Europe there were just too many young guys with time on their hands, bodies full of testosterone, and a need for brotherhood, mayhem, and money not to emulate the Angels. And they did, with a greater degree of savagery and heavy firepower than in America itself. Their actions and style revealed the new, global face of the Angels. They were no longer groups of toughs who wanted to be left alone to ride their cycles, raise a little hell, and maybe support themselves with the odd criminal action. Marlon Brando had become a ruthless criminal with expensive tastes and unbridled ambition who just happened to ride a motorcycle from time to time. If it wasn't too much trouble.

Like Angels in America and elsewhere, European biker gangs faced two kinds of challenges: from law enforcement and from competitive gangs. The biggest threat came from these other gangs, and it started in Scandinavia, the corner of Europe where you'd least expect it.

Say "Danish" in the United States and most people will picture a pastry with jam and icing on top. After all, Denmark is half the size of Indiana and has a population of fewer than six million. It's a peaceful country, generally—the home of Hans Christian Andersen—yet it has the highest number of motorcycle gangs per capita of any country in Europe and likely in the world. Not only that, but they're among the most violent of all MCs—fierce hardliners as likely to point a gun or swing an ax at you as any MC anywhere you can name. So it shouldn't be a surprise that Denmark, among the most socially progressive countries in the world, was the site of the first Nordic biker war.

It was in 1980 that a motorcycle club in Copenhagen calling itself the United MC patched themselves over to the Angels, becoming the first Hells Angel chapter in the country. Small, local MCs grew nervous. So they gathered together under the name Bullshit MC and declared themselves anti-Angels.

Their base was in an area of Copenhagen called Christiania. To give you an idea of the area, its main drag is called Pusher Street. It was like a Scandinavian version of San Francisco's Haight-Ashbury district back in the 1960s—lots of drugs (mostly grass and hash), free love, and few problems. Danish police tended to look the other way where drugs were concerned, opting to keep the cannabis trade in one place rather than have it spread all through the city. But things changed in Copenhagen with the arrival of the Bullshit MC. First came the harder drugs, followed shortly by the Angels, who, as they had everywhere else, wouldn't tolerate rivals, especially where big money was to be made.

And the Bullshit MC made a lot of money. They'd avoided direct confrontation with the Angels by making Christiania their home, and a couple of years of relative peace came and went. Eventually the inevitable happened: the Bullshits began to feel confined in their little turf. So with their war chest full of money and their numbers strong, they decided to venture out into greater Copenhagen. In September 1983 they opened a clubhouse in the city—their first wrong move. Their second wrong move was going to a Hells Angels' bar to celebrate.

War was declared. The Bullshits didn't have a chance against the Angels, although they put up a good fight—it took the Angels two years to annihilate them. The final score was eight dead Bullshits, including three consecutive presidents, which made the club's leadership inconsistent and sketchy at best. For the last six months of the fight, the remaining Bullshit guys were just trying to survive. Meanwhile, only one Hells Angel and two of their drug dealers were killed, although two innocent bystanders died in the cross fire. When police raided the Bullshit clubhouse they found the body of an unidentified biker under the floorboards. So the total body count was fourteen known dead plus dozens of others injured.

The war had been confined to Copenhagen and the Angel victory had been decisive, meaning the Bullshit members admitted defeat. The few Bullshits still kicking around were just glad to be alive. But they hadn't learned their lesson entirely, which gave rise to the second Scandinavian MC war.

Not everyone wanted to join the Angels as victors, especially the surviving Bullshits. They, along with others who disliked the Hells Angels (or perhaps just mistrusted them), chose to join the Morticians MC. For a few years the two clubs coexisted without incident, but when both clubs accelerated their transformation from guys who liked to ride bikes to criminals who liked to make big profits, the camaraderie dissolved. In 1992 the Morticians changed their name to the Undertakers MC. More important, they allied themselves with the Bandidos, who'd launched their first European chapter in Marseilles, France. Now they were the Bandidos MC Denmark.

Just to complicate things, the Outlaws landed in Oslo, Norway, and soon formed an alliance with the Bandidos. Their strongest link was their shared hatred of the Angels. And, of course, their ambition to corner and expand the drug market in northern Europe.

These moves appear to have taken the Hells Angels by surprise. Europe had once been their drug-dealing paradise, a place unfettered by serious competition. And there was a strategic factor to contend with, too. The Nordic countries were import points not only for Scandinavia and Western Europe but for the Eastern Bloc countries as well. Their newfound freedom from Communism promised a massive future market for drugs that the Angels had been ready to exploit and dominate. Now they were facing two of their most powerful rivals, gangs who weren't intimidated by the death's head patch or the reputation that went with it, and who had the same plans.

The result was inevitable.

On January 26, 1994, the first shots in the second Scandinavian drug war were fired at a Morbids MC clubhouse in Helsingborg, Sweden. No one was injured, but the die was cast. A month later another shoot-out in the same city left a Hells Angel named Joakim Boman dead. A few days after that the Angels clubhouse was struck by an anti-tank rocket. The Angels retaliated in June by shooting dead the president of Klan MC, an ally of the Bandidos in Finland. In February 1995 the war reached Norway when a shoot-out in Oslo between the Hells Angels and Bandidos ended in one biker being wounded.

Local police described these incidents as a game to prove which club was the toughest rather than a strategic effort to gain the total control each side sought. Maybe so, but it was a "game" that escalated, and that kept raising the body count.

In July 1995 the president of Bandidos MC Sweden was assassinated, which inspired the Bandidos to fire anti-tank rockets at Hells Angels prospect clubhouses in Helsinki, Finland, and Helsingborg, Sweden. The police responded to these attacks with arrests, eventually finding two Bandido members guilty: Kai Tapio Blom was given six years in prison and Antti Tauno Tapani was given four. When the president of Bandidos Finland arrived at the Helsinki courthouse for Blom and Tapani's trial, he was attacked and beaten by Hells Angels members. Time for retaliation: a few days later an Angels-owned tattoo parlor in Helsinki was leveled.

In North America, the usual approach to destroying enemy clubhouses had been to plant a bomb or start a fire. European bikers were more direct. Their favorite technique was to fire rockets at the clubs using anti-tank weapons stolen from army bases, usually in Sweden.

The war spread, with murderous consequences. On Christmas Day 1995, two Hells Angels members were beaten up by Bandidos at a nightclub in Copenhagen, signaling the beginning of the war in Denmark. Soon after, the bombing of an Angels prospect club in Hamar followed by the Angels' clubhouse in Oslo kept things going. In Helsinki one month later, an Angels-owned bar was flattened with a bomb. More retaliation: the Angels attacked the Bandidos' Helsinki clubhouse in March, shooting two members, including the vice president of Bandidos MC Finland, Jarkko Kokko. He died a couple of weeks later, and two Hells Angels prospects were convicted of his murder: Ilkka Ukkonen was sentenced to twelve and a half years in prison and Jussi Penttinen to six.

Things grew more frantic and violent. In March 1996 the Angels launched twin attacks on Bandidos at airports: at Oslo's

Fornebu airport several Bandidos were wounded by gunfire, and at Copenhagen's Kastrup airport, Bandidos returning from a weekend in Helsinki were shot while they sat in their car. Three were wounded and one, Uffe Larsen, was killed. This led to the arrest and conviction of six Hells Angels members and prospects. Five received a total of fifty-three years in prison; one was given a life sentence. Another series of clubhouse bombings was launched within weeks in Helsingborg and in southern Denmark. The clubhouse of a Hells Angels prospect club, Avengers MC, was also attacked in Aalborg, Denmark.

Through these and a subsequent series of attacks, the differences between the two enemies became apparent to police. The Angels were more methodical, more tactically proficient. They would assess the situation, weigh the risks, and proceed with some discipline. The Bandidos were, as one observer put it, more like kamikaze pilots, not giving a damn about consequences and prepared to take action right away, as though planning and second-guessing were for wimps. Or for Angels.

I can vouch for that. Among my various assignments working undercover with biker gangs, I spent almost two years as a Bandido. I've also spent nearly as long as an Angel, a Mongol, and with other clubs. I know their culture, their values, their outlook, and their attitude.

You may think all biker clubs are alike, but the differences are real, if sometimes subtle. The Angels consider themselves royalty, the guys everyone else wants to be like. That used to be the case, but it's not now and hasn't been for quite a while. Some gangs see themselves as natural enemies of the Angels, just as a mongoose is to a cobra. That's the attitude the Bandidos take. They're not royalty and don't pretend to be. They're the guys on the street outside the palace and they'd like nothing more than to kick out the king, stomp on his body, and carry his head through town on a stick.

The Bandidos will not quit. Not ever. They'll fight, if necessary, to the last man where the Angels are concerned. And the Angels are beginning to realize it.

THINGS DID NOT LET UP over the Scandinavian summer of 1996. Jan "Face" Krogh Jensen, a Bandidos member, was shot and killed in Drammen, Norway, in July; a Hells Angels supporter was shot six days later in Oslo; and two Hells Angels were shot and wounded, one in Malmö, Sweden, and the other in Denmark's Jyderup prison. The summer ended with the wounding of the vice president of Hells Angels MC Sweden in Helsingborg.

The next year reads like a casualty list from an all-out-war battleground. Which, of course, it was.

- **October 1996:** Three attacks on Hells Angels clubhouses. One in Malmö wounds twelve innocent bystanders. Three days later an anti-tank rocket is fired at an Angels clubhouse in Copenhagen during a party; full-patched Angel Louis Linde Nielsen and guest Janne Krohn are killed. (Bandidos prospect Niels Poulsen is later convicted of carrying out the attack and sentenced to life in prison.) On the 30th a car bomb explodes outside the Hells Angels clubhouse in Oslo.

- **December 1996:** Shootings of Bandidos Denmark members in Horsens and Aalborg.

- **January 1997:** Hells Angel Kim Thrysöe Svendsen is murdered in Aalborg. Thore "Henki" Holm, president of the Swedish Outlaws, and a French member are shot and wounded by a member of the Untouchables MC, a Hells Angels puppet gang. Bandidos' foot soldiers are shot in Amager and Køge in Denmark. The Bandidos respond by ordering shootings on Hells Angels members and allies in Frederiksberg.

- **June 1997:** A car bomb explodes outside a Bandidos clubhouse in Drammen, Norway. Three people die, including Irene Astrid Bækkevold, a civilian driving by in her car. A Hells Angels member is convicted of the bombing five years later. Bandido Björn Gudmandsen is killed and three other Bandidos wounded as a result of a shooting in Liseleje, Denmark. Hells Angel Vagn Smith is convicted of the murder and sentenced to life imprisonment.

Eventually the cost became too high—not in bodies but in cash. The war was expensive to maintain: weapons needed to be purchased, lawyers hired, clubhouses rebuilt. And, more important, drug profits were drying up as frightened Scandinavian users decided to do without their hash, cocaine, and meth rather than deal with armed bikers sharing a hair-trigger attitude. What's more, the Angels were aging. Many of them were outgrowing the testosterone- and anger-driven attitude they'd harbored in their twenties and early thirties. Many had families and responsibilities, not to mention gray hair and a sense of their own mortality. As a patched Hells Angel, punch-outs and shoot-outs had once been a part of life. Now they seemed more like an opportunity to lose your teeth, your freedom, and your life, which meant they probably weren't as necessary as they once seemed.

Discussions began in the United States between heads of both clubs, leading to more detailed conferences—for which Scandinavian police volunteered to provide security service so that both sides could negotiate in relative comfort. To the surprise of many, it worked.

On September 25, 1997, Danish TV news cameras captured and recorded the sight of "Big" Jim Tinndahn, president of all the Bandidos' European chapters, shaking hands with Hells Angels Europe president Bent "Blondie" Nielsen. The agreement was headline news across Scandinavia and much of Europe, like a minia-ture version of VE Day marking the end of World War II in Europe. The two clubs signed a treaty agreeing that no more chapters would be opened in Scandinavia. By the end of the 1990s both sides had broken the treaty from time to time. Denmark passed a law banning motorcycle clubs from owning or renting property for their club activities, but it was repealed on constitutional grounds.

Nothing could change a more gruesome reality. More than four hundred violent incidents occurred during the three-year battle, wounding more than a hundred people and resulting in the deaths of eleven. Many scoff at these numbers, saying that at least as many people "disappeared" during the war and that numerous attempts to wound or murder were simply never reported to police.

Surprisingly, things settled down and the truce began to hold. With small exceptions the battles ended. The police, and citizens generally, breathed a sigh of relief.

The long-term results of the second Scandinavian biker war are important to note, because more than a cessation of hostilities was involved.

First, peace reigned because the bikers essentially cut first Scandinavia and eventually all of Europe into a massive drug-filled pie, doling out slices as they saw fit. The two clubs also expanded over the next decade. Within a few years of the peace agreement, the Angels could boast eight chapters in Denmark (a total of almost

170 full-patch members), five chapters in Norway, four in Finland, and six in Sweden.

The Bandidos outdid them. Over the same period from 1997 to 2005, they registered thirteen Danish clubs, six in Sweden, five in Norway, and two in Finland. Where the Angels could count twenty-five support chapters in Denmark, the Bandidos boasted thirty support groups, called "X-Team chapters," with a membership of 350 or more. Yet each tolerated the other's breaking of the agreement. Temporarily, at least.

With both clubs solidly established in Scandinavia, they were poised to leapfrog through Europe, into Russia, and all the way to Asia. The Scandinavian police may have assumed that their security assistance during the Angel–Bandido peace talks saved lives, including those of innocent passersby, and it did. But only for a while, and only in Scandinavia. For the rest of the world it unleashed a wave of biker-driven crime that continues to roll through countries well beyond North America.

The second effect of the war was to weaken the image and, to some degree, the strength of the Hells Angels. No longer were they the irresistible dominant force among biker gangs, the club that could control whatever it chose to control wherever it chose to operate. Now it had to contend with serious opposition from the Bandidos and other gangs sworn to knock down and replace the Angels. The 1997 peace conference changed the face of biker gangs in Europe, and not necessarily for the better.

It also revealed that the parent chapters of the Angels and the Bandidos no longer exerted the total control they once had over their European chapters. This was more of a factor for the Angels than for the Bandidos. The Angels had based a lot of their recent success on top-down discipline, like a standard well-trained army.

When the generals say "Fight!" the word is passed down to the grunts in the foxholes and they shoulder their guns; when the generals say "Cease fire!" the guns are put aside until the next order. In the old days, an order from the top of the Angels was like an order from God—disobey it at your own peril. In contrast, the Bandidos have more of a guerrilla attitude: "Leave us alone and we'll kill the bastards our own way!"

Scandinavia wasn't the only place where the Angels leadership was no longer as effective. While all the mayhem was happening in Denmark, Sweden, and elsewhere, the Quebec biker war was raging in Canada, and the top Angel guys couldn't control that one, either. Plus, the Mongols were doing whatever they wanted to do in Southern California.

To anyone looking at the whole picture, the image was clear. The days of the Angels doing whatever they wanted, wherever they pleased, and to whomever they chose were over. So in retrospect, the end of the Scandinavian biker war may have sounded a death knell that keeps ringing to this day.

EARLIER, in Chapter 3, we saw the kinds of things that were going on in Holland around the same time. Nothing like the Scandinavian biker wars or the wars in Quebec was happening in the Netherlands, but somehow no bikers exceeded the Dutch in sheer viciousness, something I don't fully understand. The Dutch bikers are hard-core and ruthless. Why? Maybe it's because of Amsterdam's role as a major entry point for drugs, or the influence of the city's red-light district, where women are used and abused like so much trash. Or maybe it's because the biker tradition there stretches back so far—all the way back to that Marlon Brando movie that defined what it was to be a biker.

By the 1960s all the kids who'd seen *The Wild One* were old enough, big enough, and angry enough to live the biker life, as though the open land around Hollister, California, could be replicated among the dikes and windmills of Holland.

One of the top motorcycle clubs in Holland at the time, the Kreidler Team, were well-known for their violence. They enjoyed invading school dances and private parties, where they'd beat up boys and girls equally. Their leader was the psycho we met earlier, Big Willem van Boxtel. Van Boxtel cared little about the rest of society, and that included Sonny Barger and his boys. So he and the rest of the Kreidler Team changed their name to "Hells Angels" and adopted the HA patch without bothering to check with the home chapter. (It would never cross their mind to ask permission of anyone about anything.)

Calling themselves the Angels, authorized or not, attracted every kid in Holland who could ride a cycle and wanted to raise hell. The club spurted in size and spread well beyond Amsterdam. The American Angels weren't too pleased, of course, that a bunch of Dutchmen were roaring around the Netherlands on Harleys wearing the death's head symbol on the backs of their vests, selling drugs, running prostitutes, and generally acting as if they were in San Berdoo instead of Rotterdam. But by the time they realized they should do something about it, the Dutch Angels were too big to challenge.

It took the Americans ten years of cajoling and playing nice to convince the Dutch Angels to make things legal and sanctioned. Finally, in 1978, they became the Dutch Hells©. By that time, Amsterdam city authorities had also tried to make nice to van Boxtel, with results somewhere between tragedy and comedy.

In 1973 twelve members of the still-unofficial Dutch Hells Angels, led by van Boxtel, had been arrested for a savage beating of some young students and two of their teachers. The press had a field day reporting every little gory detail. When van Boxtel and his gang received twelve weeks in jail for assault, the pressure from the press and the public ramped up. The municipal government *must* take action. And they did: they paid about $100,000 to buy the Angels a clubhouse. In the misplaced reasoning of the municipal authorities, the Angels were merely young, energetic boys with no place to hang out and feel at home, which is why they rode around the city on their motorbikes and got into trouble. If they had a real home, a place where they could gather and talk and maybe play ping-pong, they would relax and not go around the city beating up boys and teachers and threatening to do terrible things to young girls. Not only that, the city would contribute more than $12,000 a year to making the Angels feel comfortable and secure.

The Angels, naturally, welcomed the gesture, calling their new headquarters Angel Place. They loved the idea of being a social cause, and agreed to assist the city in guiding other youngsters onto the straight path toward becoming law-abiding Dutch citizens. Within weeks—maybe even days—Angel Place became not a haven for wayward kids and an oasis of goodwill but a hellhole in which to conduct murder, drug deals, torture, and gang rape.

The patch-over ceremony, when the Dutch Angels were officially sanctioned by the U.S. Angels, was a major event in Amsterdam. At least 300 motorcycles and 150 cars formed the parade through the city. It opened eyes on every side. The Dutch Angels, now considered royalty among bikers, could hardly wait to extend their influence and build their bank accounts. The American Angels realized just how important Amsterdam and Rotterdam could be as entry points for drugs into Europe. And the Dutch citizens, watching Angels from everywhere flaunt their colors and strut with pride, wondered just what the country was in for. So, in time, did the American Angels themselves.

THE DUTCH ANGELS grew fiercely independent. Not only did they fail to work well with others, they couldn't get along very well with themselves, with regular beatings, shootings, and other bad things happening among the members. Yet it seems to have taken a while for the Dutch to recognize the threat the Angels posed. The city of Amsterdam, for example, paid the annual $12,000 fee to keep the drug-running, prostitute-pimping, girl-raping clubhouse going for ten years before it dawned that the Angels weren't at all interested in helping needy youth.

Things became more and more violent until, in October 2005, the law took charge. A thousand cops hit sixty-four locations throughout the country, arresting forty-seven Angels, most of them on weapons charges. "Weapons" doesn't begin to cover the kinds of armaments the Dutch police seized. They included grenade launchers, grenades, machine guns, hand guns, and a fully loaded flame thrower with gas and ready to go.

This, together with the assassination of Nomad leader Paul "The Butcher" de Vries for trying to rip off his brother Angels, left the club disorganized. Which was great news for the Satudarah MC. With seventeen chapters and more than three hundred members, they were a powerful presence in such a small country.

And when the massive cocaine deal that resulted in de Vries's murder went all wrong, the Satudarah were deeply interested in finding the cache. After all, some of it had been slated for them, and they'd invested a fair amount of cash to buy it in the first place. The Satudarah didn't care who killed de Vries, or even why. They wanted the drugs, and they'd do whatever it took to find them.

De Vries had shared a small house with a girlfriend, Deedee Sam. It was a nothing kind of place, just somewhere for him to keep cash, guns, drugs, and other things he didn't want in his "real" house. Shortly after de Vries was tortured and murdered, Deedee went to the house to collect her things as well as some of his assets she could claim. The door was locked when she arrived, but someone had been there before her. The interior was a wreck and everything of value was gone. The Satudarah had beaten her to it. But they weren't finished yet.

Remember the tough Indonesian kid we met in Chapter 3, the guy from Jakarta named Aditya? He was recruited after a couple of girls were sent by the Satudarah to comfort Deedee in her grief. They managed to get the name of a friend of de Vries and the hotel he was staying at in Den Haag (The Hague), about fifty kilometers from Amsterdam. They also learned that the friend had worked as a courier for de Vries and would be transporting twenty kilos of cocaine in a duffel bag on Friday, three days away.

This didn't leave much time, but they knew exactly what to do. They'd hit him just before he boarded the train. They needed a volunteer to do it, someone who couldn't be traced back to the club. No, not a volunteer; a patsy, a throwaway, someone they could use, someone who'd never be missed.

A couple of Satudarahs recalled meeting the nephew of one of the club's dealers, a tough kid who'd just arrived in town and wanted to make it big. His name, they remembered, was Aditya.

They met the kid at the uncle's house and explained what they wanted. He liked the idea. He could hardly wait to get started. It would be his entry into Big-Time Crime. Soon he'd be riding in the big cars he saw, living the good life that the top guys in Satudarah lived, lording it over ordinary people. They gave him a gun, a disguise, and instructions. They warned him not to screw up and promised $5000 in cash plus a job working in one of the brothels they owned. The instructions were simple: kill the target before he boards the train, take the duffel bag, and deliver it to the car that would meet him in front of the railroad station. Without the duffel bag he wouldn't be paid.

Oh, by the way, they added. The guy you're going to kill is a Hells Angel. When word gets around that you successfully hit a top-level Angel you'll get respect from everyone.

That's what brought Aditya to the train station with murder in his heart. He didn't get the five thousand dollars, of course. He got a bullet in the face instead.

He should have died, but he didn't. Being shot in the face means a 50/50 chance of survival, albeit at a horrific price. Beneath the skin, the bone structure of your face provides a good chance to deflect the bullet from your brain. Aditya was lucky to survive, but the bullet tore off half his face.

While he recovered in hospital, Dutch authorities decided not to pursue charges against him. Even with the video evidence from the train station, he'd been wearing a disguise and could argue it wasn't him. The Dutch might succeed in convicting him of theft of the duffel bag, but not much more—so let his home country deal with him. A murder warrant for his arrest had indeed been issued by Indonesia, which was pressing for extradition. Indonesia has the death penalty, and their case was iron clad.

Arriving back home, Aditya was charged with robbery resulting in death. He pleaded not guilty and lost his case. There'd never been any doubt. The Indonesian police had his prints, his DNA, his journal, and the bloody clothes that he and his mother had tried to hide.

The sentence was death by firing squad. Unlike much of the rest of the world, in Indonesia there is little chance for a successful appeal, and no execution date is given. You never know what night will be your last. The guards arrive after midnight, drag you from your cell, and tie you to a post facing a twelve-man firing squad.

I could find no record of Aditya's death. He may still be in a cell, waiting for the key to enter the door in the middle of the night. Or he could be in an unmarked grave by now. Who knows?

SO WHAT'S THE LESSON to be learned from all this? I can name several.

First, the Angels are no longer as feared as they once were—or believed they were—in Europe. Powerful, yes. But it's no longer just their game. The spoils, especially from drugs, are much too impressive. It's a very big pot and lots of hands want to reach into it for the gold.

Next, the Angels are no longer the toughest guys on the block. In many ways, they never were. The Mongols, the Bandidos, and others have whipped their butts when they needed to. In the past, the Angels could count on their organization and discipline to get things done, but just as the U.S. Army discovered in Vietnam, that can only go so far.

As for the Angels themselves, they're perhaps too quick to turn on their own. As we saw in Quebec and elsewhere, if you're too ruthless with your own people, they can come back and bite you. And other clubs will have nothing to do with you, except perhaps dedicate themselves to your annihilation.

Finally, any Angel needs to avoid two things over all: drawing excessive heat from the cops and losing money for the club. Had Butcher de Vries played by the rules the whole club could have made money and he'd likely still be alive today. But the same things that drive many guys to become Angels these days—greed and narcissism—overcame him and he paid for it. Painfully.

13

THE SILENCE OF THE INNOCENTS

It's difficult to discuss the Hells Angels—their violence, their disrespect for the rest of society, and their future downfall—without discussing the innocent people who've died, many of them in horrific circumstances, as a result of the bikers' behavior. Some may call their deaths "collateral damage," unintentional casualties that the bikers regret. Or not. I call them something else. Slaughter. Butchery. Repulsive. I don't have the exact word. But I do have accounts of the kinds of things the Angels have perpetrated, no doubt telling themselves "We can do this because we're Hells Angels and it needs to be done."

Nothing as terrible as innocent deaths, especially of children, ever "needs to be done." But the stories need to be told.

IN MY ALMOST THIRTY YEARS of chasing bad guys, I never worked a pedophile ring. I couldn't. After spending six months with animals who abuse children, I know I'd become a raving maniac. The only reason I discuss the cases here is to alert you to the kind of people the Angels are, and to explain why some cops dedicate their lives to bringing them down.

The Angels like to boast about their Toys for Tots runs, where dozens of full-patched guys ride their Harleys around town gathering toys for little children. It's a PR gesture—everyone knows that. It's a way to soften their image in the hope that people will think, "Gee, those Hells Angels aren't so bad. Just a bunch of guys who like riding their motorcycles. Maybe we should all cut them a little slack."

The next time you find yourself thinking that way, think of Dallas Grondalski. She was five years old. She had blond hair, big blue eyes, a smile that could melt a glacier, and a laugh that sounded like music. She'll never need toys and she'll always be five years old.

Some people say bikers' murder of children is an anomaly, an unusual event that doesn't define them. I say that too many of these "events" occur to think the Angels give a damn about the people they hurt. To the Hells Angels, the death of an innocent, whether a five-year-old girl or a fifty-year-old man, is an inconvenience—something that generates unwelcome heat from the cops, the press, and the public. No matter how much they may claim that they're opposed to this kind of stuff and how many flowers they may send to the funeral, the death of innocents as a result of their actions produces only a "Gee, that's too bad" response. In the corporate world it might be called "the cost of doing business."

Nothing illustrates this better than the tragedy of Dallas Grondalski.

IN 1986, when Sonny Barger was still in charge of the Angels' Oakland chapter, he discovered that a senior Angel named Terry

Dalton had been stealing money from the club. That was a serious deal, no matter how high up in the pecking order Dalton might have been. You don't steal from your brothers, damn it.

Sonny took the usual action. He got Dalton into the clubhouse with other Angels who knew the score and together they beat the crap out of him. Then they threw him out of the club.

According to club rules, Dalton was to be shunned by all Hells Angels. But he'd been an Angel for so long and based his identity on it so solidly that he couldn't just fade away. After a couple of months word came back to Sonny that some guys in the club were still being seen with Dalton, having a beer and going for runs together.

Sonny had to put a stop to it. He circulated a picture of Dalton to all the local chapters with a warning: stay away from this SOB.

The guys in the Vallejo chapter didn't seem to get the message, so Sonny decided another lesson was needed. He ordered the whole chapter to Oakland for a meeting, which is never a good sign. Still, the entire club showed up. The locals gave them a major beating, saving the roughest treatment for the president, who, along with a few other members of the Vallejo chapter, was kicked out of the club.

Sonny installed an Angel named Butch Lester as the new Vallejo boss. But that wasn't enough. He wanted to find Dalton and finish things once and for all. That, after all, is the Angel way.

One of the Vallejo members who'd survived Sonny's beating and purge was Billy Grondalski. Despite what he'd gone through, Grondalski ignored Sonny's orders and maintained contact with some of the expelled Angels. Why would anyone with enough intelligence to stay upright on a motorcycle risk it? Was he that dumb?

Probably not. It's not a lack of intelligence that makes people like Grondalski do stupid things. It's an excess of greed. He had his drug-dealing turf, he had earnings from the deals, and he needed his contacts to keep doing business. On the whole, he'd rather risk Sonny Barger's wrath than give up the easy money he'd been making for the past few years.

Word got back to Sonny, who hit the roof. He required total obedience. More than that, Billy's body still bore his Hells Angels tattoos. Plus, Sonny was told, he'd taken off with about $600 worth of Angel decals. The word was sent out: teach this douche bag Grondalski a lesson.

Butch Lester valued his new position as president of the Vallejo chapter. He also valued his life. So when Sonny flew into a rage over Grondalski's defiance, Lester promised to take action. It would, after all, put him in Sonny's good graces. And that could lead to a bright future as a heavyweight Angel.

Lester's girlfriend happened to be Billy's sister-in-law, which, Lester believed, would make it easy to track Grondalski down. Unfortunately for Lester, it also made it easy for his girlfriend to alert Grondalski. Whether or not she was the source of the tip, Grondalski, his wife, and their five-year-old daughter Dallas skipped town, heading north for a new life. They chose Fort Bragg, a quiet tourist town on the ocean, about 250 kilometers north of Vallejo. Their small home was nestled among giant redwood trees alongside the Noyo River. Fishing was good in the Noyo, and Billy liked to fish. It seemed a perfect spot to escape the Angels.

Billy, Patty, and Dallas arrived in Fort Bragg on October 1, 1986. Once settled in their new home, they enrolled Dallas in her new kindergarten class. Their problems with the Angels must have seemed far away. They weren't. On a visit south to visit Patty's sister, they were spotted by an Angel lookout and trailed back to their home in Fort Bragg.

Lester and the Vallejo chapter's vice president, Chuck Diaz, were assigned to do the job. Diaz, it should be noted, knew Billy's family well, including little Dallas. She knew Diaz well. She called him "Uncle Chuck."

On Sunday, October 5, Billy went into town to buy some new fishing gear. Shortly after he arrived home Lester and Diaz appeared at the front door and barged their way into the house. At more than six feet and 240 pounds, Billy was a handful. He was also tough and aggressive, not to mention protective of his family. When Billy told Lester and Diaz to get the hell out of his house and leave his family alone—which at this point included Patty's seventeen-year-old half-brother, Jerami Vandagriff—Lester shoved his .45-caliber pistol in Billy's face.

Later, Lester would claim that the gun went off accidentally. It didn't matter to Billy; the bullet entered his mouth and he fell dead on the floor.

Lester's next move was no accident. He turned to Patty Grondalski and shot her, then pursued a frantic Jerami down a hall, finally putting a bullet in his head. Now only Dallas was left.

Chuck Diaz found her hiding behind some furniture in the back room. She may have been five years old, disarmingly pretty, and a hundred percent innocent, but it didn't matter to Diaz. She was a witness. Diaz lifted her by her long hair with one hand, pulled his knife out of its sheath with the other, and began slashing the little girl's throat. Maybe the knife was dull. Maybe Diaz's heart wasn't entirely into it. Dallas bled, she gasped, she struggled, she attempted to scream. Until Lester walked over and shot her in the face. And then "Uncle Chuck" dropped her.

Other Angels helped Lester and Diaz get rid of the evidence. They destroyed the gun and burned their bloodstained clothes. The next morning Charlie Haas borrowed a truck, drove to the house, scattered gasoline, and set the house alight. But first he cut the Hells Angels tattoo from Billy's body. Later he would bring the pound of flesh back to Oakland, displaying it like a trophy.

But something went wrong. The fire never burned its way all through the house. Dallas's body and other evidence remained.

Law enforcement officers and the public were sickened, outraged, disgusted. It had clearly been a Hells Angels killing. But the Angels watch each other's backs. Usually.

Nine years after the murders, two Angels, including Haas, offered to trade their testimony for some breaks from the law. Still, it took another eight years, three trials, and more than $4 million of taxpayers' money for justice, or a close approximation of it, to be done. Lester was convicted of all four murders and received four life sentences. The prosecution could make only one murder charge stick with Diaz, but it didn't make any difference; his one life sentence will be just as long and just as effective as Lester's. By this time, of course, they were no longer Angels. That way, the HAMC could keep collecting Toys for Tots with straight faces.

I'VE ALREADY TALKED about other innocents who died because the Angels just didn't give a damn. Remember the six-year-old twin daughters of Margo Compton, shot in the head while clutching their teddy bears? And Daniel Desrochers, who was playing in a schoolyard when someone detonated a bomb hidden in a nearby Jeep?

Daniel's death had an interesting effect on the biker war raging through Quebec in the mid-1990s. Until Daniel's death, Les Hells and the Rock Machine were looked upon almost fondly by people in the neighborhood of their clubhouses, or people who secretly admired the free life the bikers seemed to enjoy. The slayings of one gang against another? A settling of accounts. Something to shake your head over when you see it on the TV news. Let 'em fight. Who really cares? Daniel's death changed all that.

The Angels and the Rock Machine should have felt at least some regret about Daniel's death. At the very least it would have been a decent PR gesture. But when Daniel's mother, Josée-Anne, expressed outrage at the idea of two warring biker gangs not giving a damn about the safety of innocent children, the Angels in full colors rode slowly by her house just as the family was leaving for Daniel's funeral. One biker lifted his hand in a one-finger salute.

If they thought this was a neat idea or that it would intimidate Josée-Anne Desrochers, they were wrong. Her fury at the Angels, the Rock Machine, and the entire don't-give-a-damn bike culture launched the Elles Angels, four French-speaking mothers as angry as any four grizzly bears whose cubs are threatened. They demanded that both police and politicians help them take back the streets. And who could disagree? How much tolerance could anyone hand to people who chose to kill each other off and rack up bystander deaths as so much collateral damage? And it wasn't even Daniel's death alone that inspired them. The death of any innocent person concerns us all.

The Elles Angels lacked colors, bikes, nicknames, and tattoos, but they were filled with determination and resolve. Their battle cry was *Nous n'avons pas peur!* We are not afraid! When the Elles Angels presented a petition to the Quebec government demanding that the hammer come down on the warring bikers, signed by more than two million Québécois, the politicians got the message. And when Josée-Anne Desrochers authored a book about her son and her response to his senseless death, *My Child Against a Bomb*, the Angels offered her $2 million to "just go away." The offer was reportedly made by an attorney associated with Mom Boucher's personal lawyer. Josée-Anne told him bluntly what he could do with the money.

As much as anyone in the Angels' history, Josée-Anne Desrochers stood up to the Angels and drew attention to all that they represented—their misplaced sense of omnipotence, their contempt for the rest of humanity, their hypocrisy in riding in Toys for Tots parades while disregarding the blood of children on their hands, their delight at humiliating anyone injured by their selfish acts.

The Angel who flashed his disgusting salute at Josée-Anne Desrochers the day of her son's funeral has a good deal to answer for. Josée-Anne and the other Elles Angels were instrumental in the passing of anti-gang legislation directed specifically at the bikers and in pressuring law enforcement authorities to cooperate in organizing special squads—which led to the convictions of hundreds of bikers.

Her efforts, and the ongoing sorrow at having buried her own child, took a toll on her. Less than ten years after the death of her son, Josée-Anne Desrochers died of cancer. She was just forty years old. Her legacy remains.

ANGELS, LIKE ALL BIKERS, want the world to see them as the ultimate macho men, proud and free individualists overflowing with bravery in the face of threat.

Tell that to Hélène Brunet.

On a sunny morning in July 2000 she was working her usual morning shift at Eggstra, a breakfast café on Montreal's Henri Bourassa Boulevard, when two regulars walked in and ordered coffee and orange juice. Hélène had avoided serving them in the past, leaving it to other wait staff. She knew their names—Normand Descôteaux and Robert Savard—and knew they were loan sharks with ties to the Hells Angels. Everyone in the restaurant knew this. Hélène didn't like bikers, especially guys like these, but on this day one of the other waitresses had left work early. She reluctantly but politely took their order.

As thirty-one-year-old Brunet leaned across the table to pour coffee, gunshots rang out behind her. She turned to see Savard slumped over the table and a man in a ski mask staring back at her, a pistol in his hand. The killer had one more target, but as he swung the gun toward Descôteaux, the muscular, two-hundred-pound biker seized the petite waitress and lifted her off her feet, using her as a human shield. Unable to move, she felt four bullets from the shooter's gun tear into her arm and leg. When the shooter fled, Descôteaux dropped her to the floor and sprinted in the other direction.

Montreal papers called it a "gangland shooting," leaving out the part about an innocent woman forced into the line of fire.

After recovering from her wounds in hospital, Hélène was not content to simply fade away, insisting that police take legal action against Descôteaux, whose lawyer dismissed her claim, saying it was an invention of the police. Eventually the case was settled out of court. For how much money? No one was talking. Whatever the amount, it was less than the damage done to the Hells Angels' vaunted reputation as Robin Hoods on wheels. They were labeled as cowards in denim.

It took a month in hospital and years of therapy for Hélène Brunet to overcome the events of that July morning. No amount of money from the court settlement could begin to pay for her pain and suffering. Her life was left in a shambles. Most of her friends deserted her, believing she'd be a target for biker revenge, and they preferred to avoid being in shooting range. Her boyfriend abandoned her for the same reason. She began sliding into deep depression and considered suicide, until she joined forces with Josée-Anne Desrochers in battling the bikers.

And the guy in the ski mask who shot her? We met him earlier: Gérald Gallant, the quiet hit man from Donnacona who got his killing contracts while seated in a pew of his parish church, and who apologized to the families of his victims when he confessed to his crimes.

There is no record of him apologizing to Hélène Brunet.

YOU SAY NO to bikers at your peril. You also break gang rules at your peril. Sound complicated? Not really.

In October 2000, about four months after Normand Descôteaux used Hélène Brunet as a shield, Francis Laforest and his wife stepped out of their house on the way to the McTavish Bistro, a restaurant in the quiet town of Terrebonne that Francis operated with his two brothers. For some time the three brothers had resisted the selling of drugs on their premises. They ran an honest business, they'd worked hard to make it a success, and they had the right and the obligation to prevent unlawful activities.

As soon as they emerged from their home, the couple were attacked by two men wearing ski masks and wielding baseball bats. While his wife screamed in fright, the men beat the thirty-three-year-old Francis over and over, leaving him broken, bleeding, and dying on his front lawn.

Officially, the murder remains unsolved. People on both sides of the law know what happened, however. Police contacts have told me how bikers wanted to deal drugs in the bistro, how the owners told them to leave and not come back, how the bikers threatened revenge and the brothers ignored them. But police don't have enough proof to win a conviction.

More important, they believe there aren't any suspects to arrest. The murder of Francis Laforest was so brutal, so outrageous that another wave of revulsion against bikers rose within the province. As the police tell me, the two bikers wielding baseball bats were at loose ends and chose to kill Laforest without permission from the gang leadership. That's a no-no. And when it produces a kickback from the public and the police, it's a serious no-no. As the police understand it, the two bikers with the baseball bats are dead.

Sounds like justice? Not quite. Michèle Laforest, mother of Francis, became involved with a victims' group that managed to have laws against bikers and their activities strengthened. She also agreed to do a number of media interviews in which she spoke out against their excesses. That's when she began receiving late-night hang-up telephone calls and saw parades of bikers in full regalia riding slowly past her home.

These are not considered empty threats. An insurance company refused to issue policies on the lives of her two remaining sons, claiming "danger to close members of their families that could put the applicants in jeopardy." That's as real as it gets.

The bistro is still going strong, and the remaining brothers still don't allow drugs to be sold there. So they won. But what a price to pay.

ABOUT A YEAR LATER, in October 2001, a biker named Benoît Guimond, who was a member of the Hells Angels farm team the Rockers, was unhappy about having to stand in line waiting for entry to an after-hours club in Montreal. Not only that, but when he reached the entrance he was told he couldn't wear his biker colors in the club. Given all the violence associated with Quebec bikers, this seems like a reasonable rule. But not to Guimond. Why, he was almost a real Hells Angel—nobody was going to treat him that way. So he stepped back, withdrew a pistol from his jacket, and began firing into the waiting crowd.

He managed to shoot seventeen-year-old Marc-Alexandre Chartrand, who later died in hospital, and wound another young man, who survived.

The remarkable thing about this incident is not that some hothead believed his association with the Angels made him invincible, but that police were inundated with witnesses who were ready to assist them in prosecuting the killer. Years earlier, no one would have seen a thing. But Les Hells had used up their goodwill with the public. Knowing he couldn't fight the charges, Guimond arrived at a police station with his lawyer and was charged with one count of murder and one of assault causing bodily harm. In April 2004 he was declared guilty and sentenced to life in prison.

These murders and so many others might be considered random acts. They are not. They represent a systematic disregard for human life that is part of the biker lifestyle established and perpetrated by the Angels.

AMONG LAW ENFORCEMENT TYPES, nothing illustrates the Angels' attitude toward others better than the fate of Cynthia Garcia. Her story has become legendary, and not because it's unique—no one really knows how many Cynthia Garcias have suffered at the whim of the Angels—but because knowledge of it is so detailed and her treatment was so brutal.

It involved the Mesa chapter of the Hells Angels and a biker named Kevin Augustiniak, a rebel without a clue. A full-patch Angel, he was charged with assaulting a woman in February 2001. Her crime was bumping into him at a party. When she failed to show sufficient respect he punched her hard enough to break her jaw. Big brave Kevin. He was charged, but walked. Sometimes justice works, sometimes it collapses. A few months later Kevin arrived at his home in Mesa to hear his neighbor making too much noise in his yard. We've all experienced it: our neighbor runs his power saw too long, or plays his music too loud, and we ask him to turn it down.

Kevin went outside to state his case. The neighbor said something Kevin disagreed with, so Kevin pointed his gun, shot him twice in the chest, then turned around and went home. The neighbor survived (barely) and Augustiniak was arrested. Good: a second opportunity to lock him up.

Instead he made bail and Cynthia Garcia's fate was sealed. She wasn't a target. The Angels likely didn't even know her. And they certainly didn't value her any more than they might value an old boot.

Into the mix comes "Mesa Mike" Kramer, one of those fools whose only goal is to become the most feared man in any room he walks into. He'd been a member of the Dirty Dozen, a gang absorbed by the Angels in the late 1990s. After several years as an Angel, Kramer appeared to be settling down. He had a job with the city of Mesa and a young family to support. Sounds promising, but his best friend happened to be the psychopathic Kevin Augustiniak.

Crazy Kevin talked Mesa Mike into heading to the chapter clubhouse for a party one weeknight. To the Angels, a party isn't really a party without women. Someone had noticed one wearing a red dress in the neighborhood and a prospect was sent to find her and bring her back for the "party." Prospects, of course, are taught to do what they're told. A few minutes later, the prospect returned with Cynthia Garcia, an attractive forty-four-year-old single mother with a penchant for drinking guys under the table.

With all her "street smarts" she still let the prospect talk her into going back to the clubhouse with him, and found herself alone with a bunch of drunk Hells Angels.

I never met Cynthia Garcia. Her orphaned children described her as a kind and gentle soul, a single mother trying to weave her way through a tough, uncaring world. She may have had social problems, including drinking and drug abuse, maybe because she wasn't hugged enough as a child. I don't care and I'm not soliciting testimonials. It doesn't matter. The only thing that matters is understanding what happened to her, and how it illustrates the cruel, pointless savagery perpetrated by a gang of cowards. In some ways they represent the Hells Angels in their truest form, without the layer of civility they like to cover themselves with from time to time.

Somewhere, sometime during the party Cynthia failed to show respect for the Angels. She may have said something insulting, in jest or seriously. Again, it doesn't matter. The logical response would be to ask her to leave, toss her out, whatever. Kevin Augustiniak's response was to knock her off the stool she'd been sitting on. Then, according to court testimony from Mesa Mike Kramer, both Augustiniak and Angel prospect Paul Eischeid began kicking her, first in the face then throughout her body, over and over again while the rest of the Angels watched and did nothing. Kramer finally took charge, ordering someone to bring a car around and dump her into it. Was he concerned about Cynthia's welfare? No, he was afraid her blood would stain the carpet permanently.

Still alive and conscious, she was dumped into the trunk of the car and Kramer, along with Augustiniak and Eischeid, drove her into the desert. Again, according to Kramer, Augustiniak decided to kill her. Kramer claimed to be under the impression they would just dump her there. Opening the trunk, they realized she was very much alive and conscious. Someone pulled a knife and stabbed her.

The others joined in. Cynthia Garcia was stabbed at least twenty-six times and her head was almost severed from her body. Then she was left for the coyotes while the Angels washed their clothes and cleaned the trunk of the car, leaving no clues.

About a month later, Kramer decided to become an informant for the police. He neglected to tell them about his part in murdering Cynthia Garcia. It took a promise of immunity for him to speak about his part in the killing.

The true extent of Augustiniak's and Eischeid's participation in the crime is unknown. Kramer was the only witness who talked. Police sources identified a biker named Richard Hyder as a fourth eyewitness—but in May 2002, Kramer was driving a truck that ran over Hyder on his motorcycle and killed him. The police officially determined it to be an accident.

Augustiniak was charged and pleaded guilty to second-degree murder. I don't know where "second degree" comes into the picture. Remember that Cynthia was severely beaten, stabbed, partially decapitated after being stuffed in a trunk, and dumped in the desert. Sounds like "first degree" to me. Augustiniak was sentenced to twenty-three years in prison.

Eischeid, the prospect, was arrested in 2003 but released on his own recognizance because he had a good job. A good job! Well, guess what? He split, went on the lam, and was caught in Argentina. I guess that means he quit his "good job." Finally he was sent back to the United States, where he pleaded guilty and was sentenced to life.

Kramer was sentenced to a five-year probation for the murder of Cynthia Garcia. As an informant for the U.S. Bureau of Alcohol, Tobacco and Firearms, he was given a new identity and a substantial amount of money.

Richard Hyder's death was forgotten. Hyder wasn't the first or the last to be murdered by his own club. The Angels have a long history of eating their young. Some of these murders have become infamous for their brutality, but many are single, random acts of violence that go virtually unnoticed by both the public and the cops.

14

FIGHTING BACK

For most of their history, the Hells Angels considered themselves untouchable. They had the support of celebrities, the tolerance of the general public through intimidation, the legal tactics of expensive lawyers, and the frustration of law enforcement officers who found it difficult to penetrate the biker culture.

Things have changed. In more ways and to a greater extent than the Angels themselves know.

True, they can still boast top-level legal representation, and they bring in tens of millions of dollars each year from the usual illegal antics. But they can no longer count on the support of celebrities like Mick Jagger or Hunter S. Thompson, or the tolerance of the general public who once thought of them as merely guys raising hell. Police forces have been remarkably successful in infiltrating the biker gangs, and many law enforcement agencies are now armed with tougher laws to deal with gang activities. And although the Angels can boast a few sharp minds in managing some of their business activities, they lack the vision and leadership power of a young Sonny Barger.

And let's not forget their direct competition from MCs like the Mongols and street gangs like MS-13. These organizations won't be intimidated by the Angels, and they won't let aging bikers prevent them from taking charge of business wherever and whenever they choose.

As if this weren't enough to knock the Angels off their self-appointed pedestal, now they have to pay attention to people in the know, like me, who are dedicated to exposing the Angels for people who *should* know. Like you.

MOST OF US are fighting the good fight not for money or fame, but because it's the right thing to do. We also know the risk we're taking in opposing the Angels, who don't exactly welcome criticism of any kind from any source. One of the loudest and most effective voices belongs to Agent K, who signs himself as Tom Jones (fans of the original *Men in Black* movie will recognize the reference) on his blog Gangsters Out (Gangstersout.com).

In 2009, Jones started the site as a safe place for Canadians to out neighbors suspected of being in organized crime. Since then it's had almost six million visitors.

Thousands of people who are alarmed about the kinds of things done by the Angels and their brothers on bikes read Gangsters Out. They trust Agent K and look to him for news and updates. He gets beneath the newspaper reports and deals with the kind of rough reality that the broader media can't—or won't—handle for fear of being sued or maybe even attacked by the bikers. Nothing scares this guy, as you can tell by reading any of his blog posts. Like the story of Bob Roth.

In late October 2012, just outside of Ranfurly, Alberta—a place so minuscule Google Maps doesn't bother labeling it—somebody cut a man's head off and left the rest of his body in a ditch. The head was discovered in a garbage bag tossed into an Edmonton alleyway. Police refused to identify the victim at first, but an anonymous blogger did it for them.

The victim was Robert John (Bob) Roth, a fifty-four-year-old laborer from Lloydminster, Alberta, about three hundred kilometers southeast of Edmonton. Apparently Roth had been a friendly soul whose biggest flaw was an addiction to cocaine. With his identity revealed, others began to fill in the story behind his gruesome death. Roth had bought cocaine from the White Boy Posse, a neo-Nazi gang who push drugs for the Angels. When Roth got over his head and couldn't settle his debt, the thugs made an example of him. It took six weeks for the Edmonton police to confirm almost everything that had already become widely known.

Why the delay? The Edmonton police have a reputation for withholding information from the press, as though the public either doesn't care or doesn't need to know what the taxpayer-funded law enforcement people are up to. Some privacy is necessary in police work, but many believe the Edmonton cops go too far.

It all reflects a rising tide of gang violence in western Canada, and especially in Alberta's northern reaches. What's the cause? In part it's the massive oil sands projects in the area, which have given rise to a boom-town atmosphere in places like Fort McMurray. There's a lot of money to be made there if you're young and adventurous and don't mind working twelve-hour shifts. But when your shift is over or you have a three-day break, what do you do? If you go looking for booze, drugs, or girls, you're the demand. The supply comes from gangs, most of whom are centered in Edmonton and funnel their supply in from the nearest port city, which happens to be Vancouver.

The White Boy Posse with their use of Nazi symbols has found some degree of acceptance, or at least tolerance, in many small northern Alberta towns. When police finally made arrests linked to Roth's death, they tied at least two other murders to the Angels puppet gang. A thirty-five-year-old man named Bryan Gower was found shot twice in the head near Kitscoty, another small Alberta town. In announcing the discovery of Gower's body, the police said they were treating his death as "suspicious." Two bullets in the head? No weapon around? Yeah, I guess that sounds suspicious. The Posse were also charged with the murder of Lorry Ann Santos, an innocent mother of four whose mistake was to answer a knock on her front door. That's when she was shot. The White Boy Posse thought her place belonged to someone else, suggesting they aren't the brightest Nazi medal at the flea market.

"They're a bunch of whacked-out, socially awkward kids with these bizarre, racist ideas," says Tom Jones/Agent K. "They want to sell drugs, so they go to Hells Angels and say, 'We'll kiss your butt and sell your drugs to make a commission.' They're losers." Apparently the Posse entered Roth's hometown of Lloydminster after another Hells Angels puppet group, called the Baseball Team, got busted. As Jones puts it, they pretended to be "just a group of guys playing baseball."

Jones takes anonymous tips from people across North America. "When I get a tip, I always check it," he says. "I Google the name to find a media report or a court record" to confirm the report. In the case of Bob Roth, Jones was contacted by an acquaintance of the victim and told Roth's name and location. Which was enough for Jones to access Roth's brother's Facebook page, where he found a memorial photo of Roth. This may not be the stuff of *CSI*, but it was good enough for Jones, who dismisses criticism of his tactics and goals.

"People can argue the integrity of the investigations as much as I do," he says, "but they can also argue that [police are] suppressing crime statistics. The guy on the street or relaxing in his home in suburbia has no idea of the scope of some of the crimes these guys are committing." He supplements information in his blog with an updated online registry of gang emblems, confirmed gang members, and the occasional law officer who likes to use bondage gear.

Tom Jones himself is a bit of a mystery. He calls only from pay phones, which are difficult to find these days—more difficult than biker gang members, at least. He writes about seven hundred posts annually, keeping tabs on the intricate network of gangs operating in western Canada and elsewhere, most of them dedicated to drug dealing. The whole business leads up to and through the Hells Angels, "the largest criminal organization and cocaine importers in Canada." The operation is consistent. "Everywhere we look, it's the same thing, the same puppet clubs, and the same driving force behind them." He encourages the outing of drug dealers and traffickers that neighbors want removed from their community, and advises people to "rat on the rats."

He's also not hesitant about commenting on events related to the Angels—including their Mafia links, primarily in Montreal. He was among the first, for example, to claim that the Hells Angels were behind the stunning murder of Rizzuto clan members, more specifically that the Angels had encouraged and perhaps even contracted the smaller D'Amico family in Granby, Quebec, to carry out the killings. The Angels and the Rizzutos have, of course, been closely linked in the Quebec drug trade for many years.

"The rationale behind my theory was simple," Jones wrote. "The Hells Angels are compulsive liars and consistent betrayers. They are taking over the drug trade all over Canada. It was strange that no one was claiming responsibility for the Montreal murders. Back in Ireland, someone always claims responsibility for the murder. It is the Hells Angels that lie and deny every murder they commit. Sometimes they even attend the funeral of people they have been accused of hiring the hit on."*

Jones claims that the sniper shot that took out Niccolo Rizzuto in his own home, in front of his family, was more of a military than a Sicilian hit. So was, he notes, the 2011 firebombing of a Montreal funeral home that the Rizzuto family favored. Things may be even more complex than that: Jones has also blogged about a Calabrian family in Hamilton, Ontario, being responsible for the hits.

"Since the Hells Angels have a huge control of the drug trade in Ontario, it would make sense that they would align themselves with families there," he says. "It also makes sense that if the Rizzutos were supplying the Bloods and the Rock Machine cocaine, they would want to put a stop to that. The Angels supply the Crips, after all."

The outrage that Jones/Agent K expresses is in part owing to the fact that he addresses events the mainstream media soft-pedals or skips over entirely. Of course, he doesn't have to deal with libel threats to the extent that national media outlets do. But nor have his claims been seriously challenged. Clearly, he remains in tune with the goings-on in the darkest side of the underworld in Vancouver and beyond. Consider the following revelations.

Ashley Machiskinic, who I talked about earlier, was a beautiful twenty-two-year-old First Nations woman whose life literally came crashing to the ground in a laneway behind a scuzzy Vancouver hotel. She'd battled drug addiction for some time without success, but no one who knew her believed she committed suicide by

---

* gangstersout.com, October 4, 2012.

leaping out of an upper-story window of the hotel. For one thing, she landed on her back, facing the hotel, which means she would have jumped backwards, which is not very likely. "One witness claims the person threw her shoes out the window after she fell, which would also imply she was thrown out," Jones wrote, adding this statement from a women's group: "There's been a few women lately thrown out of Vancouver hotel windows, at the Balmoral, the Regent, women missing fingers, wearing wigs because their heads have been shaved."* Jones suggested that the women were killed in a highly public way by drug dealers who wanted to send a message about what would happen to women if they don't pay off their drug debts.

"That sounds an awful lot like what's happening in Prince George, where people will have fingers cut off for a drug debt and have been found chained in the basement of crack houses tortured for drug debts," Jones comments. Drug dealers in that city, he suggests, do a brisk trade each Thursday, the day after "welfare Wednesday," and boast of profits as high as $15,000 a month. Their collection methods can be brutal. So who's responsible for these horrific acts?

"Let's face it," he says. "We all know who supplies the crack for East Van."

It's not just the Angels' criminal mayhem and violence that raises Jones's hackles. It's their over-the-top, juvenile behavior, as if they're celebrities parading their lifestyle before the public. In other words, people like Hap Porteous.

Porteous, a full-patch Angel, likes to hang out and have his photo taken with real-life celebrities like Fergie and Rihanna. Whether he buys his way into their company or they honestly

---

believe their careers will be enhanced by befriending such people is beside the point.

Porteous, performing under the name Hal Heffner, became famous for making and distributing a rap video in which he glorifies the biker/gangster lifestyle. Cute. The video opens with the tinted window of a white Rolls-Royce sliding down to reveal Porteous, who beckons to an awestruck teenage boy. The boy sets his bicycle aside and climbs into the limousine with the rapper, who introduces him to men dressed in gangster-style attire. The "lyrics" Porteous delivers, often over footage of mounds of cash, include lines like "I solve all my problems with a loaded gun," "Double-cross me and you'll run for your life," and "Basically my attitude is fuck authority." Not all that different, perhaps, from standard gangster rap, except that Porteous is no actor assuming a fictitious role.

The video included roles for two of his confederates, Angels Rob Shannon and Jody York. The men, who ran a trucking company out of Langley, B.C., were indicted in 2008 for running a cross-border drug trafficking operation on behalf of the Angels.

"This bust involved the seizure of more than 1,700 pounds of cocaine, 7,000 pounds of marijuana and about $3.5 million, according to the U.S. Attorney's office," Jones reports. "They were taking BC Bud into the U.S. and bringing back cocaine as payment."

Another cross-border drug ring tied to the Angels was busted in 2011. "Randy Jones, a full-patch member of the Whiterock Hells Angels, was implicated as well as his brother Trevor, who was charged but has yet to be extradited," Jones reported. "The U.S. indictment claimed the operation was run out of a strip club in Surrey called T Barz, run by the Hells Angels." (The club's name has since been changed to Shakerz.)

It was a smooth and sophisticated operation. Cash earned from the sale of the marijuana was transferred to Southern California and used to purchase large amounts of cocaine. The cocaine was then smuggled back into Canada through the United States to Trevor Jones. According to sources, the ring was transporting and distributing a thousand to two thousand pounds of marijuana and a hundred to two hundred kilograms of cocaine each month.

In November 2011 yet a third ring was smashed. "This ring was tied to our own local Larry Amero in Montreal," Jones explains. "He's the high-profile member of the Angels Whiterock chapter who was shot in Kelowna with Jonathan Bacon. This was another huge cross-border drug trafficking ring tied to the Hells Angels. They were trucking BC Bud across Canada and smuggling it into New York and California, bringing back cocaine as payment." Jones estimates that this third ring had the capacity to import and distribute about seventy-five kilograms of cocaine each week.

"These three rings show a clear pattern," he adds. "When one was busted the operation continued, because the Hells Angels own all the B.C. grow-ops and control all the Canadian crack dealers. It's impossible to document all the drug busts tied to the Hells Angels of late, but these three recent drug rings establish the pattern."

Without saying it, Jones suggests that the Angels-dominated cross-border drug traffic is a game of whack-a-mole—knock one ring down and another pops up nearby. What makes it all possible is the Hells Angels' control of the marijuana source, especially in B.C., and their extensive contacts in the United States that enable them to move cocaine up from South America.

Agent K's blog could easily be taken as loose commentary on events reported in the media—arm's-length opinion pieces implying underground connections from someone whose criminal activities amount to no more than stealing a candy bar from the neighborhood drugstore. Now, I don't know if Jones ever stole a candy bar, but I do know that at one time he had very good connections with the biker crowd. I say "had" because he surely doesn't have good relations with them now. In fact, he receives threats on a regular basis, which proves that much of what he writes is true.

In late 2013 he wrote about someone who not only said Jones was wrong but called him a rat, adding, "I hope you die a slow and painful death."

"So which is it?" Jones responded. "I'm wrong or I'm a rat? Those are two very different accusations."

The threat had been based on Jones's claims that the White Boy Posse is associated with the Hells Angels, and that they sell drugs and commit murder. "If I'm right, and the real concern is that I'm ratting them out, then that delusion needs to be addressed," he added. "People who sell crack, commit murder, and steal cars are rats. Not the people who report them to the police."

The people he writes about in his blog, he points out, are drug dealers. "I don't want anyone to shoot them. That's the Belfast way. I'm simply following the rules of engagement. In times of war you warn your enemy before you fire upon them. That gives them the opportunity to stand down before they get killed."

Agent K just wants the dealers to stop and the Angels and their cohorts to go back to riding their motorcycles—which was what they originally wanted to do, remember? "I want them to wake up and smell the coffee and take a look at what they're doing to other people." He encourages whomever he can reach through his blog to "rat out" the drug dealers, especially those connected to biker gangs. That's a tall order—no one has to be told what bikers tend to do to people who testify against them—but he also makes a strong case for it: ordinary people shouldn't have to live in fear of

Harley-riding brutes who feel they haven't received enough respect or that they can abuse women or push drugs with impunity.

"One day, like it or not, we'll all stand accountable for our choices," he says. "Martin Luther King was right: anyone can be great, because anyone can serve. The shallow, selfish lives these clowns are obsessing over are so pointless. There is no joy or happiness in that."

He adds one more observation: "When I was a kid, I used to read Alan Watts. He was into Zen. He claimed that the literal translation of the Greek word *to sin* was to miss the mark. If our goal in life is to find true happiness, then *to sin* would be to miss that mark like an archer misses his target. I believe people are free to choose. I just think those half-wits [drug-dealing bikers] are missing out on a much more rewarding life someone else had planned for them."

Still, it's difficult to believe Mom Boucher would ever be able to grasp the point.

15

RACISM AMONG THE ANGELS:
REAL OR IMAGINARY?

B ack in early 2011 a guy named Jesse James got himself into a lot
of trouble by being remarkably stupid. James was married to a
genuine movie star, an honest-to-god celebrity who's both bright
and beautiful, although some may have questioned the "bright"
part when they learned more about James. Her name is Sandra
Bullock, and although she could presumably choose any guy she
wanted, she chose James. Okay, maybe there was something else
going on between them. It doesn't matter. For several reasons,
much of the discussion about her and James involved James's use
of Nazi symbols.

James fancied himself a biker. Personally, I think he just liked
the idea of being considered part of the biker culture; it would help
support the outlaw association of his name. One of the celebrity
magazines ran pictures of James giving a Sieg Heil! salute while
wearing some Nazi material. The woman in his life before Bullock
came along, Michelle McGee, was frequently photographed
wearing a Nazi hat and a swastika armband. Some of James's friends

defended him. "He's into history," one of them said. "The swastika deal is just to scare people. It's part of biker culture."

"Into history"? Maybe someone should tell James who won the war and why it was fought and what the Nazis stood for. That's "history."

Nearly fifty years earlier, Hunter S. Thompson talked about Nazi regalia worn by the Hells Angels, which seemed to fix them in everyone's mind as right-wing radicals closely akin to the KKK and similar groups. But are they?

Let's face it: one way to both outrage and intimidate "ordinary people" is to wear things considered naturally evil, like a Nazi swastika or the German Iron Cross. It's a way to declare that you're a badass, or want to be. It's a way to piss people off, and it dates back to the 1940s and 1950s, long before the Angels existed. Remember that a lot of early MC members were war veterans who returned to America ready to raise hell. A lot of them brought back captured Nazi paraphernalia and wore them as trophies for a while. Only when it became clear that people were shocked by the sight of them did the one percenters adopt Nazi symbols. Sonny Barger himself explained it by saying, "This stuff—iron crosses, the Nazi insignia, the German helmets—that's to shock people. To let them know we're individualists."

In fact, the use of such symbols appears to be dying out. You see them less and less with the major gangs like the Angels, Bandidos, and Mongols. For one thing, these gangs don't need them to outrage or intimidate anymore. It's gone out of fashion, according to Tom Barker, a professor of criminal justice at Eastern Kentucky University who studies motorcycle gangs. The reason? Barker claims that it's simply a matter of marketing strategy. The Angels, Bandidos, and Outlaws have established chapters around the world, including Germany, where the symbols are outlawed.

So does limiting the use of Nazi symbols signal a more tolerant approach toward other races? Not a bit.

There's always been a connection between motorcycle gangs and white supremacy. The five major MCs in North America—the Angels, Bandidos, Outlaws, Mongols, and Pagans—refuse membership to African Americans. It's an interesting approach since the Bandidos, and to some extent the Mongols, were born in reaction to the Angels' not allowing Latinos into their gang. There are exceptions, but they're rare. Declarations of White Power are common among MC gang members, and among those who profess to admire them. Michelle McGee, the former girlfriend of Jesse James, sports two tattooed letters on the back of her legs: W and P, standing for White Power.

THE RACIST ELEMENT in the Hells Angels and other outlaw MCs cuts both ways: white supremacists join the one percenters and the outlaw gangs join the racist organizations. One glance at the symbols and language shared by both groups reveals the connection. More than once, a link has been made between outlaw gangs and prominent racist groups like the Ku Klux Klan.

In June 2006 members of the Imperial Klans of America followed their leader, a guy named Ron Edwards, to the Barbarians' annual biker reunion at the Mendon racetrack in northwest Ohio. One of the IKA members invited to speak to the bikers began by raising a clenched fist and shouting "White power!" He went on to urge the crowd to stand up for the white race so that their grandchildren would have white kids to play with. He also suggested that cleaner air, less crime, and less garbage would mean that America would require fewer non-whites. The Barbarians didn't seem to disagree with the idea; they gave the

IKA an award for being the largest organization to attend the event.

While the traffic seems to move both ways—bikers looking for white supremacist groups and racists searching out biker groups for support—it's usually the racists doing the most recruiting. Stormfront, probably the largest neo-Nazi site on the internet, hosted a white nationalist barbecue as part of the July 2009 Northwest Harley Weekend. The website has fostered a bikers' user group known as Aryan MC, and a White Pride Riders group has shown up on Bikers-Or-Not, a bikers' social networking site.

In Canada, the most prominent racist group on bikes has to be White Boy Posse, based on their name alone. Well, at least they're upfront about it. Too bad they're not reasonably bright as well. These are the guys, remember, who knocked on the door of a suburban Saskatoon home one morning in September 2012 and shot dead Lorry Ann Santos, a young mother of four. The Posse members had gone to the wrong house in the wrong part of town. The Edmonton cops raided their clubhouse to find, in addition to the usual harvest of cash, drugs, and guns, a wide collection of Nazi paraphernalia. The Posse, of course, is a puppet gang of the Angels.

So are the Angels racist or not? The answer appears to be yes, but likely no more or less than other bikers. The joys of the open road and living wild, unlimited by such mundane things as social approval and the law, is kind of a natural right-wing attitude on its own, and the extreme fringes of the right wing have always been racist in nature.

Of course, the idea that Hells Angels and their offshoots, puppets, and rivals have any deep political philosophy to espouse or even describe is a laugh. They're apolitical by nature. I have no idea how many Angels, for example, vote in elections at any level, but it's difficult to envision them registering and showing up at a polling booth. Their racist attitudes represent a rejection of anyone who doesn't fit the accepted stereotype of a gang-related biker. Asking if the Angels admit blacks or other visible minorities is like asking if the Bloods or Crips welcome southern whites into their organization. For whatever reason, white boys tend to ride motorcycles. So do a lot of Latinos and, in western Canada, a growing number of Asians and East Indians. But blacks? Hardly ever.

AS I SAID, there are exceptions to the Angels' whites-only rule, and none is bigger or badder than Greg Woolley. Woolley grew up in a rough neighborhood in North Montreal. He started his own gang, the Syndicate, before he was twenty years old, so you know what he had planned for his life. Later he joined the Rockers as their only black member, and became well known when Maurice "Mom" Boucher chose him to watch over his son, Francis. This brought Woolley into Boucher's inner circle. In Canada, that's just about as high as you can go with the Angels, and the fact that Woolley is black made it all the more impressive.

So what was Woolley's secret? The same as anyone else's who has risen through the Angel ranks: he was smart, mean, and vicious. And it took all three of those qualities to enable him to beat not one, not two, but three murder convictions.

In the first trial, a jury acquitted him and four other Angels of killing Rock Machine member Jean-Marc Caissy. That was impressive enough to earn Woolley his full-patch status. The other two murder raps he beat were for the assassination of Pierre Beauchamps, another Rock Machine member. Woolley's first trial ended with a hung jury, and the second one led to his full acquittal in 2005.

A few months later his luck ran out when he was caught with a gun while trying to board a flight out of Montreal's Trudeau airport. Things were rough for Woolley in prison. He was no model prisoner, and when he became eligible for parole the parole board rejected his first application. Noting Woolley's quick temper and history of violence behind bars, where he enjoyed considerable influence over his fellow prisoners, the board wrote, "No matter where you find yourself in custody, the power conferred on you by your official status among bikers, and implicitly as the head of street gangs, is of such a scale that no [rehabilitation] program can sufficiently protect the public from the risk you represent."

In August 2012, not long after Woolley's eventual release, "Big" Chénier Dupuy was shot to death while sitting in a parked car in east-end Montreal. Dupuy was head of the Bo-Gars street gang, whose members are aligned with the Bloods gang in the United States. Word has it that Dupuy slapped Woolley in the face during an Angels-sponsored summit at a bar in Ste-Adele, a pretty little town in the Laurentians north of Montreal. The meeting had been aimed at getting several of the street gangs together under the Hells Angels banner. After publicly humiliating Woolley—which was either incredibly brave or incredibly stupid—Dupuy stormed out of the meeting along with Lamartine Sévère Paul. Both men claimed they'd never work with the Angels, and they were right: Paul was shot soon after Dupuy died.

Wherever the investigation into Dupuy's murder may lead, no one has heard the last of Gregory Woolley, who picked up the nickname Picasso along the way. He has too much ambition and too much power to quietly fade into the woodwork. As I discussed earlier, the police crackdown on biker gangs in Quebec, as well as infighting among the Mafia, much of it aimed at the Rizzuto family, has left a power vacuum in the region's drug trade. Bikers, street gangs, and the fractured Mafia organization all want the biggest piece of it, and Woolley is as well positioned as anyone to seize it. He could become a poster child for the Angels as a way of proving they aren't racist. But don't count on it. They don't care what you and I think about their racial attitudes.

WHATEVER MAY BE HAPPENING in North America, things are becoming clearly racist in Europe. Is this a strictly regional thing or a global situation? Either way, it has a chance to spread, and with wide-ranging consequences.

Consider Denmark, the quiet, peaceful little country that, as we saw earlier, is home to some of the most violence-prone bikers in the world. Beginning in 2008, Danish Hells Angels began recruiting prospects to "rid Denmark of the Muslim menace." Other biker gangs, up against the Angels for control of the Western European drug trade, started signing up new Muslim members to help "eliminate those who want to eliminate us." This racist attitude in the land of the Danes may be surprising to us, but it's not a big shock to people who know the Danes well. Especially the Danes themselves.

Jacob Holdt, a well-known Danish photographer, documented racism in the United States in the 1970s. By 2008 he was ready to publicly declare, "Denmark is today more racist than America." The country has Europe's most stringent immigration laws, and its government insists on monoculture and assimilation. The last time an outbreak of Hells Angels violence occurred in Denmark was in 1996–1997, when the Angels fought a prolonged battle with another traditional gang, the Bandidos. But the latest Angels conflict in the country is with Black Ghost, whose members all have immigrant backgrounds. The Angels claim they're fighting to protect Denmark from the "jackal mentality" that "characterizes" Arabs and Muslims.

So are the Angels encouraging or reflecting this racism where Muslims are concerned? Or is it a matter of dealing with competition? At least some Danish law enforcement officials consider it's the latter, suggesting that the Angels are motivated less by skin color or religious faith than by the ongoing battle over control of Denmark's, and the Western European, drug market.

ANGELS IN THE SUNSET?

Did the conformist society of the 1950s and the upheavals of the 1960s really give rise to the Hells Angels and the biker culture they inspired? I leave it to the sociologists to figure that one out. I'm spending my time tracking the imminent demise of the Hells Angels, not as an organization that represents some of the most pervasive and violent criminal acts of our time, but as a group that seems lost within the very culture they invented.

We've seen that one of the attractions of the Angels a generation or so ago was the sense of freedom, rebellion, and (in its widest definition) romanticism they inspired. You rode your Harley-Davidson wherever the road and your interest took you. You were a band of brothers as tightly devoted to one another as a combat platoon in any war you could name. You feared no one, you intimidated everyone, and you enjoyed the benefits that came along with it, including sex, drugs, rock 'n' roll, and adulation.

Where are those Angels now?

Some are shells, like the Sonny Barger we met at the opening of this book. Some are languishing in jail, watching their lives ebb away. Some are married with children whom they wish to protect from the same kind of scourge they once created. Some, of course, are dead at the hands of rivals, as a result of road accidents, and even at the hands of their own gang brothers. Some have moved so far beyond the biker identity and into the big business of international crime that they resemble the original Angels the way Donald Trump resembles your local slum landlord.

And some are none of these things.

Like George Christie.

Christie had once been the number-two man in the entire Hells Angels organization. Actually, the correct descriptor is "corporation"—the Angels long ago sought incorporation, just like Exxon or Coca-Cola or any business operation looking to protect its interests and identity.

Anyway, whatever Sonny Barger couldn't get done, George "Gus" Christie could. Christie had two qualities that tend to be scarce among Angels and other bike gang members generally: charm and intelligence. It's all relative, of course. How much charm does it take to kick the head of those you've knocked down because they didn't show you enough respect? How much intelligence is required to ride an overweight and badly designed motorcycle on a highway through the southwestern American desert?

Christie had a little more of both, which I suppose made him unusual in the biker culture. He used them to climb up the Angel ranks while avoiding, for the most part, serious criminal charges. He was also pegged as a dove in the various biker encounters in Southern California, usually between the Mongols and the Angels. George preferred to talk things over with a beer and some barbecue rather than beat each other's brains out. As a result, he managed to achieve two goals that most Angels have little hope of attaining: age sixty-five and retirement.

Given his high profile, however, the law couldn't allow it. I suspect it also bugged the law enforcement types in and around Ventura, California, where Christie lived and worked all his life, that they'd failed to wipe him out or at least put him away. He'd been charged in 1987 for solicitation to commit murder. He was acquitted. Ten years later he was charged with conspiracy to sell prescription drugs and (this was the heavy charge) filing a false income tax return. He fought these as well, until a long stint in solitary confinement and the offer of a deal from the prosecutor persuaded him to plead no contest.

Ten years after that, as a result of the Black Rain operation, he was charged with conspiring to firebomb two Ventura-area tattoo shops (Christie made a living from his own tattoo parlor called the Ink House). According to the police, Christie wanted to put his competitors out of business. Their case was reportedly based on the claims of two guys who set the fires and were offered leniency if they claimed Christie was behind it.

Throughout the lead-up to the trial, some people tried to paint Christie as Robin Hood, a likable guy mixed up with lowlifes, a colorful character who wasn't nearly as bad as the law painted him. A family man with a wife, kids, a mortgage, and a business. They neglected to mention that Christie was convicted of shepherding his own son into dealing drugs, leading to the young man's conviction on the charges.* And that he'd spent more than forty years as a higher-up in one of the most violent

---

* Tracy Wilson and David Kelly, "Hells Angels Leader, Ex-Wife and Son Get Probation in Drug-Selling Case," *Los Angeles Times,* April 18, 2002.

biker gangs in the world. I don't think he has a halo and I don't think he deserves one.

Christie and an Angel named Kyle Gilbertson faced six counts of conspiracy that could have sent both men away for life. Gilbertson, incidentally, didn't fit the stereotypical Hells Angel image: he held a full-time job as an air traffic controller. (You have to wonder how pilots and passengers would feel if they knew that the voice talking them down through the clouds belonged to a full-patched Angel.)

The case never made it past the prosecution's opening statement. Had it gone forward, former Bandidos president George Wegers and former Mongols MC member Al Cavazos would have both testified *for the defense*! Instead, Christie and Gilbertson agreed to a plea deal. It took six months for the sentencing to come down. Christie was given a year in jail.

FOR THE ANGELS to survive, they'd need more than one George Christie in more than one location around the world. Instead they have people like Allan Potter and Bradley Summers, two Angels wannabes in, of all places, St. John's, Newfoundland. They were arrested in July 2013 for committing a drive-by shooting. Now, drive-bys have to be the simplest method of committing a potentially fatal crime: you don't need strategy, tactics, or much planning. All you need is a car, a gun or two, and an address. A little intelligence helps as well. Potter and Summers lacked two out of four: they shot up the wrong house.

A few weeks later, four Canadian Angels were arrested in Pontevedra, Spain, in connection with a yacht holding about five hundred kilograms of cocaine. All four Canadians were known to police. The yacht had sailed directly from Colombia, and for six weeks it had been under surveillance by the Spanish police, the

U.S. Drug Enforcement Agency, the RCMP, Europol, and France's tax authority.

I don't know much about smuggling drugs, but it seems to me that a boat sailing across the Atlantic from Colombia just might attract attention from the law, especially if a known Hells Angel is on board. Of course, maybe a hundred other drug-filled yachts made the crossing safely, and this was the one that was caught. But I suspect that the truth involves increased pressure from the police, supported with more technical assistance (surveillance and communication) than the Angels may have known.

Pushback against the Angels and other gangs is building in Europe. The Angels may remain stronger there than in North America—that's Agent K's opinion, in any case—but cooperation among European law enforcement agencies is tight and impressively effective.

Sometime before the massive cocaine seizure in Pontevedra, Spanish police conducted thirty-one simultaneous early-morning house raids and arrested twenty-five Angels in the process. Charges included drug trafficking, trafficking in human beings, extortion, money laundering, and corruption, and were based on an investigation stretching back two and a half years. The operation involved more than two hundred officers and was focused on the island of Mallorca, more a luxury tourist destination than a gang site. The Angels had just opened a new chapter on the island, working hand in hand with chapters in Germany and Luxembourg. Several cars, motorcycles, and weapons were seized, along with computers, laptops, mobile phones, and electronic devices. These latter no doubt represented treasure troves of information for more police raids and more charges.

I was impressed with two things about this Spanish raid.

The first was the wide cooperation among all the police forces, including Interpol. I'm not suggesting that they're any more or less competent than the FBI, DEA, RCMP, SQ, and other agencies. Only that this represents a serious determination to control if not destroy the Angels (and other MCs) in Western Europe. I suspect that the days when the gangs could run amok from Dublin to Düsseldorf are long gone.

I was also impressed by the amount of planning that went into the raid, which again indicates a serious approach to the problem. The Angels may consider this and the cocaine bust in Pontevedra as merely a cost of doing business. It may be much more than that.

The Angels are losing their leadership, their ability to intimidate, and their unique identity. No one, including me, is suggesting they'll vanish tomorrow. But they're a mere shell of the organization they once were. All shells, by definition, are empty, and most are eventually discarded.

IN *Beyond Good and Evil*, Friedrich Nietzsche wrote, "He who fights with monsters should look to it that he himself does not become a monster. And when you gaze long into an abyss the abyss also gazes into you." I and many others have been gazing into the abyss of the Hells Angels for several years now. And of course we've all asked ourselves, What caused them to become the people they are?

The answer is complex, and stems as much from society as it does from the bikers themselves. I think it reflects how we treat the disenfranchised. It could be argued that those of us who are affected by the Angels are simply reaping what we've sown. Hells Angels members may be considered dangerous now, but at one time they were all lost children, and no one stepped up to help them. Think of Sonny Barger. Picture him as a child abandoned by his mother and stuck with a violent drunk for a father. How else could he have turned out?

But does this justify the man he became and the kinds of things he did as a gang member? What does his background have to do with his actions as an adult?

I think it has everything to do with it. When I first infiltrated biker gangs, I knew nothing about them. It turned out to be the toughest assignment I've ever had. Not because of the danger, but because of the influence of being, even temporarily, a part of their culture. I almost became what I beheld, and it scared me to death.

I discovered they were a lot like me, without the murder and mayhem of course. Now, long gone from the biker environment, I watch the corruption trials on TV, the stories of senators and other public officials cheating the public and stealing everything they can. I add them to stories of crooked lawyers and bad cops, drone attacks on civilians and prisoner abuse in Abu Ghraib, pedophile priests preying on children and porn magnates making millions by exploiting young women.

Recently I heard about governments in a so-called free society spying on their citizens through social networks. It all makes me wonder if I spent thirty years, endured two failed marriages, and invested large chunks of my life chasing shadows. And I ask myself if it was all worth it.

Law enforcement people are now debating whether to make the bikers' patches illegal. It's a big deal to them. If the police can show that a club is a criminal organization, wearing a sign of belonging to that group becomes a crime. Sound like a good idea? Not necessarily.

The patches let the police know who is a legitimate member. They can count the number of members by counting the patches, they can identify bosses, and they can spot prospective members.

Without the patch, all members would become virtually invisible. Are there a hundred of them? A thousand? Ten thousand? Who would know?

The primary problem isn't the patches. It's the people—the ones whom the Angels and others count on. No biker could infiltrate legitimate businesses without the help of real estate agents, bankers, lawyers, and others who jump aboard just to make a few bucks. The helpers go all the way from crooked business people and legal types down to the sad sack in the basement, watching pornography in the dark. Are we in another basement, doing other things to help the Angels? When we're asking where the Angels came from, we might also ask ourselves where we're coming from.

AND THE CORNER may have been turned.

One of the things that characterized the Hells Angels as little more than an organized gang of misfits was their lack of sophistication where strategy was concerned. They reacted instead of planned. If another gang or another gang member insulted or threatened an Angel, the Angel struck back, almost always with heavy support from the rest of the gang and sometimes all the way up to Sonny Barger or Gus Christie or whoever's approval was needed to make a serious dent in the other guys. "You whack me, I whack you back harder" was all the tactics the Angels needed or used.

This, of course, was not an effective approach to dealing with the Angels' ultimate enemy—law enforcement agencies at all levels. Sure, now and then someone like Mom Boucher would make a stupid call, like ordering the Angels to kill two correctional guards, chosen at random, just to prove a point. The victims weren't cops, but they were close enough for real cops to take offense and run down the shooters. They also, eventually, ran down Mom Boucher.

He's staring at a gray stone wall today (when he's not ducking other inmates intent on winning macho points by giving him a beating) and for a long time to come.

But that's not sophisticated strategy. That's schoolyard stuff. Fighting back in a sophisticated manner means doing it so quietly that the enemy doesn't realize he's been had until the hammer drops. That's how the RCMP, FBI, and other law enforcement groups used me—to enter the bikers' inner sanctum with my eyes and ears open, ready to feed what I learned back to my handlers.

The side of the Angels more focused on building a criminal organization—one that demands more than the ability to stay upright on a moving Harley-Davidson—appears to understand the importance of this strategy. More disturbing, they may know how to apply it effectively.

In the autumn of 2013 the Canadian press was full of shocking stories out of Montreal, all connected with a man named Benoit Roberge. I know Benoit well. Of all the people I worked with in law enforcement, he was one of the best, most trusted officers in the province, a guy who led the police in their efforts to crack down on biker gangs. Yet in October 2013 he was charged with gangsterism, obstructing justice, and breach of trust, all based on alleged actions connected with the biker gangs he was assigned to cover. This, I told myself when I first heard of his arrest, is a major mistake. Somebody screwed up; it couldn't be Benoit. But it was. In March 2014 Roberge pleaded guilty to participating in the activities of a criminal organization and breach of trust.

How could this be? No one knew more about biker gangs, and no one was trusted more by the law enforcement agencies dedicated to busting them, than Benoit Roberge. He'd immersed himself as deeply into the biker gang culture as it was possible to go without wearing an MC patch. He went to biker funerals, bugged biker hangouts, and testified at biker trials. He was the first police officer to recognize the inevitable war that was brewing between the Angels and the Rock Machine, and the deaths it would cause. When he tried to warn the Sûreté du Québec, they laughed at him. They stopped laughing when the bodies began piling up and the scope of the war became obvious. More than any other individual, Benoit Roberge was responsible for obtaining the wealth of information on Angel activities that Dany Kane provided.

Dany Kane trusted Benoit. So did René Charlebois, who was serving a life sentence for being an Angels hit man when he escaped from prison in September 2013.

Benoit was a cop, but he was a "good cop," a guy who would give you his word and keep it. Everyone trusted and admired him, including me. He earned my admiration for the way he handled the bikers. We worked together and respected each other's opinions and abilities. The idea that Benoit Roberge, whose wife is a Crown prosecutor assigned to probe organized crime in and around Montreal, would deal with the Angels was as likely as my being elected prime minister.

So what really happened?

The headlines shouted "Cop Dealing with Biker Gangs Goes Bad," or something along those lines. In his March 2014 court appearance, Roberge admitted that he'd provided information to René Charlebois through a go-between, whose identity was protected by court order. The impetus for this, Roberge claimed, was a threat made to him by the go-between that if he didn't cooperate a member of Roberge's family would be harmed (Roberge is married with two children).

In early September 2013 Charlebois called Roberge from a minimum-security facility—a curious place for a man serving a life sentence. The purpose of his call was to inform the recently retired Roberge that he'd recorded conversations between the two men in which Roberge had provided Charlebois with secret police information. During the telephone call, Charlebois attempted to blackmail Roberge into helping him launch a new drug-distribution network in Montreal. When Roberge balked, Charlebois simply walked away from the prison. The go-between contacted Roberge while Charlebois was on the run, then alerted police to the recordings. Hearing the news, the SQ set up a sting operation, offering to sell Roberge the recordings for $50,000, and Roberge's response led to his arrest.*

I can't help believing there's more to this story beneath the surface. Through all my work with various police agencies operating in Quebec, I was aware of the competition, the jealousy, and the outright loathing between some members of the law enforcement groups involved in controlling the bikers. There were frequent speculations about certain individuals and what they were up to in their dealings with the Angels and others.

That speculation was easily sown because agents were given a lot of discretion in how they dealt with the bikers. They needed that freedom. Opportunities to pick up data and run down evidence often came up unexpectedly and with a very short window of opportunity. The top guys were granted the right to do cash deals up to a $10,000 limit.

Add to that the nature of the relationship between the law and the bikers. Imagine the pressure you can lay on a biker—who may be facing ten or twenty or more years in a maximum-security prison—when you offer the chance for a lighter sentence, or no prosecution at all, in exchange for information that could land a

---

* Paul Cherry, "Former Montreal Cop Benoit Roberge Pleads Guilty in Hells Informant Case," *Montreal Gazette*, March 13, 2014.

much bigger fish. Maybe that fish isn't a biker at all. Maybe it's a pain-in-the-ass cop who needs a lesson.

Speculation? Maybe, but it's no more speculative than some of the stuff foisted on viewers by the CBC-TV's *The Fifth Estate* when it covered Roberge's arrest and the charges he faced. During the show Roberge was quoted as saying, "They'd like to see me dead. They want to send me to jail, but I'm not going down alone."*

The media made a big deal about Roberge having enjoyed something called "high living," which made me laugh. A lot of his work tracking the bikers involved sitting in a car and watching a door for four, five, eight hours at a time, waiting for someone to emerge. Nothing I ever saw suggested he was leading anything other than the kind of middle-class life you'd expect from a sergeant-detective.

Here's something else to ponder: Benoit started visiting René Charlebois in 2009, after Charlebois had been given a life sentence for murdering a police informant for the Angels. Benoit, the story goes, had been trying to persuade Charlebois to provide information to the police from behind bars. Was there a quid pro quo? After all, Charlebois had been transferred to a minimum-security facility, which was far more comfortable than the maximum-security place where people like Mom Boucher will be living out what's left of their lives. It was also easy for Charlebois to walk away from. Cornered in a cottage southeast of Montreal ten days after escaping, Charlebois committed suicide, leaving a note drawing attention to the audiotapes that reportedly led the police to lay charges against Benoit Roberge.

There's a lesson to be learned from this, no matter what the

* Julia Sisler, "Accused Ex-Cop Benoit Roberge Vows to Name Names in Hells Angels Case," CBC News, January 22, 2014.

outcome. Whatever went down with Benoit Roberge and whoever may have manipulated things, it suggests that the Angels are fighting back in a sophisticated manner. They have learned from their enemies. The most devastating damage to the Angels, and to all biker gangs, has been done not by other gangs but by cops finding a way to get inside their organizations. I know; it was once my job. The way I see it, the Angels have become sophisticated enough to employ tactics and strategies that are similar to the ones used by the police. This kind of action is not the stuff of a gang of toughs on some beat-up Harley-Davidsons. It's the act of an organization looking beyond the next street battle or drive-by shooting in order to reach its goals. That's what the Angels have become: a group of guys with clear criminal intent who are dedicated to achieving new heights in gathering big dollars—tens of millions of dollars—through any action they choose, especially if it involves drugs, prostitution, extortion, and slavery. And they intend to do it on a global scale.

If they succeed, they will have established an evil empire—one whose existence and power we tolerate at our peril.

AS THIS BOOK, the third and last in the Biker trilogy, draws to a close, I admit to feeling another sense of loss. Finishing my recollections of and observations about bikers and their activities is like ending a criminal investigation, leaving mixed and contradictory emotions. When I went undercover to track biker gangs and gather information for police, the hardest part of the job was extracting my character on the last day. As I watched the world I'd created self-destruct in the rear-view mirror, I would tell myself, "You made it out and now you're going home." I should have felt elated, but I didn't. I just felt empty.

I knew what would happen after I left. At six o'clock that morning SWAT teams would kick down the targets' doors. Flash and smoke grenades would be going off to cover and confuse. Among the shouts and noise would be the wail of frightened children running in all directions from the breakfast table, their mothers scrambling to gather them in their arms, the mothers themselves as frightened as the children but not permitted to show it. The cops in charge of securing the premises would be tackling and holding them, sometimes by the hair. Anyone could be going for guns or trying to destroy evidence or dispose of drugs. The biker coming downstairs carrying a gun, sometimes still in his underwear, would see it all in a glance. He'd know enough to drop his weapon and raise his hands before Sergeant DoRight sees the gun and makes a fatal decision.

That's your legacy, I would tell myself. That's what you're leaving behind. Some of those families had you over for dinner. You know the children by name, and during all the long months you spent undercover, they served as a substitute for your family, remember them? And don't give me that crap about working for the greater good, and how you're saving the kids from growing up in a world of crime and violence. That's all bullshit. Kids know what they know, and you know what you know. Soon the bad guy knows the truth. He trusted you and accepted you, was maybe good to you, and now he's paying the price. You befriended him and then you betrayed him. That's the whole story right there. Okay, that's your job, that's what you do. Everything else is fluff. Like a homicide cop who's seen too many bodies, you lose your sensitivity, part of your humanity. It's the easiest thing in the world to rationalize, isn't it? You didn't ask the bikers to do what they did. That was *their* choice, not yours.

HERE'S WHAT I THINK after all those years of watching, listening, acting, and recording:

The biker cop and the outlaw biker should be viewed as two sides of the same coin. The fate of each party is dependent on the other. After years of playing the game of chasing and hiding, accusing and denying, threatening and agreeing, cops and bikers begin to merge and their lives intersect.

Clothes don't make the man? Yes they do, to a certain extent. You form your first impression of someone by their appearance, and that impression affects your whole attitude toward the individual. If you have a high school–aged daughter, you'll know exactly what I mean when she brings home her first boyfriend.

Working with law enforcement groups and biker gangs means blending totally into the biker gang environment. Suits and ties are not required. You start by building peripheral friendships with non-members just to have someone to talk to and sit with when you're in a biker bar. Many of these second-tier guys are hard-riding old-timers, living the biker life and surviving the best they can. When you start hanging with these guys, you get a totally different perspective of the biker lifestyle. You don't want to start talking drugs or guns with them. They won't listen. They've survived too long to engage in idle chatter about such things. They spend their time sitting around, drinking beer, and telling colorful stories about runs, parties, and the good times they used to have that, in truth, probably weren't that good. You listen to their stories carefully and pick up key words, like drug names or club parties or anything that's illegal or shows club friendship. You respond. You build trust. You get them to like you, and they become your vehicle into the target clubs.

All the while, two undercovers are in the bar to watch your back, so they too have to blend in perfectly with everyone else.

They're not there only to save your butt, of course. They're also the watchers, the ones who'll verify whatever you report in your notes at the end of the night. It's not that they don't trust you, it's just that they don't trust you. Their job is to have a good time, and since they don't deal with the most dangerous characters and situations, the ones you're constantly aware of, it can skew their view.

For the first years of my career working to bring down the worst of the bikers, I honestly believed I was a shadow warrior with a mission to aid society. But after time passed and after participating in dozens of court cases, I began to realize that I was just a cog in a big machine, and that my work was really of little consequence. There will always be bad guys, and there will always be people paid by society to keep the bad guys in check. But when you're all used up, you're put on the FBI's Most Unwanted List, and it's over. Just like that. You're left to return to your life and try to get back to being ordinary Joe Citizen. Return to your roots and look for acceptance. Unfortunately, everyone has moved on with their lives, and after a few hours visiting your friends and catching up on the news you missed, you leave. It's not that they don't want you. It's just that they don't know you. There isn't any room in their life for you.

So when you leave your hometown, you feel cast loose and totally adrift. The sea is vast and your ship is small and the shoreline soon disappears. The trauma may be over, but it's never really gone. Now it has a name: PTSD. We all know about it where war veterans are concerned, but there's no PTSD help for agents. You're on your own.

The decisions you make within the first year will determine whether you survive or not. This is the period when cops eat their guns or ex-agents go rogue, returning to the character they were supposed to shed. Many keep the identity they assumed while undercover and, with nothing else to replace it, they stay bad. Others write books and relive their experiences, waiting for their true identity to return and rebuild itself. Books mean editors and publishers and a host of "regular" people to deal with. Slowly you become reinserted back into the mainstream. You are neither a criminal nor a fully innocent and naive citizen.

You're a hybrid, and that's not bad, all things considered.

I'VE WRITTEN ABOUT the Bandidos, the Outlaws, and now the Angels. I'm finished with them all.

I've learned a lot during my years of researching and writing about them. I'd like to say that I wish them well, but I don't. Sonny Barger and his buddies may be able to blame their Angel identity and adventures on the actions or inactions of others, and with some people they'd make a strong case. But that's where it ends.

A rabid dog may have been abused, and we can feel bad about it.

But when it's running down the street, foaming at the mouth, we know what must be done, and we do it.

Or we should.

INDEX